Here I Am

365 Devotions for Teens

Natalie Dorland

 **Pacific Press®**
Publishing Association

Nampa, Idaho | Oshawa, Ontario, Canada
www.pacificpress.com

Cover design by Steve Lanto
Cover design resources from iStockphoto.com/610445216
Interior design by Kristin Hansen-Mellish

The author assumes full responsibility for the accuracy of all facts and quotations as cited in this book.

You can obtain additional copies of this book by calling toll-free 1-800-765-6955 or by visiting http://www.adventistbookcenter.com.

Library of Congress Cataloging-in-Publication Data
Names: Dorland, Natalie, author.
Title: Here I am : 365 devotions for teens / Natalie Dorland.
Description: Nampa : Pacific Press Publishing Association, 2018.
Identifiers: LCCN 2018024956 | ISBN 9780816364084 (pbk. : alk. paper)
Subjects: LCSH: Christian teenagers Prayers and devotions. | Devotional
    calendars—General Conference of Seventh-day Adventists.
Classification: LCC BV4850 .D67 2018 | DDC 242/.63—dc23 LC record available at https://lccn.loc.gov/2018024956

July 2018

Dedication

This devotional book is dedicated to all of my youth at the Puyallup Seventh-day Adventist Church and Northwest Christian School, whose lively conversations and thought-provoking questions inspired many of the topics in this devotional. Know that each one of you has made a difference in my life during my years of ministry with you; and I hope that through our many Bible classes, Sabbath School discussions, Pathfinder campouts, Friday chapels, Week of Prayers, youth vespers, baptismal studies, counseling sessions, and other God-moments that I've left a bit of Jesus with you too. I want nothing more than for each of you to develop your own relationship with Jesus, follow the Holy Spirit's call in your life, trust the Father's plan, and meet me in heaven if I don't see you again on this earth.

I want to thank my family for their encouragement throughout the writing process. Your prayers, ideas, love, and support helped make this book happen. You have never ceased to believe in me, and you encouraged me to follow God's call to ministry.

Introduction

This devotional isn't like other devotionals you may have read. Yes, it has 365 entries, one for each day of your year. But it's different because I expect you to make it personal. There are spaces for you to contemplate your relationship with God, track your growth, write your prayer requests, and dig into your Bible. There are a few things to note if you want these devotions to be meaningful for you.

First, these devotions are designed to be personal. Yes, you could read some of the stories with your friends or family, but on the whole, this book is designed to help you grow as an individual in your one-on-one relationship with Jesus. So pick a time that works for you to read these devotions, a time when you can be alone, not distracted by other people or things. For some people, this is in the early morning when they first wake up. When I was in high school, I usually did mine at night, since that's when my brain was most focused and I could concentrate on what I was reading or praying about.

Second, find a place to do your devotions that makes you feel comfortable. If you like to be warm, pick a blanket that you can always use during devotions, or make yourself a cup of tea or hot chocolate. If you prefer crisp mornings, try reading in a chair on your back porch, or open the window to your room for some fresh air. Whatever your preferences are, make yourself comfortable so that the things around you won't distract you.

Next, pick your Bible. Any version will work, but I prefer picking a version that is both easy to read and also has been translated accurately into my language. For example, though the King James Version is traditional in many churches, we don't speak in this way today, so it isn't the easiest to read. Some of my personal favorites are the New King James Version and the English Standard Version. Do some research on your own and pick a version of the Bible that fits you, and stick to that as you go through your devotions. When you come to places where you have questions or would like another perspective, try another version of the Bible and compare the two translations of the story.

Most importantly, make spending time in prayer a part of your daily devotions. Your relationship with God is meant to be multifaceted, just like your relationships with your friends, the person you're dating, your grandparents, or the neighbor next door. Your journey with God will be dynamic and alive—so don't limit it to one mode of communication! Try prayer, Bible reading, daily devotions, music, time in nature, journaling, art, and other things to grow in your walk with Jesus.

And lastly, make a commitment to God as you go through this devotional. If you skip a day on accident, don't beat yourself up over it. Instead, pick it back up again and keep going. Your relationship with God is something in motion, and the way you express praise and prayer may be different on some days than others. Listen to God, communicate with Him, and develop a plan that works best for you!

Be Doers

But be doers of the word,
and not hearers only, deceiving yourselves.
—James 1:22

Welcome to 2019! A new year has begun, and you are picking up a new devotional book. Perhaps this is the first one you have ever read, or maybe you are an avid reader of devotional books. Either way, this book is meant to help you on your daily walk with God. Every step forward in life matters, and I have personally prayed over this book, hoping that God would bless and spiritually grow every young person who reads it.

James 1:22 gives a challenge to Christians that I would like you to make your "mission statement" for 2019. Be a *doer* of the Word, not just a *hearer*. Hearers sit and listen in Sabbath School, attend church, and are fine enough people. However, if you are only a hearer, you do not put anything you are learning into practice. If there is a plate of your favorite meal in front of you, are you going to eat it or just look at it? Be a *doer*. Eat the meal; do not just stare at it.

Young people have a great potential for being influencers of change in the world. You might think it is the older people that really make a difference, but believe it or not, the voice of a teenager is much more powerful! If you were to get up and deliver a sermon at your church or start a small group Bible study or begin a community outreach program, it would shake the church into action in amazing ways! When people see a youth following God's call in their life to do big things, they will jump on board and support you!

As you walk the halls of your school this year, sit in church, or attend programs and hang out with friends, choose to be a *doer* of the Word. Live out your walk with God in your daily life, not just once a week at church. By *doing* God's Word, you can change the world!

Hitting the Refresh Button

"For I know the plans I have for you, declares the LORD,
plans for welfare and not for evil, to give you a future and a hope."
—Jeremiah 29:11

The spinning circle of a website refreshing is enough to cause stress in most people. We are accustomed to having everything at our fingertips, with instant access to all our heart's desires. While it is annoying to need to hit the refresh button, the reward is always worth it because you reach your intended destination online successfully!

The beginning of a new year is a great time to hit the refresh button on your life, especially your spiritual life. While nothing physically changes from December 31 to January 1, the significance of a new year triggers a desire within to start over and do better in the new year. We set goals, aim higher, and try to become healthier, happier people.

Once again, it is time to hit your refresh button. What is your destination? Where is it you want to be in life thirty years from now? Where do you want to be in your relationship with God? How do you imagine success? What expectations do you have for yourself or for God? How do you plan to hit the refresh button on your spiritual life and grow in Christ this year? Use the lines below to ponder these questions and write your spiritual goals for the new year:

_____

_____

_____

_____

_____

_____

_____

_____

How to Read the Bible

*"This Book of the Law shall not depart from your mouth, but you shall meditate on it day
and night, so that you may be careful to do according to all that is written in it.
For then you will make your way prosperous, and then you will have good success."*
—Joshua 1:8

One way to grow in your relationship with God is to have meaningful encounters with Scripture. The Bible is God's Word to us, His message. This Book holds life-giving secrets, so learning how to read it is important.

Have you ever heard of the word *exegesis*? The word is Greek, and it means "explanation." Essentially, *exegesis* of the Bible is interpreting it and learning the meaning of the passage. *Exegesis* focuses on the ancient text itself and what it means. Another important word, *hermeneutics*, is the theory and methodology of interpreting Scripture. So *hermeneutics* is the way you interpret the text. Although these big words may seem overwhelming, they can help you build a foundation for how you will study the Bible.

The Bible was written primarily in two languages, though a third language is used briefly. Hebrew makes up most of the Old Testament, though a small part is written in Aramaic. Both are Semitic languages, Hebrew being more Canaanite, and Aramaic being more Afro-Asiatic. The New Testament was written in Greek, an ancient language spoken in Asia Minor and used by scholars. Both Hebrew and Greek are still spoken today in their modern forms. You can think of it like the differences between reading Old English and street slang today—they come from the same original language but are spoken and understood very differently.

So when you approach a book of the Bible that you want to read, pay attention to where it is in the Bible. Is it in the Old Testament? Then its stories will be influenced by a Hebrew mind-set, with the cultures and customs of the time period influencing the way the author writes what God was inspiring them to say. Research when the book was written and what audience it first spoke to, and pay attention to the cultural nuances described in it. This will help your study of the Scriptures flourish beyond just a surface reading of verses, and you will delve into the Word with eyes wide open.

It Is All About Jesus

And the Word became flesh and dwelt among us, and we have seen his glory,
glory as of the only Son from the Father, full of grace and truth.
—John 1:14

It is all about Jesus. The entire Bible. Everything is all about Jesus. It is a new year, and you have a new chance to start over and make things right with Him. You have a chance to grow, learn, change, discover, and be everything you were ever made to be!

From Genesis to Revelation, the whole of Scripture points to the moment when Jesus hung on the cross. At that moment He conquered the devil forever, He won the war, and He made a way of salvation for us. Genesis begins with a fallen world in need of His saving grace. Exodus through Deuteronomy shows us the desperate search for morality and a relationship with the Creator that the Israelites went through in becoming "His people." The whole of the Old Testament shares story after story revealing sin's true nature and humanity's need for a Savior to take away this horrible sin problem. The Gospels of Matthew, Mark, Luke, and John tell us parables, miracles, and lessons from Jesus' life that reveal the character of the Savior who came down to earth to complete His mission. And the rest of the New Testament shares experience after experience of how life-transforming following Jesus can be. The struggles, victories, and theological questions still point to Jesus and a desire to be closer to Him.

So as you begin this year, I challenge you to read through your Bible. You can do it in one year by reading three to five chapters a day, and it is worth making the time for! Your life will be transformed. Your picture of God will be transformed. And your relationship with your Savior, Jesus Christ, will be transformed. God will become more than just the thing you talk about once a week in Sabbath School class. He will become the very air you breathe, the one you focus all your attention on, the whole point of your life! He will give you purpose, motivation, and excitement. A life with Him is thrilling! So hit the ground running, and commit yourself to Him this year.

Salvation Is Simple

"For God so loved the world, that he gave his only Son, that whoever believes in him should not perish but have eternal life. For God did not send his Son into the world to condemn the world, but in order that the world might be saved through him."
—John 3:16, 17

Study, take a test, get straight A's, become class president, work on the school leadership team, play sports, write killer essays, and get a great scholarship. Doing well in high school is grueling! You work all day long, and probably long into the night, trying to ace high school. You are told that in order to do well in life, you have to get good grades, all while learning life lessons and growing into a productive and successful young person.

Salvation is sometimes presented like the academic ladders we climb to succeed in school and a future career. You have got to go to church, know all the right answers in Bible class, always be kind, put others first, and understand Revelation in order to get into heaven. Your parents may have grown up in a generation saturated with the importance of works to get into heaven. Yet the Bible tells a different story: salvation is simple. The work is not on your end; that's God's responsibility.

John 3:16, a famous verse you probably memorized as a kid, explains the simplicity of faith in Christ and the salvation He gives us. Read verses 15–17: "That whoever believes in him may have eternal life. For God so loved the world, that he gave his only Son, that whoever believes in him should not perish but have eternal life. For God did not send his Son into the world to condemn the world, but in order that the world might be saved through him."

It is simple: salvation is a free gift. We do not have to "earn" our way into heaven. Our acts of goodness come as a result of our acceptance of that gift and the way we want to live our lives in response to God's outpouring of love on us!

The Story Begins

In the beginning, God created the heavens and the earth.
—Genesis 1:1

Throughout this book you will see a few running themes, all focused on drawing you closer to God. One of these running themes will be picking a story from every book of the Bible and focusing on how its message can benefit our walk with God today.

The story begins in Genesis 1:1: "In the beginning, God created the heavens and the earth." Before anything else, God existed. Before the universe, before life—in the beginning, God was. A Creator Being whose voice caused elements to combine and become matter. A Higher Power whose breath *is* life—and His words become living things. The universe was on His lips.

The book of Genesis tells the story of the beginning of the world, from its creation to the people God chose to use on earth. The first part of the book is all about God's relationship with the world and those He created, who sadly turned away from Him and chose to sin. The second part of the book hones in on a specific person, Abraham, and his descendants whom God chose to work through.

Throughout the book of Genesis, there is one common thread that we find near the beginning. When God creates people, He makes us "in his own image" (Genesis 1:27), meaning we are supposed to reflect the character of the Creator in the world. He gives us a special power that previously only He had—we are able to create life. As you read through Genesis, you will see how the devil tempted humans to thwart this power and sometimes use it in incredibly sinful ways, going against God's purpose for His creation.

Yet in the middle of this confusion and chaos in Genesis, there is a moment of hope: "I will put enmity between you and the woman, and between your offspring and her offspring; he shall bruise your head, and you shall bruise his heel" (Genesis 3:15). At this moment, God promises a Redeemer will come and crush the devil's head, meaning he will be eternally defeated by Jesus' death and resurrection. As you read the dramatic stories in the book of Genesis, you can be encouraged by those two main themes: (1) we are created to reflect the character of God, and (2) the Redeemer has already come, so we are saved from evil forever!

Proclaiming Christ

Some indeed preach Christ from envy and rivalry, but others from good will.
The latter do it out of love, knowing that I am put here for the defense of the gospel.
The former proclaim Christ out of selfish ambition, not sincerely but thinking to afflict me
in my imprisonment. What then? Only that in every way, whether in pretense or in truth,
Christ is proclaimed, and in that I rejoice. Yes, and I will rejoice.
—Philippians 1:15–18

Have you ever listened to a preacher and wondered what the true motivation for the sermon was? All preachers are human, and sometimes they fall into the trap of speaking on a topic with an ulterior motive rather than because they were moved by Christ to do so. It is easy to jump on the bandwagon of naysayers and critique them for what they preached about, but Paul has an interesting perspective to share here in Philippians.

As an apostle, Paul was frequently criticized. In addition, he had been imprisoned, beaten, and persecuted for proclaiming the gospel of Christ on his missionary trips. In this letter to the believers in Philippi, he makes the point that some people preach about Christ with an ulterior motive. However, does Paul get upset at their preaching? Nope. Instead, he rejoices! Above all else, he wants Christ to be proclaimed. At that time in history, most of the world did not yet know the good news about Christ. They had not heard the stories about this Man of Nazareth. They did not know about the Man who had healed the sick, helped the needy, stood up to Pharisees, and even raised the dead. News about Jesus, King of the Jews, who died on a cross and was raised again to life in three days, had not spread around the world, so Paul was eager for any word about Christ to get out there!

Today we need to take his message carefully. It is important that we seek to uplift Christ in our words and actions. Our focus should be on having a relationship with Him and spreading His love to a world in need. I hope that you will choose to be one of the ones who proclaim Christ out of a heart of goodwill and will rejoice when Christ's name is preached!

Basics for Belief: Theology

Therefore let us leave the elementary doctrine of Christ and go on to maturity.
—Hebrews 6:1

What is *theology*? This word means "the study of God." *Theos* means "God" in Greek, and any word with *-ology* on the end means "the study of" something. Theology is the way that we learn about and experience God intellectually. We use the beautiful minds He created us with to study Him and learn more about Him. As you grow in your own experience with God this year, we'll have a few sections of this devotional dedicated to expanding your own theology. Forming a foundation for your basic beliefs is important in helping determine how you relate to the world around you.

Let's start with natural theology. Natural theology is a combination of philosophy and theology that gives arguments for the existence of God based on things you can experience in nature or facts you can observe. It uses human reason to try to prove God's existence and define His attributes.

General revelation, on the other hand, is knowledge about God that any person can experience. This would include your conscience, the ability to tell between right and wrong. It includes the laws of nature that we observe in the universe, which tell us about God's wisdom, power, and greatness.

Can you think of ways you have already used these two types of theology in your system of belief? Have you ever marveled at the detail on a butterfly's wings and thought about the amazing Creator we have? Observing the laws of motion or the intricacies of the human body can give us a glimpse into God's desire for order and perfection as well as His attention to detail. Maybe you have even had a philosophical conversation with a friend that led to each of you understanding a bit more about God and His role in your lives. As you begin your journey with Him this year, commit yourself to watch for evidence of Him in the things you see around you every day. His fingerprints are everywhere!

Reckless Love

There is no fear in love, but perfect love casts out fear. For fear has to do with punishment, and whoever fears has not been perfected in love. We love because he first loved us.
—1 John 4:18, 19

Oh, the overwhelming, never-ending, reckless love of God. Oh, it chases me down, fights 'till I am found, leaves the ninety-nine. I could not earn it, I do not deserve it, still You give Yourself away. Oh, the overwhelming, never-ending, reckless love of God."

These lyrics, written by the worship band Bethel Music, have echoed in hearts around the world. Sometimes Christians are raised to think that they must earn God's love and that His favor and blessings come as a result of our good behavior and always doing what is right. While these actions will lead to fewer negative consequences in life, they will not earn us God's love.

The crazy part about God's love is that it is truly reckless, as the song says. God goes against the grain of what love typically looks like in our world. He seems to love more fiercely and deeply despite how far we run from Him. His love is so powerful that it can pull us back from the darkest places. He does not look at us with anger and judgment in His eyes when we mess up. Instead, He sees us as His broken children whom He wants to wrap His arms around, dry our tears, and comfort us through the pain we bring on ourselves. His heart is overwhelmed with love for us, so He does crazy things to get us back!

God's love is not something you need to worry about earning. It is already there for you no matter what you have done. It is reckless because it will chase you down those dark alleys and into those places you do not want anyone to see you go. His love will fight against all the evils around you to win you back.

Jesus Gives Me Hope

"And you will feel secure, because there is hope;
you will look around and take your rest in security."
—Job 11:18

A relationship with Jesus will change your life in ways you cannot imagine. By picking up this devotional every morning, you are taking one step in your journey of building a meaningful relationship with Him. Each month there will be at least one "Jesus Gives Me . . ." devotion for you to read through, and today we're starting with hope!

A relationship with Jesus has given me hope in the darkest times. When I was broken up with unexpectedly in college, Jesus became the source of my hope in a better relationship in the future. When I watched a little boy pass away from a stroke, I had to hold on to hope in Jesus that the resurrection would be soon! When I was writing this book, I had to keep my hope in Jesus that He would give me inspiration to fill each page. Jesus' hope can carry you through anything.

Hope is more than just a feeling you get in your heart when you hear some good news. It is a choice to look forward and trust that God is in control, especially when you cannot see what is next. When you come to what seems like a wall that is blocking your path, hope in Jesus that He will get you over it. When you cannot understand why people are acting in such an unkind way, Jesus will give you hope of better friendships down the road. When a certain teacher seems to want to fail you in their class, hope in Jesus to help you study hard and pass the class anyway. As you continue to grow in your relationship with Him, what do you need hope for right now? Take a moment to journal and pray about it below:

_____

_____

_____

_____

Double Black Diamonds

"Even to your old age I am he,
and to gray hairs I will carry you.
I have made, and I will bear;
I will carry and will save."
—Isaiah 46:4

My father taught me to ski when I was very little. I remember going down the bunny slope with him slowly, very slowly, with him encouraging me to keep trying. He corrected me when I had improper form. He helped me up when I fell down. He caught me if I was going too fast and lost control. Then one day I was able to fly down the mountain right beside him.

Now that I am an adult, skiing with my family is a treat. At the end of one ski trip, we split off into smaller groups to head back to the place we were staying. As my group was on our way back, we accidentally took a wrong turn and ended up going down one of the hardest runs in the area! Since none of us are pros at skiing, it took us a while to get down the mountain. There were lots of tumbling, sliding, rolling, and falling and a few screams too! But we knew we could not give up; we had to keep going and make it to the bottom, or we'd be stuck on the mountain with no way out.

Skiing through life can be difficult. You might take a wrong turn and get into a situation that feels like a double black diamond ski slope. That ski slope could look like a party you were invited to, knowing there would be alcohol present. It could look like the class you chose to skip out on. It could look like the time you said nasty things about that one person. But it could also look like this: Your Father catching you when you go too fast, picking you up when you fall down. Your heavenly Dad skiing right beside you, encouraging you on as you slowly navigate through your teenage years. You might not have picked the slope, but He will be right there with you through the whole thing.

Interpreting Scripture

All Scripture is breathed out by God and profitable for teaching, for reproof,
for correction, and for training in righteousness,
that the man of God may be complete, equipped for every good work.
—2 Timothy 3:16, 17

Understanding the Bible is essential to a thriving intellectual relationship with God's Word. Yes, any person can read it and gain a blessing from it whether they have formal theological training or not. But if you want to go deep into the Word, you have to know how to approach it and read it.

First, we need the Holy Spirit. He is the only one who can truly help us interpret what we are reading in Scripture. Next, we need to pay attention to the context and time frame that Bible stories were written in. Ask yourself what cultural setting the story happens in and what audience is being written to.

When I was on a mission trip to the Dominican Republic in high school, I had to speak Spanish if I wanted to communicate with anyone at the church I spoke at. I had taken two years of Spanish in high school, but I still did not know very much. While I knew enough conversational language to get by, I definitely did not have a deep understanding of the language or culture that I was visiting. Having a knowledge of those things can be extremely helpful in communicating effectively and building relationships with people.

The Bible is the same way. To understand it deeply and build a relationship with God through His Word, you must be led by the Holy Spirit and take time to study it. God will communicate with you through the Bible if you just take the time to open its pages and dive into its message.

When God Burns

And the angel of the LORD appeared to him in a flame of fire out of the midst of a bush. He looked, and behold, the bush was burning, yet it was not consumed. And Moses said, "I will turn aside to see this great sight, why the bush is not burned." When the LORD saw that he turned aside to see, God called to him out of the bush, "Moses, Moses!" And he said, "Here I am." Then he said, "Do not come near; take your sandals off your feet, for the place on which you are standing is holy ground." And he said, "I am the God of your father, the God of Abraham, the God of Isaac, and the God of Jacob." And Moses hid his face, for he was afraid to look at God.
—Exodus 3:2–6

Moses is a man whose biblical narrative constantly amazes me. His life was so unique. He started out as a Hebrew slave's baby, then was adopted by the Pharaoh's daughter. He was raised both by his own mother then in the palace as a young prince. Eventually he killed a man and ran away to the desert to escape execution. The first forty years of his life were incredibly tumultuous, and yet God orchestrated his existence in order to build a nation.

For all the fame and glory Moses gets, he was a flawed individual. His life is proof that God can use anyone to do His work. When God appeared to Moses through a burning bush, Moses must have been filled with awe. God called to him in a miraculous way, proving His power. Moses' life had been riddled with powerful individuals seeking control over his life, yet God's call would be one of freedom. God would use Moses to lead Israel out of slavery and into the Promised Land of Canaan!

Your God is powerful, and He has a plan for you. Take the sandals off your feet and stand in His presence today. When God calls, pay attention! He will make His presence known in your life and set you on a path to freedom from all that oppresses you!

Basics for Belief:
Special Revelation

"He is your praise. He is your God, who has done for you
these great and terrifying things that your eyes have seen."
—Deuteronomy 10:21

In our last "basics for belief" devotional, we discussed general revelation and natural theology, which both look at the things observed in nature that show evidence of a Creator. Today we'll explore a new term: *special revelation*. This is another theological idea that refers to knowledge about God that comes through supernatural means. Some examples of this would be when Daniel received visions from God or when King Nebuchadnezzar, an unbeliever at that time, was given dreams by God.

Special revelation is when miracles, things outside of the laws of nature, happen or a discovery of God's truth through things outside of what human logic understands occurs. Scripture is also special revelation because God communicates with us through the Bible! If we were to identify who in the Godhead is most involved in special revelation, it would probably be the Holy Spirit. He is the one who enters into human affairs and pierces the human heart with conviction. Jesus' life on earth would also be a very real example of special revelation, when God literally came to earth in human form and performed miracles that revealed His divinity before our very eyes.

Have you ever experienced God through special revelation? Has He shown Himself to you in a special way? While God does not speak to everyone in such a direct way, you would be surprised how many people have experienced a miracle. In your next Sabbath School class or youth group meeting, ask how many people have witnessed a miracle or know someone who has. Share your stories and encourage one another with these experiences of God!

Holy Temples

Or do you not know that your body is a temple of the Holy Spirit within you, whom you have
from God? You are not your own, for you were bought with a price. So glorify God in your body.
—1 Corinthians 6:19, 20

What does it mean to live a holy life? Typically, you'd think *holiness* means moral perfection. And since God is morally perfect, that makes sense—mostly. However, there is more to holiness than just following the rules—that's not really the essence of its meaning and purpose at all.

God's holiness is something so good it actually has the power to harm us. But that has nothing to do with God; it is simply because we are unholy, imperfect, impure beings. In the Old Testament, whenever God's presence was among men, such as in the tabernacle or the temple, it was highly guarded. You could not walk into God's presence after burying a dead relative because you had touched something unclean, and in a sense, its impurity had contaminated you. Think of it like having a cold. You get a cold from germs, so washing your hands is important to keep germs away. Likewise, God gave the Israelites instructions on how to cleanse themselves after coming in contact with something unholy. The reason for the prescribed cleansing was that if they walked into God's presence while impure, they would die. Impurity cannot exist in God's presence because He is completely perfect and pure. So anything that goes against that would be obliterated instantly.

However, because God wanted to connect with His people, He made a way for sinful humanity to approach Him. When Jesus came to earth, He touched the people Israelites considered impure and unclean based on the Old Testament rules. Jesus transformed the idea of how impurity transfers by showing that since He is perfect and holy, anything He touches takes on His holiness. Instead of the uncleanness of the lepers transferring to Jesus, holiness works the other way around—His holiness cleansed the lepers and healed them, making them clean and able to enter into God's presence!

So your holiness is not based on what you do to make yourself clean and morally pure in God's eyes. It comes from Jesus transferring His holiness to you. That's what it means to be a temple of God.

Eating With Sinners

Now the tax collectors and sinners were all drawing near to hear him. And the Pharisees and the scribes grumbled, saying, "This man receives sinners and eats with them."
—Luke 15:1, 2

One Sabbath morning I stood near the back of the church, watching as everyone sang and enjoyed the beginning of the service. One older gentleman in the congregation came through the doors and came over to greet me before sitting down. About three rows in front of us was a very overweight woman wearing somewhat revealing clothing. The man leaned over to me and commented nastily, "She should cover up in church. Does she not know how ugly she is? I do not want to have to see that in church." I was shocked and firmly expressed to him that speaking that way about another person was completely inappropriate.

This situation reminded me a bit of how the Pharisees and scribes sometimes grumbled about Jesus and the company He kept. They did not like the fact that He always hung out with people they considered the worst of sinners. And worse, He ate with them, something they thought should be reserved for people who are clean and good! Eating with sinners was like accepting and befriending them.

While we might laugh at the Pharisees and scribes who missed the point of Jesus' ministry of love, how often do we do the same thing? Have you ever gossiped about someone? Do you criticize people for what they wear to church or who they hang out with? Sometimes we do not accept the people who are on the fringes of church life because we are afraid of how our reputation might look if we associate with them. Jesus did not care about these social constructs. He broke every rule to meet sinners where they were and draw them to Himself and His holiness. We should strive to draw others closer to Christ as we draw closer to Him ourselves.

The Letter of the Law

*"If you obey the commandments of the LORD your God that I command you today,
by loving the LORD your God, by walking in his ways, and by keeping his commandments
and his statutes and his rules, then you shall live and multiply, and the LORD your God
will bless you in the land that you are entering to take possession of it."*

—Deuteronomy 30:16

*L*aws are usually important things meant to keep us safe and keep life in our towns running smoothly. Sometimes, though, laws can seem downright ridiculous and make you wonder what happened to make them need that law? Here are a few funny ones I found:

- In New Hampshire, USA, you will get a violation if you attempt to collect seaweed at night.*
- In Toronto, Canada, you may be fined up to $5,000 if you have more than two garage sales in one year.†
- In Fresno, California, USA, you are not allowed to annoy lizards in a city park.‡

These laws are both hilarious and confusing. Who was collecting seaweed at night? Why only two garage sales per year? And those poor lizards must have had a rough life if a law needs to be written for them!

Do God's laws ever seem ridiculous to you? We often call the Ten Commandments "laws," but each one of them was set up to protect us from hurting ourselves or others. All God's laws originate from a place of love. He wants us to keep His laws so that we can have a better relationship with Him and, as a result, a better relationship with those around us also.

Keeping God's laws will not get you into heaven. Assuming that is like saying turning in your homework will pay for your hot lunch bill; the two do not equate! Jesus gives you salvation and promises you heaven. You do your homework to get an education, learn more, and, yes, get good grades, but ultimately to graduate with a degree that shows you have learned a lot! Likewise, you follow God's laws so that you can live a moral life, happy and free from worry because God has given you the keys to live it successfully.

---

* Emmie Martin, Christina Sterbenz, and Melia Robinson, "The 17 Strangest Laws in America," *Business Insider,* updated Mar. 6, 2015, http://www.businessinsider.com/strangest-most-ridiculous-laws-in-america-2015-3.

† "Six Strange Canadian Laws Still on the Books," CTV News, updated Aug. 4, 2017, https://www.ctvnews.ca/canada/six-strange-canadian-laws-still-on-the-books-1.3533115.

‡ "Dumb Laws in California," Dumb Laws, accessed May 27, 2018, http://www.dumblaws.com/laws/united-states/california?page=20.

Climbing Walls

The LORD upholds all who are falling
and raises up all who are bowed down.
—Psalm 145:14

A school was built near the house I grew up in, and since the school was on a hill, there were some cement walls with fences at the top that supported the soil where the playground was built. As a kid, I loved to climb up on top of those walls with my friends and walk along the cement blocks, high above the grass and sidewalks below. Holding on to the fence and keeping your balance was the only way to keep from falling. Looking back now, I realize that climbing those walls was probably dangerous!

Recently my mom saw a little girl playing with her mother at those same walls. The little girl ran up the hill and climbed up onto the first wall, hold-

ing the fence as she walked along. The wall rose higher and higher, and so her mother followed below her, watching her daughter's every step carefully. As the little girl reached the other end of the wall, her mother asked whether she needed help getting down. Her high-pitched voice gave an emphatic, "No!"

Kids love to do things all by themselves, and that's how they learn. But all the while that little girl's mother was ready to catch her if she fell off the wall. God is always watching and waiting. He is ready and willing to catch us when we fall. Even when we insist on trying things on our own, His arms are always ready. He walks with us as we try new things and figure out life. What wall did you climb today? If you are having trouble seeing a way to get down from the problems you created for yourself, trust God and jump into His arms! He will catch you and help you recover from the ordeal you put yourself through.

The Nicodemus Dilemma

Jesus answered him, "Truly, truly, I say to you,
unless one is born again he cannot see the kingdom of God."
—John 3:3

Nicodemus was a Pharisee who had watched Jesus' ministry from a distance. He heard about the things Jesus was teaching, and he was curious what this Man was all about. One night Nicodemus met with Jesus and asked him a life-changing question: "Rabbi, we know that you are a teacher come from God, for no one can do these signs that you do unless God is with him" (John 3:2).

By calling Jesus "Rabbi," Nicodemus was attributing Him the respect of being a teacher of the Jewish religion—an element of respect most Pharisees did not give Him. In response, Jesus tells Nicodemus that humans must be born again. Naturally, Nicodemus asks, "How can a man be born when he is old? Can he enter a second time into his mother's womb and be born?" (John 3:4).

Jesus' laughter probably floated softly into the night after this question. Of course, being born again does not mean a literal, physical birth! Jesus clarifies in John 3:5 that you have to be "born of water and the Spirit" to enter God's kingdom. Today we recognize this as baptism—the public act that shows you have chosen to follow God with your whole life—and accepting His Spirit into your heart to guide you.

If you have been baptized, you may remember what it felt like to go under the water and the excitement you felt after your baptism. But as the days passed, was anything that different? Being born again is not about instantly being a different person; it is about the trajectory of your life. It means you have made the choice to walk toward Jesus instead of away from Him, even when you mess up.

Basics for Belief: Canon

For whatever was written in former days was written for our instruction,
that through endurance and through the encouragement of the Scriptures we might have hope.
—Romans 15:4

Have you ever thought about reading the Bible Jesus would have read when He was on earth? It is possible, you know! The Old Testament in your Bible was translated from the Hebrew Scriptures, which were put together by Jewish religious leaders long before Jesus ministered on earth. These Scriptures were considered holy to the Jewish people, and they were taught in every home and synagogue. Jesus would have grown up very familiar with the stories of the Old Testament and the traditions handed down from generation to generation.

When the entire Christian Bible, Old and New Testaments, is put together, it is called the "canon of Scripture." This term *canon* comes from the Greek word κανών, which means "rule" or "measuring stick." Christians in the fifth century A.D., after Christ was on earth, brought together the books of the Old and New Testaments into one canon of Scripture, or the Bible. During the Council of Trent in 1546, the Hebrew Scriptures and the gospels and letters of the New Testament were confirmed as canon.

Throughout the hundreds of years that theologians and church leaders debated which books should be included in the Bible, God led. Ultimately, we believe that the Bible is inspired by Him and that He led those leaders to pick the texts He had inspired and preserved for thousands of years so that you and I could read them today. Your Bible is incredible. It has survived wars, harsh weather conditions, and thousands of years of history. Yet you are able to have it on your shelf today and pick it up to read anytime you want! Take a moment now and do that.

Martin Luther King Jr. Day

*But if you show partiality, you are committing sin
and are convicted by the law as transgressors.*
—James 2:9
*Our lives begin to end the day we become silent
about things that matter.*
—Martin Luther King Jr.

Martin Luther King Jr. was a man who shook the world. Through peaceful protest, he stood up against racism and preached about a day when a black child and a white child could be friends in the same classroom and be presented with equal opportunities. He dreamed of a day when there would be no more segregation based on the color of someone's skin. He prayed for a time when people would be judged by the content of their character instead of their appearance or country of origin.

Is our world becoming better or worse in this regard? It is easy to want to say, "Oh, the world is better now! We do not have segregation laws anymore, there are not slaves anymore, people can go to any school they want, we all have equal opportunities no matter what our skin color." And in some places, yes, this is true. But in many places, it is false. And we as Christians cannot be silent about this. As King's quote reminds us: silence about what matters is unacceptable.

It is time to do your part to make it better. Cross cultural barriers and befriend people who do not look or talk like you. Speak up when you see injustice. Be like Jesus, unafraid to confront the issues in His society, working to find ways to fix them.

Lithium-Ion Gods—Part 1

"You shall have no other gods before me."
—Exodus 20:3

Throughout this book we'll look at the heart of the Ten Commandments God gave to Moses on Mount Sinai and what they mean for us today. The commandments are the guidelines for what it means to live a holy, God-led life. Keeping them is not just about following an old set of rules our parents taught us as kids; it is about loving God. We keep the commandments to show Him our love and to let His love shine through us to the world.

The first thing to note about the Ten Commandments is their order. They start by talking about our relationship with God. The first four directly deal with loving God. The last six deal with our relationship to other people on this earth and loving those around us. Following these principles leads to a happy, healthy, well-balanced life.

Today let's start with commandment number one: "You shall have no other gods before me" (Exodus 20:3). If you keep reading, you will see that this instruction ties in very well with the second one in this list. The Israelites who were raised in Egypt lived in a society that had a very different set of religious ideas than they did. The Israelites were monotheistic, meaning they believed in one God. The Egyptians surrounding them were polytheistic, believing in many gods. Idols, temples, and religious rituals of these religions were constantly in their view in Egypt. Tomorrow we'll discuss this in more detail. For today, I want to encourage you to journal about these questions:

1. What does it mean to you to "have no other gods" before our God?

_____

2. How do you think our current society relates to the societies of the Israelites and Egyptians?

_____

3. What are today's "other gods" that influence society in large ways?

_____

4. What specific "other gods" influence your life and your relationship with God?

_____

Lithium-Ion Gods—Part 2

"For you shall worship no other god, for the LORD,
whose name is Jealous, is a jealous God."
—Exodus 34:14

When the Israelites escaped slavery in Egypt, they had an identity crisis. These Israelites had never traveled outside the land where they grew up. Their whole life had been in service to Egypt. They could hardly comprehend freedom. Part of their identity crisis meant they struggled in their relationship with God. Suddenly He had whipped them out of their crisis in a grand display of His miraculous power. Why would God need to ask them to have no other gods before Him? Would it not be obvious He was the greatest of all?

Despite God's displays of love and protection, the Israelites very quickly became nostalgic about their days in Egypt. People often revert to what is most familiar. While Moses was up on Mount Sinai, what were they doing in the valley below? Creating an idol! That's one reason God gave the commandment to steer clear of any other gods. Worshiping other gods was clearly something they struggled with, so He gave an instruction to avoid it.

Today we are not surrounded by a culture that worships entirely in one religion. There are hundreds of religions in the world today, and much of the society surrounding us is more secular than religious anyway! So does this commandment still apply?

It does, because we have replaced gods made of stone and wood with gods made of fame, fortune, and lithium ion. We idolize Instagram models and Snapchat stars who share glimpses of their fabulous lifestyles. And secretly, we do want to be like them. We want to have rich lives, be able to buy and do anything we want—without consequences. Our devices and desires have become our idols.

Have you ever thought about how to curb the influence these things have on you? Take a few moments now to ignore the electronics and the world you access through them and analyze how your connection to them influences your connection to God. Taking time away from your "other gods" to connect with the one true God is worth the relationship you will build with Him.

High Sun

Every good gift and every perfect gift is from above,
coming down from the Father of lights,
with whom there is no variation or shadow due to change.
—James 1:17

When light from the sun is blocked, shadows are created. They cast an image on the ground, an outline of something, only darker and less defined than the object itself. However, when the sun is directly above you at noon, there are no shadows. When the sun is high in the sky, nothing blocks its path, and no sideways shadows are seen.

Shadows in life can be moments of doubt or fear, times when we are sad about something, or times when we have pushed God away. When we do not let Him near, the shadows start to creep in and take over, growing longer as the day wears on.

What is blocking your Light Source today and causing shadows to be cast on your path? What is standing between you and a thriving relationship with God? Take a moment and write them here:

_____

_____

Recognizing what is creating the shadow is the first step in making it disappear. If you choose to elevate Christ and put Him first, the things blocking your Light Source will be forced to disappear. Nothing can stand in the way of Christ and His powerful presence! He is our "Sonshine," and when we choose to keep Him high in our life, like the sun at noonday, then the shadows in our path will disappear!

In the Wilderness

And all the people of Israel grumbled against Moses and Aaron.
The whole congregation said to them, "Would that we had died in the land of Egypt!
Or would that we had died in this wilderness!"
—Numbers 14:2

Have you ever opened the book of Numbers voluntarily? If you skim through its pages, it sounds like a really boring book with a really boring name. Why would you read about math if you do not have to, right? But check out the original Hebrew name for this book: *Bamidbar*, meaning "in the wilderness." That sounds epic! A journey through Numbers reveals tragedy and triumph, and most of all, a God who continued to love and lead His people even when they forsook Him repeatedly.

This book in the wilderness begins by organizing and counting up the people by families and clans and giving them a few more life pointers before leaving the region around Mount Sinai. As the Israelites start their journey, there is enthusiasm in the air—finally, they were traveling to the Promised Land! However, only three days into their journey, the grumbling and complaining started. If you have ever gone backpacking for three days, you can probably relate! Your legs are sore, you wonder whether you will ever really reach your destination. Whose idea was this anyway? The Israelites blamed Moses for their discomforts, and they wanted to go back to Egypt. Chaos ensues after twelve spies go into the land of Canaan to scout it out, and all but two come back with bad stories. Because of their lack of faith in God's ability to conquer the land for them, He lets them have their consequence: wandering in the wilderness for forty more years.

However, through all their grumbling and complaining, God remained faithful to them. He let them make their own choice to walk away from Him, but He still took care of them even while they did that. He provided them with miracles, such as manna from heaven and water from a rock. In the final section of the book, God even uses Balaam, a man trying to pronounce curses on Israel, to offer a blessing over them. By the end of the book, they have reached the end of the forty years in the wilderness, and it is finally time for all of them to enter the Promised Land.

God gives us chance after chance when we mess up, and despite the many times we try to push Him away, He *still* comes after us, provides for us, loves us, and protects us.

Lord of the Sabbath

On a Sabbath, while he was going through the grainfields, his disciples plucked
and ate some heads of grain, rubbing them in their hands. But some of the Pharisees said,
"Why are you doing what is not lawful to do on the Sabbath?" And Jesus answered them,
"Have you not read what David did when he was hungry, he and those who were with him:
how he entered the house of God and took and ate the bread of the Presence,
which is not lawful for any but the priests to eat, and also gave it to those with him?"
And he said to them, "The Son of Man is lord of the Sabbath."
—Luke 6:1–5

Keeping the Sabbath is a cornerstone of Adventist faith and tradition. However, do you think we sometimes turn it into a day of dos and don'ts in order to please our own agenda of holiness? Think about why you choose to keep the Sabbath and why your parents have said they choose to keep the Sabbath. Do not let it be just another day for you, but rather, let it be a time of special communion with God. Rather than a day of dos and don'ts, view it as a day of worshiping and rejoicing!

Jesus flipped the Jewish view of the Sabbath completely upside down when He was on earth. The religious leaders had turned it into a day that had so many rules, people hardly knew what to do to keep it correctly! It was probably a very frustrating time to be one of God's chosen people. Jesus viewed the Sabbath in a much more practical way, and He wanted it to be a day of experiencing time with God, not stifling it. So on the Sabbath, He let His disciples pick grain and eat it. When the Pharisees got upset about this, Jesus' response showed His place as the Son of God and His original intent for the Sabbath. He did not care about a tiny movement like picking grain that could be perceived as "work." He cared much more about spending time fellowshiping with His disciples! His proclamation "The Son of Man is lord of the Sabbath" showed His true purpose: to reclaim the day that belonged to Him and turn it from a day of rules and regulations to a day of joy and fellowship. Choose to spend this Sabbath with Jesus this week!

Basics for Belief: Text

And we impart this in words not taught by human wisdom
but taught by the Spirit, interpreting spiritual truths to those who are spiritual.
—1 Corinthians 2:13

How deeply do you think about the words you use when you text a friend? Do you sometimes sit there and go back and forth between different ways to say the same idea? The words you choose to use matter. And the order you place your ideas in, as well as your style of writing, say something about how you are thinking and what you want the reader to understand or perceive about your message to them. I hope that you do not think this in-depth about every text you send! But understanding how language is used can not only change the way you communicate, it can also completely transform your understanding of the Bible!

Every book of the Bible is written in a different style. If you were to examine the grammar and syntax of a section of Scripture, you would understand something deeper about the author's intent in that passage. Grammar is analyzing the structure of a language, and syntax is looking at how words are arranged in a sentence. Since the Bible is written in Hebrew, Aramaic, and Greek, theologians like to study these original languages to understand why biblical authors chose to say things the way they did. If you want to get deeper into biblical translation and understanding the original language, you do not need to know Greek, just go to a site like biblehub.com and search for the passage you are interested in! Study guides can give you insights into Scripture you may not have seen before.

Here are a few things you can do to study a Bible text in depth: Choose words that are important to the meaning of the story, like verbs or significant nouns. Then search a Greek or Hebrew lexicon, dictionary, or concordance to figure out the range of meanings that word has in its original language. Figure out how many times a word is used in your text, that book, or the entire Bible—this might show you how important its meaning is to the author! While God did not dictate word-for-word every sentence of the Bible, He certainly inspired authors to phrase things in certain ways. And understanding why will enrich your reading of Scripture. Pick your favorite passage and give it a try!

We Believe: *Sola Scriptura*

Every word of God proves true; he is a shield to those who take refuge in him.
—Exodus 30:5

Sola scriptura! Essentially it means "only Scripture!" The Seventh-day Adventist Church believes that the Bible is the Word of God and is above all other writings about God.

Where did this idea of "the Bible only" come from? It was born out of the Protestant Reformation, which occurred during a time when many churchgoers could not read the Bible for themselves but had to rely on priests to read and interpret its meaning for them. Can you imagine going to church and having no Bibles to read? Or even if there were Bibles, only having them in a language you did not know? That's what it was like for many Christians in the Middle Ages. Unfortunately, not all priests were honest, good folk, and because people were forced to rely on them to tell them what the Bible said, essentially, they could make it say whatever they wanted! Many people were deceived because they could not read the Bible for themselves. Instead, they relied on tradition and the local priest or bishop as their sources of knowledge about God and religion.

Because so many people were being led astray by traditions that had no basis in the Bible, some Protestant Reformers were called by God to carry forward the message that the Bible should be the only source of authority on God, faith, and religion. This movement led to the many translations of the Bible that we have today!

This is what the Fundamental Beliefs of Seventh-day Adventists, or the bases for our faith, says about the Bible:

The Holy Scriptures, Old and New Testaments, are the written Word of God, given by divine inspiration. The inspired authors spoke and wrote as they were moved by the Holy Spirit. In this Word, God has committed to humanity the knowledge necessary for salvation. The Holy Scriptures are the supreme, authoritative, and the infallible revelation of His will. They are the standard of character, the test of experience, the definitive revealer of doctrines, and the trustworthy record of God's acts in history. (Ps. 119:105; Prov. 30:5, 6; Isa. 8:20; John 17:17; 1 Thess. 2:13; 2 Tim. 3:16, 17; Heb. 4:12; 2 Peter 1:20, 21.)*

---

* Seventh-day Adventist Church, "The Holy Scriptures," in *28 Fundamental Beliefs* (General Conference of Seventh-day Adventists, 2015), 3, https://szu.adventist.org/wp-content/uploads/2016/04/28_Beliefs.pdf.

The Seventh Hour

The official said to him, "Sir, come down before my child dies." Jesus said to him,
"Go; your son will live." The man believed the word that Jesus spoke to him
and went on his way. As he was going down, his servants met him and told him that his son
was recovering. So he asked them the hour when he began to get better, and they said to him,
"Yesterday at the seventh hour the fever left him." The father knew that was the hour when Jesus
had said to him, "Your son will live." And he himself believed, and all his household.
—John 4:49–53

*A*t the seventh hour, a child was saved. The man who brought news of his son's impending death to Jesus was a Jewish official, not a common citizen. He had heard of this Healer, this Jesus of Nazareth, and he already believed this Man would save his son. It was this official's unwavering faith in Jesus that ultimately healed his son. When Jesus spoke with the man, his belief was instant. He needed no prodding, no convincing, no miraculous sign. Before he even knew whether his son was healed, the verse tells us he believed the word Jesus spoke to him. Before he saw the sign . . .

How often do you ask God for a sign proving His reality to you? We are not very good at having faith in things we cannot see. Incredibly, this official believed in Jesus *before* he witnessed a sign or a miracle. Jesus said his son would be healed, and he believed. Others in his household also believed because they saw the healing taking place and then discovered it happened at the exact time the boy's father had talked to the Healer.

Belief sometimes seems to be easier for those who have no prior experience. For those who were raised in the church, sometimes it is hard to believe in miraculous events because they do not happen every day. However, do not let your desire for an obvious sign be what holds you back from having a dynamic, faith-based relationship with Jesus. Have faith that what He has spoken in His Word will happen! His promises will be fulfilled, and He will take care of you.

His Great Nation

"For what great nation is there that has a god so near to it as the LORD our God is to us,
whenever we call upon him? And what great nation is there,
that has statutes and rules so righteous as all this law that I set before you today?"
—Deuteronomy 4:7, 8

The Old Testament book of Deuteronomy begins with Moses recounting the travels of the children of Israel after escaping Egypt. He tells the story of their entire journey up until that point, reminding them of God's faithfulness even when they turned away from Him, over and over again throughout their forty years in the wilderness! Moses gives this long address to the people right before they finally enter the Promised Land.

The book is filled with stories, laws, instructions, and a final send-off where Joshua is appointed as the new leader for the children of Israel. The book ends, sadly, with Moses' death on top of Mount Nebo, which overlooks the Jordan River where the Jewish people would cross and enter the Promised Land. However, Moses' statement in chapter 4 reminds them of the whole purpose of his long speech. Moses knows their mission: to be a nation that reflects the power and intimacy of their God. The nations around them worshiped multiple gods made of wood and stone, idols that could do nothing for them. The Hebrew God was not confined by geographical location, and He lived among the people—completely different from any of the other gods of the religions around them!

This God that led the Israelites is the same one who wants to have a close relationship with you as well. He wants the people around you to be amazed at a God who is near whenever you call on Him. He wants your relationship with Him to inspire others to follow the same path in their hearts and open their lives to Him as well. Give Him a chance to lead you!

Praise Him

A key part of your growing relationship with God is learning to express emotion to Him and not being afraid to say anything to Him. He can handle it all! A great way to start doing this is by reading through the Psalms. So today read the following psalm, pray, reflect.

As a deer pants for flowing streams,
    so pants my soul for you, O God.
My soul thirsts for God,
    for the living God.
When shall I come and appear before God? . . .
These things I remember,
    as I pour out my soul:
how I would go with the throng
    and lead them in procession to the house of God
with glad shouts and songs of praise,
    a multitude keeping festival.

Why are you cast down, O my soul,
    and why are you in turmoil within me?
Hope in God; for I shall again praise him,
    my salvation and my God.

My soul is cast down within me;
    therefore I remember you. . . .
By day the Lord commands his steadfast love,
    and at night his song is with me,
    a prayer to the God of my life. . . .
As with a deadly wound in my bones,
    my adversaries taunt me,
while they say to me all the day long,
    "Where is your God?"

Why are you cast down, O my soul,
    and why are you in turmoil within me?
Hope in God; for I shall again praise him,
    my salvation and my God (Psalm 42).

Puppy Love

He shall cover you with His feathers,
and under His wings you shall take refuge;
His truth shall be your shield and buckler.
—Psalm 91:4, NKJV

A viral video that circulated on Facebook a few years back caught my attention. A mama dog had just given birth to a litter of puppies and appeared tired, though excited, about the new lives she had just brought into the world. Sitting in a chair nearby was her proud owner. One by one, the mama dog gently picked up the puppies and brought them over to her owner, placing them in her arms. Once all the puppies had gingerly been given to her owner, the dog rested her head on her owner's stomach, the puppies crawling all over her face and the owner.

At that moment the mama dog showed how much she trusted her owner. It was as if she was recognizing that parenting is a huge responsibility, and she did not want to do it alone! She wanted her master to help her take care of them. She trusted her master with the most important thing in her life: her babies.

There are two things we can take from this story. First, we should trust God with the most important things in our life. Our vulnerable points should be trusted to Him because He can handle them far better than we can. Second, this is much like what parents do when they dedicate their child to God in a church. If you were dedicated as a baby, take a moment to thank your parents for raising you in God's love. If you do not have that kind of family life, remember that God is your ultimate Father and that His love is far more fulfilling than anything this earth can give.

Joshua's Exaltation

"And when the soles of the feet of the priests bearing the ark of the LORD,
the Lord of all the earth, shall rest in the waters of the Jordan, the waters of the Jordan
shall be cut off from flowing, and the waters coming down from above shall stand in one heap."
—Joshua 3:13

After the death of Moses, the traveling nation of Israel probably felt in disarray. God had been preparing Joshua for this time, training him under Moses and giving him leadership abilities to bring the people successfully into the Promised Land. In order to establish Joshua as the new leader of Israel and give the people confidence in him, God did a miracle at the Jordan River to remind them of His great power. His choice of a leader for the people would bring them through every hardship of entering Canaan.

If you read the whole chapter of Joshua 3, you will witness God give Joshua a special assurance in verse 7. The Lord tells Joshua that He is going to do this miracle of parting the waters of the Jordan as proof to Joshua that God is with him, just as He was with Moses. So Joshua did as God asked and told the priests to carry the ark of the covenant and then stand in the waters at the edge of the Jordan. When they did, the waters stood still, and they walked across on dry ground!

This moment probably reminded them of the story their parents and grandparents had told about coming out of Egypt. God had made a way through the waters of the Red Sea for their parents, and now He was making a way through the waters of the Jordan for them. It was a special way for God to remind them of His power and of His love and continued presence in their lives.

God can always stop the waters, but sometimes He asks us to walk through them to grow stronger. At other times, He holds back things that could destroy us so that we can see His power and presence in our lives. Those moments should assure you that God cares about you as an individual and that He is willing to do big things to keep you safe and close to Him.

Love Languages: Words of Affirmation

Love is patient and kind; love does not envy or boast; it is not arrogant or rude.
It does not insist on its own way; it is not irritable or resentful.
—1 Corinthians 13:4, 5

Since this is the famed month of love, we will be going through Gary Chapman's five love languages this month. You can read more about all five in his book *The 5 Love Languages*. (He has even written a version specifically for teenagers.) Do not worry, you will not get cooties reading about love. You will end this series better prepared to show love to people in your life because the love we will talk about is not only the romantic kind. Understanding people's different love languages can help you show anyone that you care about them—whether it is your boyfriend or girlfriend, your parents, or even your siblings.

The first love language is Words of Affirmation. People who have this as one of the top ways they feel loved will recognize how important words are to them. Compliments that are given from the heart mean everything! Saying "I love you" out loud, as well as telling that person the reasons why they are special to you, are important. On the flip side, insulting or unkind words will leave them broken and hurt. And while they may not want to hold grudges, they will likely have a hard time forgetting unkind words.

Showing love to someone whose primary love language is words is not hard. Writing an encouraging letter or leaving a kind voicemail will go a long way in showing this person you care. Talking about how you feel and affirming them when they do something well will let them know how important they are to you.

Think about people in your life that you love. Who among these people do you think has Words of Affirmation as a primary love language? Maybe your mom appreciates when you compliment her. Maybe your best friend thrives when you encourage him or her before a sports game. Maybe your brother needs to hear how proud you are of him. Figure out who your Words people are and find a creative way to show you love them through your words this week.

The Other Woman on a Bus

Therefore, my beloved brothers, be steadfast, immovable, always abounding
in the work of the Lord, knowing that in the Lord your labor is not in vain.
—1 Corinthians 15:58

She was the other woman on a bus. Her name was Claudette Colvin, a 15-year-old girl living in Montgomery, Alabama, in the 1950s. As a kid, you probably colored pictures of Rosa Parks sitting on a bus, protesting bravely against segregation laws. Claudette's story starts months before Rosa Parks's bus encounter but is not as famous. Hers is a great story to remember during Black History Month because she was a teen who made an impact on her world!

Claudette was a typical teenager, struggling to deal with the fierce segregation laws in America in the mid 1900s. On public transportation, in restrooms, restaurants, and schools, black and white people were separated. Signs and laws indicated segregation based on the color of a person's skin. One day a teenager decided to stand up for what was right by not standing up.

As Claudette was going home from school one afternoon, she paid for her bus ticket just like everyone else and found an open seat. When a white passenger got on the bus and wanted her seat, she refused, reminding the bus driver of her constitutional right to sit anywhere on that bus, regardless of the color of her skin. The teenager was arrested for violating segregation laws, but her courage to defy racism was one of the tipping points in changing segregation laws in her town.

Teens can make a difference in social and political change. Going against the crowd and standing up for what is right is something God often encourages. Although official segregation laws from the 1900s may no longer exist, racism, sadly, does. Let the past be a lesson for the future, and be a part of the change. Rely on God to show you ways you can use your voice to make a difference in your community.

I Say, Arise!

Then he came up and touched the bier, and the bearers stood still.
And he said, "Young man, I say to you, arise." And the dead man sat up
and began to speak, and Jesus gave him to his mother.
—Luke 7:14, 15

ain is a little town in the northern part of Israel, not too far away from the Sea of Galilee and the Jordan River that runs south of it. Jesus took His disciples there to minister, and as always happened, a crowd of curious people followed Him. On their way into town, they came upon a funeral procession that was taking the body of a dead young man to his burying place. His mother was already a widow, and now her only son had died. In Israel at the time, that would have left this woman socially helpless. She would have no place in society and no one to take care of her. The Jewish society was patriarchal, mean-

ing the man was the head of the house and a woman had no status unless she was linked to a man's household. That's why divorce, death, and adultery could be so disastrous for women. Jesus treated women differently; He noticed them and took care of them. Jesus knew that this woman would become poor and destitute unless she had a man in her life to take care of her. So He took compassion on her and did something miraculous!

First, Jesus spoke to her and told her not to weep. Every time Jesus even speaks to a woman in the Bible, it is revolutionary because rabbinic Judaism did not permit men to speak to women. Next, Jesus spoke, and the young man rose from the dead! Jesus gave him back to his mother—He gave them both a second chance. Jesus was revolutionary in the way He cared. Be revolutionary in the way you care for those around you. Pay attention to those with "low social status," and find ways to raise them up like Jesus did.

Blood Transfusion

But as it is, he has appeared once for all at the end of the ages
to put away sin by the sacrifice of himself.
—Hebrews 9:26

February is American Heart Month, which means it's a time dedicated to awareness of how to have a healthy heart and blood supply. Regular exercise, healthful eating, staying away from drugs, and living a sexually abstinent lifestyle until marriage are all important to maintaining health. Your blood is the life-juice of your body. You can get by without your appendix, spleen, and other small things in your body, but without your blood, you will not be alive. It carries life to every part of you, from your brain to your toenails. If you were to choose to risk your heart and blood's health by using needles to inject drugs into your system, not exercising, risking getting STDs, or eating garbage, the health of your blood would decrease dramatically, and it would, in turn, cause your whole body to suffer as well!

Some people who have unhealthy blood or perhaps lost a lot of blood because of an injury need a blood transfusion. They need good blood from another person in order to continue living. Donating blood is giving life to another person.

When Jesus died on the cross for us, it was the ultimate blood transfusion. When God the Father looks at us, He does not see our sinful blood running through our veins, tainted with all the painful things of this world. Instead, He sees the blood of Christ—perfect and pure, healthy and strong, with life-giving power in it! Choosing to accept Jesus' death for your sins on the cross means accepting this blood transfusion from God. You are accepting that Christ takes your place and that His perfection covers up all your imperfection. He gave His life as a sacrifice for us. Have you accepted a blood transfusion from God today?

Gideon

And the LORD said to him, "But I will be with you,
and you shall strike the Midianites as one man."
—Judges 6:16

You will notice that there are stories from every book of the Bible throughout this book. Seeing the whole history of the Bible and recognizing the value of each book and its message can help you grow in your relationship with Christ.

The book of Judges is a messy book. Full of blood, guts, and gore, it's not one for the queasy. As you read Judges, it may feel as if God has left the Israelites in chaos. In truth, the book is written that way on purpose. The stories in Judges are meant to serve as a warning of what happens when you turn away from God. That's why the book is so violent and disturbing. When we leave God's direction, there are consequences. And yet story after story in the book mentions the Holy Spirit's presence in the lives of the judges God chose to work with.

One man who tried his best to follow God in a time when following Him was unpopular was Gideon. His story begins in Judges 6, which starts by saying, "The people of Israel did what was evil in the sight of the LORD." Gideon, another young person used by God, was called to save Israel from the Midianites, who were constantly attacking them. God asked him to go against his own family by tearing down his father's altar to Baal and his idol of Asherah. He famously asked for multiple signs, which God patiently gave him. Eventually, Gideon conquered the Midianites with only three hundred men. In order to conquer, he had to make a difficult decision—Gideon had to choose between his family and God.

God does not often cause division between family members. Ideally, He wants families to be united, loving, caring toward one another, and respectful. But that ideal also includes Him. When a family has deliberately chosen to walk away from Him, yet one member in that family still has their heart turned toward Him, He wants to redeem that one. Such was the case with Gideon, and perhaps with you also. God does not ever want you to disrespect your parents or rebel against them. He wants you to put Him first. And if your family is not willing to follow Him, then you need to make that choice for yourself. Find spiritual mentors. Get your own Bible, and make time for your relationship with God. He is your number one priority. And by your witness, maybe your family will one day follow Him too.

Love Languages: Acts of Service

Let love be genuine. Abhor what is evil; hold fast to what is good. Love one another with brotherly affection. Outdo one another in showing honor. Do not be slothful in zeal, be fervent in spirit, serve the Lord. Rejoice in hope, be patient in tribulation, be constant in prayer. Contribute to the needs of the saints and seek to show hospitality.
—Romans 12:9–13

The second of the five love languages we will look at is Acts of Service. This way of showing love to someone goes right along with the famous phrase "Actions speak louder than words." *Doing* things is essential to show love for someone with this love language. If you have this love language, you will recognize how good it feels when someone does something nice for you or helps you with a project you need to complete.

Suppose one of your parents has this love language. Try making dinner for that parent, doing chores that are not your responsibility or without being asked, fixing something that belongs to that parent that is broken, or helping that parent with a task he or she is doing—it will go a long way in showing you care. Ask questions about how you can help or what things the parent needs to finish so that your parent can relax.

In the Gospels, Jesus gives plenty of examples of how to show love through acts of service. He healed people. He also did miracles so that they could eat food when they were hungry. Much of His ministry revolved around the love language of service. One of the most humbling examples of His love was when He washed His disciples' feet. During Jesus' era, it was customary for a servant to wash people's feet when they stepped into an Israelite home. When Jesus got down on His knees and washed the others' feet, it was an act of love they would have clearly seen—their Lord humbling Himself to the level of a servant. What is one act of service that you could show to someone in your family or a close friend this week?

The Idol or the Image

"You shall not make for yourself a carved image, or any likeness of anything that is in heaven above, or that is in the earth beneath, or that is in the water under the earth. You shall not bow down to them or serve them, for I the LORD your God am a jealous God, visiting the iniquity of the fathers on the children to the third and the fourth generation of those who hate me, but showing steadfast love to thousands of those who love me and keep my commandments."
—Exodus 20:4–6

Why do you think the second commandment is so important to God? Well, at the time God wrote this commandment, the Israelites were literally worshiping an idol they had made. They were longing for Egypt, missing the familiarity of their comforts there. So Aaron had the people bring all their gold jewelry and golden objects to create a golden calf. Then the people worshiped it! The whole time Moses was on Mount Sinai, God knew what was going on down below, but He did not reveal the extent of Israel's sin until Moses got close to the bottom and could see what was going on. Moses' reaction was genuine— he smashed the Ten Commandments because of his disappointment in not only the people he was trying to lead but also his own brother!

God knows that it is hard for us to understand His presence in our lives when we cannot see and touch Him like we can the people and things around us. That's partly why He warns against idols. The things we are drawn to on this earth may seem wonderful and lovely, like technology that enhances our lives or education that will get us the perfect job someday. All these things can become our idols if we do not keep our focus on God.

We were created in His image, and God does not want us turning to any other image for life. Worshiping another image is the ultimate gut punch to God—it would be completely disrespecting the fact that He made us so carefully and precisely in His image. He made us with the purpose of bringing glory to Himself and having His character shine through us. Is there anything standing as an idol between you and God? Pray and ask Him to show you how to get rid of that idol in your life so that you can focus completely on Him.

She Is Not an Object

When she rose to glean, Boaz instructed his young men, saying, "Let her glean
even among the sheaves, and do not reproach her. And also pull out some
from the bundles for her and leave it for her to glean, and do not rebuke her."
—Ruth 2:15, 16

Ruth was a young Moabite woman who had married into an Israelite family. Sadly, her father-in-law, her husband, and her brother-in-law all died in Moab. Ruth and her mother-in-law, Naomi, traveled back to Naomi's former hometown of Bethlehem. When they reached the town, they had no social status because they were both widows. Somehow, they found a place to live, and Ruth went to work doing what the poorest in society did: gathering the leftovers from the harvest that Jewish farmers were required to leave for the poor. Seemingly by chance (though really through God's providence), Ruth began gleaning in Boaz's field. He turned out to be a relative that took care of Naomi and Ruth, eventually marrying Ruth. Ruth and Boaz were the great-grandparents of King David and were included in the lineage of Jesus!

In our verse from chapter 2 of the book of Ruth, Boaz is talking to his young men. Moabite women were often seen as scandalous foreigners, women of no value or worth, and sadly, many foreign women were taken advantage of sexually because they were deemed more like an object to a man than a human being. Boaz was a man of God, though, and he chose to protect Ruth to the best of his ability against sexual assault. That's why he instructs his gleaners to leave her alone and let her glean. He did not want any man to see her as an object to be used.

Young men, be the kind of gentlemen that Boaz was. He stood up for the rights of women, he took care of the women in his life, and he protected them. Treat the women in your life with respect—they are not objects.

Young women, you are not an object. Do not let any man treat you as one. Also, be kind to and thankful for the men around you who treat you like the woman of God you are. Be OK with them holding doors for you and being protective of you; it does not make you a weak woman! Being a strong man or a strong woman is about being OK with who God made you to be, respecting the other gender, and following God's principles in every circumstance.

Intercession

For there is one God, and there is one mediator between God and men, the man Christ Jesus,
who gave himself as a ransom for all, which is the testimony given at the proper time.
—1 Timothy 2:5, 6

Did you know that prayer is one of our human superpowers? God created us with a few unique things that help us tap into His supernatural world, and one of them is intercessory prayer. The word *intercede* means "to do something on behalf of someone else." So intercessory prayer is asking God to do something on behalf of someone else. This form of prayer is one of the most selfless things you can do as part of your spiritual life. Praying for other people is not just something we do to be nice when someone is sick; it actually can have the power to change someone's life.

Have you noticed anyone at school or church youth group that seems to be struggling? Maybe they're having issues with their home life, or struggling with their belief, or physically hurting from some medical problems, or emotionally in pain due to being left out or bullied. How can you intercede for that person? Aside from taking action and being a good, supportive friend for them, you can also do intercessory prayer on their behalf. Sometimes they may be too spiritually or emotionally weak to pray for themselves, so they need you to pray for them.

When Jesus was on the cross, He gave us a great example of intercessory prayer. He prayed, "Father, forgive them, for they know not what they do" (Luke 23:34). As the soldiers cast lots for His clothes and the Jewish religious leaders mocked Him on the cross, Jesus prayed for them. He interceded on their behalf and asked that God forgive the very people killing Him.

Take Jesus' example to heart and pray for even the people you do not get along with. Pray for those who hurt you. Pray for the people who get on your nerves. Pray for your competition in sports. Pray for the teacher whose class you hate. Pray, and see how praying changes not only your attitude about the people and situations around you but also situations in their lives! God just might surprise you.

Love Languages: Receiving Gifts

"If you then, who are evil, know how to give good gifts to your children, how much more will your Father who is in heaven give good things to those who ask him!"
—Matthew 7:11

Your primary love language is the one that makes you feel appreciated, cared for, and valued by people in your life. If your biggest language of love is Receiving Gifts, do not think that means you are a selfish person! Having this love language does not make you greedy or desiring of too much, it just means you feel loved when someone gives you something that has some sort of sentimental value. Likewise, if you have a loved one who has this as their primary way of feeling loved, when you give them a thoughtful gift, they will get great joy from it!

Gifts that are thrown together or not thought through can be very hurtful for this person, making them feel as if you do not care enough about them to take the time and show it. Forgetting a birthday or significant life event hurts. But remembering it and being creative in giving a gift or gesture of love will be something they never forget! If you are not sure what makes a good gift, know that it is not about the price. What makes a good gift is something that took time, thought, effort, or special consideration of that person's likes and dislikes. Did you have a conversation where they casually mentioned a concert they would like to see or a book they have been meaning to read? Get them tickets to the concert or a signed copy of the book! Did they mention a place they have been wanting to visit? Make reservations or plan a time to go and give them a card that explains the details of what you will be doing. Surprising gifts are impactful. Handmade gifts are thoughtful. Giving them something and saying "I saw this and thought of you" will make them feel so loved!

God gave us the greatest gift of all: salvation through Jesus Christ. And He did not stop there! Every day He wants to shower gifts of blessing on you. Watch for those gifts, and thank Him for the many ways He shows His love to you.

Here I Am!

*And the L*ORD *called Samuel again the third time. And he arose and went to Eli and said,*
*"Here I am, for you called me." Then Eli perceived that the L*ORD *was calling the boy.*
Therefore Eli said to Samuel, "Go, lie down, and if he calls you, you shall say,
*'Speak, L*ORD*, for your servant hears.' " So Samuel went and lay down in his place.*
—1 Samuel 3:8, 9

When the future prophet Samuel was just a boy, God had not spoken to anyone in Israel in a long time. The beginning of 1 Samuel 3 tells us that the "word of the LORD was rare" and that there were no frequent visions being had by anyone. Eli was the high priest, and he was getting old. Samuel was sent there as a boy to learn how to become a priest as well. God chose Samuel, and one night He called with an audible voice to him. Samuel heard the voice, but because he "did not yet know the LORD," as verse 7 says, he did not understand that the voice could be God talking to him! After running to Eli a few times, Eli realized God must have picked someone to talk to again. When Samuel responded to God as Eli instructed, God revealed a lot to him, which can be found in verses 11–14. (Read the whole chapter.)

God does not discriminate whom He calls based on age. As you will discover throughout this book, God often calls youth to do big things for Him. You, as a teen, have the most potential for greatness with God because you have not yet been hardened by the world. You have seen enough to know that it is an evil place in need of God's love, you sense the desperation for justice in our communities, and you can make a difference. Pay attention; God might be calling to your heart. Listen carefully; what is His voice saying? When He calls you, answer Him and give Him your everything. God uses young people! He turned Samuel into a great prophet who helped deliver His people from the Philistines and anointed the first two kings of Israel. Could it be that God has that kind of a miraculous life in store for you? Listen for His voice.

Date Your Worth

So Jacob served seven years for Rachel, and they seemed to him
but a few days because of the love he had for her.
—Genesis 29:20

You are a person of value, and yes, God wants you to be happily married someday! Some people meet their future spouse, and that's the only person they ever date—a beautiful happily ever after story! Unfortunately, that's rare. Most people go through a few dating relationships before finding their spouse. So how do you find someone worth dating?

First, do not jump into a relationship just because you have a crush! Realizing your worth and value as a daughter or son of God is so important! If the person you are interested in is playing the field and showing interest in multiple people, they probably are not someone you should get into a relationship with. When someone worth dating comes along, that person will have eyes only for you, and it will feel safe and right to get into a relationship with him or her. But take your time; there is no need to rush! You do not need to date in high school; it's probably a good idea to wait until college. But since I know every high school student is obsessed with the idea of a boyfriend or girlfriend (I definitely was in high school), we'll talk about it a few times in this book!

Hold your head high with confidence, and know your worth as a child of God. The right relationship will come along at some point, and most importantly, God will be at the center of it. That's how you know it's true love! If your significant other wants to honor and serve God alongside you, they are a much better dating option than someone who could care less about religion and spirituality. You both may have different ways of connecting with God, and that's fine. High school is a time of growth, and it's normal for everyone to be at a different point in their relationship with God. So be patient and wait, take your time, and do not jump in headfirst when you have a crush, or it will hurt! God wants you to be happy, and if you wait on Him for the right moment to start dating, it will be worth it.

Church History—William Miller

Commit your work to the LORD, and your plans will be established.
—Proverbs 16:3

William Miller was a young man serving in the military when he wrote these painfully honest words:

Annihilation was a cold and chilling thought, and accountability was sure destruction to all. The heavens were as brass over my head, and the earth as iron under my feet. *Eternity!—what was it? And death—why was it?* The more I reasoned, the further I was from demonstration. The more I thought, the more scattered were my conclusions. I tried to stop thinking, but my thoughts would not be controlled. I was truly wretched, but did not understand *the cause.* I murmured and complained, but knew not of whom. I knew that there was a wrong, but knew not how or where to find the right. I mourned, but without hope.*

In 1816, as he continued his search for assurance in his faith, he spent two full years searching the Bible for answers about God, and he became particularly interested in the prophecies of Daniel. In 1823, he began to share his views with friends that Jesus' second coming would be very soon!

One summer in 1833, William promised God that he would preach the message of the Second Coming and his Bible discoveries—but only if he was directly asked to preach. To his surprise, about half an hour later, his nephew knocked on his door and invited William to preach! While William Miller was not correct about everything that he preached, he did begin the movement of believers that turned into the Seventh-day Adventist Church. Because he was willing to let God use him and because he was unafraid to speak the truth about what he learned from the Bible, God started a movement of people preaching about Jesus' soon return!

Today is William Miller's birthday. As you grow in your own relationship with Christ, study the Scriptures with the veracity of William and see what God shows you. He may use those moments to call you to a life of work for Him! You never know what God has in store!

---

* William Miller, *Miller's Works: Views of the Prophecies and Prophetic Chronology*, ed. Joshua V. Himes (Boston: Joshua V. Himes, 1842), 10, 11.

Simeon the Teacher

Now there were in the church at Antioch prophets and teachers,
Barnabas, Simeon who was called Niger, Lucius of Cyrene,
Manaen a lifelong friend of Herod the tetrarch, and Saul.
—Acts 13:1

*A*n early painting of Jesus and the apostles in a Coptic Christian Museum in Egypt depicts Jesus more accurately than most ancient (and current) paintings do: Jesus and the men around Him have dark skin. Jesus was of Middle Eastern descent, so His complexion was likely darker than most pictures make it out to be.

During the reign of the powerful Middle Ages Roman Christian Church, depictions of Jesus and the apostles were painted with light skin, reflecting

the lighter complexion of the painters and churchgoers in that area of the world. This led to the thousands of famous pictures of Jesus and the disciples we have today, often depicting them all with light skin. The followers of Christ were of varied backgrounds, so as the gospel spread, believers with Europeans' lighter skin, others with a Middle Eastern complexion, and some even of African descent joined the Christian movement.

Simeon called Niger was a teacher in the early Christian church. *Niger* means "black," so it is possible that he was of African descent. He taught with Paul and Barnabas in Antioch, preached God's message to the Gentiles, and converted many people to Christianity. Clearly, God calls people from every race and background to accept His salvation and work for His cause.

The Jerusalem Council

"Simeon [Peter] has related how God first visited the Gentiles,
to take from them a people for his name."
—Acts 15:14

As the Christian church began to grow and people from many different countries were baptized into the faith, a problem arose in the Jerusalem church. Believers there had grown up in the Jewish religion, with all of its customs and cultural beliefs. Jerusalem Christians thought that Gentiles converting to their Christianity needed to follow the Jewish customs as well, even though Christianity was meant for the whole world—not only Jewish people. Some Jewish Christians were racist toward Gentiles. Therefore, the apostles had to step in and talk with one another and the church about how to solve these problems. Simon Peter was one of the apostles at this Jerusalem Council.

In Acts 15, the apostles addressed the racial issues facing the growing Christian church. During this meeting, Peter shared the signs and wonders that God was doing among the Gentiles. Beginning in Acts 15:7, Peter describes how God first visited the Gentiles and called them to be a part of His people. He shared that God's message was not only for one race but for all and that God would build His church in every area of the world, with people from every race as a part of it.

Today, racial tensions continue to be a sensitive topic. The early Christian church dealt with racial issues, but they got through it and survived as one body of believers. Respect is essential. Choosing to be brothers and sisters of one faith, though we may not all look the same, is the only way we will get through the rest of the issues the devil has to throw at us. Let Jesus give you wisdom as you navigate through racial issues in your school and church. Do not be afraid to stand up for what's right, and represent Jesus accurately in your context. He will bless you for it!

Jesus Gives Me a Purpose

The LORD will fulfill his purpose for me;
your steadfast love, O LORD, endures forever.
Do not forsake the work of your hands.
—Psalm 138:8

I firmly believe that God has a plan for every single person on this planet. No matter the story of how you came to be here, God has a plan for you. In high school, above all else, I wanted every student in my school to know that God had a plan for their life. I believe God knows what He is doing and that everything is under His control. If you are willing, He will lead you down the best path for your life. Trusting Him may seem hard at first, but doing so is worth it.

When I was in college earning two degrees, I could not see how God would ever get me through it. I asked Him constantly what the plan for my life was, but He did not show me. However, He did inspire me to pray a different prayer:

"God, open the doors, and I will walk through. Close them, and I will walk away."

I have prayed this prayer through every hardship in life, and it is a powerful prayer that He answers every time! He did not show me the plan, but He began opening and closing doors. Some were hard to accept as they shut. Others were exciting to see open. Though I could not see what was on the other side of these opportunities, I saw God leading in incredibly powerful ways in my life, taking me on a journey I never expected.

I dare you to pray that prayer today. Invite God to open and close doors in your life, and see where He leads you. He might not show you the future, but He will help you step through those doors one by one, and you will begin to see the amazing purpose He has for you unfold!

Love Languages: Quality Time

Two are better than one, because they have a good reward for their toil. For if they fall, one will lift up his fellow. But woe to him who is alone when he falls and has not another to lift him up!
—Ecclesiastes 4:9, 10

To show the love language Quality Time, you must be intentional. You have to live it! People who have this love language feel most loved when you spend time with them and give them your undivided attention. So, hanging out while your brother plays video games might seem like a great way to show him you love him through quality time, but really, that's just time spent around each other, not *quality* time. *Quality* time may be going outside and playing a one-on-one sport together or talking about your favorite memories from a family vacation.

Loving someone through the language of quality time is all about intentionally planning moments together where your sole focus is that person. If your best friend has this love language, plan regular time that you can spend together nurturing and growing your friendship. Being there for your friend during a stressful time of need and listening to what your friend is going through will help that person trust you and know that you really do care about him or her.

Author Gary Chapman offers four tips for this love language:

1. Look the person in the eye while the person is talking.
2. Keep yourself away from distractions. Focus on the person during a conversation.
3. Listen to the person talk about their feelings. Try to put yourself in their shoes and figure out what emotions he or she is experiencing.
4. Wait to talk. Never interrupt!*

God definitely has the love language of Quality Time. He wants our undivided attention every day. Find moments throughout the day when you can give God your undivided attention and receive that attention from Him as well! Take a short walk around the school field and pray, or spend a few moments between classes reading the Bible. That quality time will pay off in the form of a deep and meaningful relationship with God!

---

* Gary Chapman, "Speaking the Love Language of Quality Time," The Five Love Languages, updated Jan. 26, 2009, http://www.5lovelanguages.com/2009/01/speaking-the-love-language-of-quality-time/.

I Will Make Your Name Great

"And your house and your kingdom shall be made sure forever before me.
Your throne shall be established forever."
—2 Samuel 7:16

King David was a man after God's own heart but also a man of great bloodshed. He fought many battles and killed many people. Because of the violence in his life, God did not allow David to build Him a temple. Instead, in 2 Samuel 7, God made a covenant with David. God loves to make covenants, and when He does, He always keeps them—so pay attention anytime you see God making a covenant in the Bible! Watch for how it will be fulfilled!

In 2 Samuel 7:8–16, God promises David many things. He says He will make David's name great, he will have rest from his enemies, and most special of all, David will have a son. But David already has several kids! Why is this son important? The son God spoke of was Solomon, the one God appointed to build His temple. In these verses, God promises to raise up this son to build the temple, to establish David's kingdom and throne forever, and to form a relationship with this son. God describes this relationship as one of "steadfast love" (verse 15), and He states that His steadfast love will never depart from him. God will still discipline the son when he sins, but He will never take His love away from him. God promises to be a father to him and never let him go.

God has made this same covenant with you as well. He promises to give you His steadfast love forever, the kind of love that will never leave you, even when you are running away from Him with all your might. God will be the Father who never leaves you, the Best Friend who never betrays you, the one who raises you up and gives you a great name. Trust in His steadfast love and His ability to make you great.

God and Guns

Then Simon Peter, having a sword, drew it and struck the high priest's servant
and cut off his right ear. (The servant's name was Malchus.) So Jesus said to Peter,
"Put your sword into its sheath; shall I not drink the cup that the Father has given me?"
—John 18:10, 11

What do you do when there is a school shooting on the news? Like many students, you are probably both enraged and nervous. A police officer who attends my church assured me that worry is not the answer to these problems. The reason school shootings hold a prominent place in the news is because they are sickening acts of violence.

Unknown to many, the Seventh-day Adventist Church has an official position on automatic and semiautomatic assault weapons. As a denomination that promotes nonviolence, the Seventh-day Adventist Church firmly states that "with public safety and the value of human life in mind, the sale of automatic or semiautomatic assault weapons should be strictly controlled."

How much worse might this situation have been if Peter had a gun in the following story? "Then Simon Peter, having a sword, drew it and struck the high priest's servant and cut off his right ear. (The servant's name was Malchus.) So Jesus said to Peter, 'Put your sword into its sheath; shall I not drink the cup that the Father has given me?' " (John 18:10, 11).

If you want to read more on the church's official stance, look at the official statement "Ban on Sales of Assault Weapons to Civilians" released by the General Conference on July 5, 1990, at the Indianapolis General Conference session, which is posted on the Adventist.org website at https://www .adventist.org/en/information/official-statements/statements/article/go /-/ban-on-sales-of-assault-weapons-to-civilians/.

Jesus wants us to be people of peace and love, promoting kindness and helping one another through hard times. Do not fear mass shootings, and trust Jesus' attitude of nonviolence.

Dr. Lottie Blake

I can do all things through him who strengthens me.
—Philippians 4:13

Lottie Blake was a young African American Adventist woman who had big dreams of becoming a missionary doctor. She did not let the tides of racism in America's Deep South hold her back from pursuing the dreams God had placed in her heart. She pushed against the odds of being a female pursuing a career in medicine during a time when females in medicine were still rare. Yet she studied hard and became the first African American Seventh-day Adventist to become a doctor. In 1901, she began her practice in Birmingham, Alabama, the only female African American doctor in the whole city. God blessed her efforts and rewarded her heart for service in huge ways. Lottie went on to become a missionary, spreading God's message of love and healing through many different countries.*

When God has a plan for your life, He gives you the strength to follow that path, even if everything is stacked against you. He worked through Lottie as a young woman, using her to make a major impact on the world and also to pave the way for other young people to follow her example of service. In the same way, He wants you to pave a way for others to follow as well. His strength is what will carry you through every moment of hardship, doubt, and frustration. When you feel like others refuse to see your potential, He will be the one cheering you on and reminding you that He has a plan.

What will it take for you to give your everything to God and trust Him to take care of your life? What will it take for you to answer His call on your heart to have a deeper walk with Him? What will it take for you to walk through the door that is open before you in order to take the path He has prepared for you? Trust. Have faith. Do not give up hope. You can do all things through Him who gives you strength!

---

* "Black Seventh-day Adventist Firsts," BlackSDAHistory.org, accessed June 19, 2018, http://www .blacksdahistory.org/special---black-sda-firsts.html.

1,000 Betrayals

Now King Solomon loved many foreign women, along with the daughter of Pharaoh:
Moabite, Ammonite, Edomite, Sidonian, and Hittite women, from the nations concerning
which the LORD had said to the people of Israel, "You shall not enter into marriage with them,
neither shall they with you, for surely they will turn away your heart after their gods."
Solomon clung to these in love. He had 700 wives, who were princesses,
and 300 concubines. And his wives turned away his heart.
—1 Kings 11:1–3

The love of Solomon, the wisest man in the world, was surely intoxicating. However, the women who married him were essentially just pieces of property, traded by their fathers to a powerful king as a peace treaty. In essence, Solomon's 700 wives were representatives of 700 contracts. Likely all the women of his harem felt unimportant, forgotten, left behind. Flashy new wives came in all the time. It was an insane way to live, but very common in his day. Harems were normal in the culture of the Middle East during Solomon's reign. Why did God allow him to make such promiscuous choices? Because God is a God of choice. Unfortunately, these women turned Solomon's heart away from God. First Kings 11 talks about Solomon's worship of Ashtoreth, Milcom, Chemosh, and Molech, gods of the regions around Israel.

God's response to Solomon's betrayal may seem harsh, but remember that God appeared to Solomon twice, asking him to not go after other gods. Twice, God asked that Solomon stay loyal in his relationship. Still, Solomon betrayed his God. So God allowed kings around Israel to harm the Israelite nation because of Solomon's sin. And he warned Solomon that because of his choices, the kingdom would be torn away from his family during his son's reign. The book of Ecclesiastes records Solomon's reflection on his sin and repentance. Despite the wisdom God gave him, Solomon still chose to turn away. How much better if he had not turned away from God!

God gives each one of us a choice. Will we turn to the gods of sex, money, and power and let them rule our lives? Will we allow relationships and electronic devices to determine our life path? Or will we stick to God's statutes and stay loyal to Him? Solomon's solemn ending reveals what happens when you choose to live a life directly against what God has warned you of. You have a choice to follow or to turn away. Which choice will you make?

We Believe: Three in One

Then God said, "Let us make man in our image, after our likeness."
—Genesis 1:26

The second of the Fundamental Beliefs of Seventh-day Adventists states this: "There is one God: Father, Son, and Holy Spirit, a unity of three coeternal Persons. God is immortal, all-powerful, all-knowing, above all, and ever present. He is infinite and beyond human comprehension, yet known through His self-revelation. God, who is love, is forever worthy of worship, adoration, and service by the whole creation. (Gen. 1:26; Deut. 6:4; Isa. 6:8; Matt. 28:19; John 3:16; 2 Cor. 1:21, 22; 13:14; Eph. 4:4-6; 1 Peter 1:2)."*

How on earth does the doctrine of the Trinity work? Understanding a Triune God is extremely confusing for singular beings! Let's start with some science: God exists in a dimension beyond us. We know this because we cannot see Him, touch Him, or hear Him out loud on a daily basis, yet we have evidence of Him and are able to have a relationship with Him. So if you believe that God is real, you know He must exist in some dimension beyond you. In order to understand these dimensions, we have to start at the beginning.

The first dimension on paper can be drawn by a single line. That line is all that exists in 1-D. In 2-D, you can draw a shape on flat paper, like a circle, or a square, or a stick figure person! But in 3-D, you can build a box, a person can walk around in space, and you can build objects with multiple sides. The square in the second dimension cannot imagine what a box in the third dimension looks like. But because we exist in 3-D, we get this concept easily!

So you can imagine how God exists in some dimension beyond us that we cannot quite imagine or understand. But one way you can think of the Trinity is using that box example. God is like the box, which has six separate squares but is still one box. God also has three separate Persons/Personalities—the Father, Son, and Holy Spirit—but is still one God, one Being. He is three in one! And *you* can have a dynamic relationship with *Him*!

---

* Seventh-day Adventist Church, "The Trinity," in *28 Fundamental Beliefs* (General Conference of Seventh-day Adventists, 2015), 3, https://szu.adventist.org/wp-content/uploads/2016/04/28_Beliefs.pdf.

The Kingdom of Mustard

And he said, "With what can we compare the kingdom of God, or what parable shall we use
for it? It is like a grain of mustard seed, which, when sown on the ground, is the smallest of all
the seeds on earth, yet when it is sown it grows up and becomes larger than all the garden plants
and puts out large branches, so that the birds of the air can make nests in its shade."
—Mark 4:30–32

Jesus told parables, or object lessons drawn from stories, as a way to help people understand deeper theological topics. Jesus spoke in ways people could relate to, using things that were a part of their everyday lives. Every time someone saw or planted a mustard seed, they would automatically be reminded of Jesus' parable about the kingdom of God. His storytelling was simple but clever!

Spreading the message of the kingdom of God on earth was one of Jesus' most important teaching missions while on earth. He wanted humans to understand that we can be a part of that kingdom now; we do not have to wait for heaven to join in. Like the mustard seed, which starts small and grows large, the kingdom of God starts in the heart of one person and grows into a large body of believers through shared testimony and experiences. The symbol of tree branches sheltering birds was a familiar analogy for the Jewish people, reminding them of passages in the Old Testament that talk about trees symbolizing kingdoms that provide shelter.

In the same way, life in God's kingdom means you will be safe and protected under His care. Your experience with Him is to be shared with others so that they too can join in the kingdom, be safe in Jesus, and share His love with even more people. God is a place of safety, and He is the one you can run to when you need to escape.

Love Languages:
Physical Touch

Let love be genuine. Abhor what is evil; hold fast to what is good.
Love one another with brotherly affection. Outdo one another in showing honor.
—Romans 12:9, 10

The story of the prodigal son returning home to his father gives a great example of how love can be shown through physical touch. Do you remember the first thing the father did when his prodigal son came home? "And he arose and came to his father. But while he was still a long way off, his father saw him and felt compassion, and ran and embraced him and kissed him" (Luke 15:20). The father missed his son so much that he embraced him as a way of showing his love and affection for his boy.

In a romantic relationship, the love language of Physical Touch makes sense: you show love through things such as holding hands, hugs, kisses, back rubs, and holding each other every chance you get. But how can you show love to someone who has the love language of Physical Touch that you are not in a romantic relationship with?

Think of how much your mom might love shoulder rubs after a long day at work, or how your sister loves giant hugs after school. Friends that constantly touch your arm or give you a playful whack in the shoulder may have the love language of Physical Touch. Men often have physical touch as a primary love language, and that's why it's an important part of a marriage relationship—and also why it is important to have boundaries and save certain parts of this love language only for marriage!

When you have had an argument with a family member, sometimes words do not help you make up, but a long hug might.

Passing On the Cloak

Then he took the cloak of Elijah that had fallen from him and struck the water, saying,
"Where is the LORD, the God of Elijah?" And when he had struck the water,
the water was parted to the one side and to the other, and Elisha went over.
—2 Kings 2:14

At some point those who have mentored you must move on, and you must take on new responsibilities. At some point, you will need to make big decisions on your own, without the help of those who have guided you. Yet I am sure, as a young person, that excites you! Many teens long for the day when responsibilities will finally be theirs and they can finally explore the freedom and independence that comes with them.

Elisha was a young person who trained under the great prophet Elijah, who had a stellar career serving God and doing His miracles. The last day Elijah was on earth, Elisha's friends received a prophecy from God that Elijah would be taken away from him. Two times young prophets told Elisha to be ready, and his answer is rather humorous: "Yes, I know it; keep quiet" (2 Kings 2:3). It's as if he was in denial: "I know guys, leave me alone. Stop talking about it. I do not want to get emotional." Finally, Elijah and Elisha crossed the Jordan, and Elisha watched as Elijah was taken to heaven with chariots of fire. Then Elisha let the sorrow of losing his mentor hit. Tearing his clothes, Elisha picked up Elijah's cloak that had fallen nearby. Following Elijah's example, Elisha struck the water and asked, "Where is the LORD, the God of Elijah?"

That day God performed a miracle for him, launching him into his career as a prophet. You have mentors now that you should learn from; these teachers and adult leaders around you will not be there forever. At some point you will need to be the mature one, you will need to make the decisions, and you will need to be the spiritual leader. God entrusted a young person, Elisha, with that responsibility. He has probably already placed some responsibilities on your shoulders as well. Take these years of learning to get whatever you can from the mentors around you, and take charge of the tasks you have been given to lead!

Bad Days

*"Come to me, all who labor and are heavy laden, and I will give you rest.
Take my yoke upon you, and learn from me, for I am gentle and lowly in heart,
and you will find rest for your souls. For my yoke is easy, and my burden is light."*
—Matthew 11:28–30

Bad days happen. They do not feel good. Siblings fight. Surgeries do not go as planned. Grandparents get cancer. Pets die. Friends leave you out. Parents get divorced. Teachers give you a bad grade. You do not make the soccer team. Your friend gets the job you wanted. Bad days just happen!

One day a student of mine came in for baptismal studies and opened up about the terrible day she was having. Many things had happened in her life recently, and she lived in silent pain, not sharing her struggles with her classmates or friends. So we talked about everything that had happened. Then, instead of jumping into our baptismal study that week, we decided to do a little "soul nurturing" together instead.

In building your own relationship with God, you can find vitality in reading Scripture. The Bible often echoes the circumstance you are going through and gives you answers from God for that moment. Thankfully, that was the case on the day of our Bible study! We started sharing our favorite verses, and I let her flip through her Bible until she found a text she liked, then we read it together. I pulled out a sticky note, and we started jotting down the favorites that we read so that she could look them up later and read them again. We found the book of Psalms to be especially comforting on a bad day. As you read the book of Psalms, you can feel the author's emotions. You can scream at God, praise His glory, and ask Him one hundred questions all in one psalm! They are perfect for the days when your faith is wavering and you are unsure about everything in life.

What was incredible was at the end of our thirty minutes reading together, we could hardly believe how fast the time had passed! By the end of those thirty minutes, my student was happy again, excited to go about the rest of her day. Her bad day was gone, God had cured it with Scripture! I believe that's possible for you too. If you are having a bad day, take a bit of your lunch break to read a few Psalms, and get some peace from God's Word.

Women's History Month: Deborah the Prophet

And she said, "I will surely go with you. Nevertheless, the road on which you are going
will not lead to your glory, for the LORD will sell Sisera into the hand of a woman."
Then Deborah arose and went with Barak to Kedesh."
—Judges 4:9

Welcome to Women's History Month! In March we will look at a few women in the Bible whom God used in amazing ways. The norm in biblical times was for women to be quiet members of society, tending to their home and their husband. Women did not usually hold important positions and were not usually allowed to make big decisions without a man. At certain times a woman had no social status at all without a man in her life to take care of her. So when God chose to use women outside of this norm, take notice! He loves to use both women and men in extraordinary ways that are countercultural to make a difference.

Deborah was a prophetess in the days of the judges of the Old Testament. She was considered a woman of high intelligence, close to God, and a warrior for ancient Israel. Deborah took her place as the fourth judge to rule over Israel after Joshua's death. She would sit under a palm tree and prophesy to God's people.

After the death of Ehud, the previous judge, the Israelites once again did evil against God's command. An army commander named Sisera oppressed the people for twenty years, so they finally cried out to God for help. God called Deborah to lead them. She sent for a man named Barak and told him God's command to take thousands of soldiers out to meet Sisera and defeat him. But Barak was afraid! He said to her, "If you will go with me, I will go, but if you will not go with me, I will not go" (Judges 4:8). Deborah went with Barak, but she told him that because of his cowardice, God would use a woman to defeat Sisera. Sure enough, a woman named Jael killed him with a tent peg! You can read the whole story in Judges 4, 5.

If you feel like you are on the outskirts, not in the popular crowd, or not part of the group of people who make decisions and lead people, fear not. God used two women, Deborah and Jael, to fulfill His mission in Israel at a time when women were not usually given that kind of respect or power. God loves to do big things through unexpected means. Take courage and be unafraid of the tasks He lays before you—He will make a way!

The Chronicles

So all Israel was recorded in genealogies, and these are written in the Book of the Kings of Israel.
And Judah was taken into exile in Babylon because of their breach of faith.
—1 Chronicles 9:1

The Old Testament we have in our Bibles today is not in the same order that the books appeared in the Hebrew Scriptures. This is important to note when you start reading 1 and 2 Chronicles. Originally these two books were one long book, a story recapping everything that had happened in Israel's history.

The first book of Chronicles that we have starts out with long lists of genealogies. While lists of names might seem very boring, the genealogies follow two very important families. One of them follows the lineage of the priests, beginning with Aaron and his sons. The other lineage is that of David, whose lineage would produce the promised Messiah. If you go to the beginning of the New Testament, you will see a similar list tracing Jesus' lineage, which came through King David! So 1 Chronicles ultimately points to Jesus, the Messiah!

Are you starting to get the sense of how every book of the Bible was carefully written to point to one common goal—Jesus? While the entire Bible is a collection of books written across different cultures, with stories thousands of years apart, God inspired all of them to have a common theme of pointing forward to the coming of the Messiah—the One who would redeem all humanity from the evil of this planet. First Chronicles gives this hope, promising that the Messiah will come through David's lineage.

You can hope in that promise because it was fulfilled about two thousand years ago! A baby was born from the line of David who became a King for God's people, establishing His kingdom on earth. His kingdom might not be one with soldiers and walls, like most earthly kingdoms. Instead, He invites you to be a child of His kingdom, spreading His message of salvation to the whole world!

The Runner

For he has said, "I will never leave you nor forsake you."
—Hebrews 13:5

Zoooom! *Whooooosh!* I am winning! I bet you can't catch me!" His energized little voice rang out on the school field. His feet ran faster and faster as he raced around the outskirts of the grassy play area. Once we reached three-fourths of the way around the field, he slowed down, out of breath. He kicked at the gravel on the path next to the field and told me how he always had to run laps because he talked too much in class. And so began my friendship with my little first-grade running buddy.

He was a good kid, with lots of energy and a big heart. He was not usually mean to the other kids, but he got in trouble a lot for talking too much or not standing in line. Whenever he got in trouble and had to run laps at recess, he would let me know so that I could come out and run with him. It became our "thing." We would run as far as he could around the field before getting out of breath, then we would walk a bit while he told me about his day or what was happening in class.

I learned a lot about his heart from those running conversations, and those moments reminded me of our relationship with God. We all sin and mess up at some point, but does God ever leave us alone? Nope! He is always right there with us, listening to our troubles. He still lets us have the consequences of our actions, but He will run with us every step of the way. If you are going through a rough patch, remember that you are not alone. God is right there with you, and you can trust Him to never give up on you—even when you have given up on Him. Trust His love for you, and trust His plan, even if it's plan B, or even plan Z! God can work with anything, and His love for you is tremendous.

Jesus Gives Me Goodness

And I am sure of this, that he who began a good work in you
will bring it to completion at the day of Jesus Christ.
—Philippians 1:6

oodness. You might think the most common way it is used in the Bible is to express how you need to be a good person and follow God's commands to be good, but that is not the case! A relationship with God is not dependent on you or your ability to be or not be anything specific at all—other than choosing to be a child of God. In your relationship with Jesus, He does something incredible for you, He gives you *His* goodness. Because He is good, we are able to benefit from His goodness. That godly goodness shines through your life to bless others around you, not because you are good or holy but because He is good and holy and does a good work in you! "And I am sure of this, that he who began a good work in you will bring it to completion at the day of Jesus Christ" (Philippians 1:6).

Read Psalm 23—it is all about God's care for you. Verse 6 says, "Surely goodness and mercy shall follow me all the days of my life, and I shall dwell in the house of the LORD forever." God's goodness is something that follows you, flows through you, and is evidence of His presence in your heart! When you have accepted Jesus' sacrifice for you and given your life to Him, the Holy Spirit does something incredible within you and gives you the ability to be *good* and share that goodness with people around you. Galatians 5:22 mentions that the fruit of the Spirit, or evidence of the Holy Spirit in your life, includes goodness! Goodness is something that can only really come from God.

Our Old Testament friend Moses asked God a bold question: "Please show me your glory" (Exodus 33:18). And God's response was this: "I will make all my goodness pass before you and will proclaim before you my name 'The LORD.' And I will be gracious to whom I will be gracious, and will show mercy on whom I will show mercy" (Exodus 33:19).

I am jealous of Moses' experience at that moment. He got to see God's goodness and glory (and God's back!). What is incredible is that this experience was not meant for Moses only. God wants you to experience His goodness as well. Through daily relying on Jesus and asking His goodness to shine through you, you will begin to see what God is doing in those around you, and you will see His goodness through them!

Spontaneous Joy

This is the day that the LORD has made;
let us rejoice and be glad in it.
—Psalm 118:24

Have you ever gone searching for joy? Have you ever spontaneously decided to go somewhere or do something for the sole purpose of being happy? Day-to-day responsibilities can be stressful, and it is easy to let the things that are weighing us down steal our joy. God has surrounded us with blessings, and sometimes it is a good idea to just step back and look for the joy.

One morning my mother asked God to bless her with joy on a day when she really needed some. In the afternoon she went for a drive with my dad through

the country, and as she gazed out the window, she saw a majestic eagle flying high above the car. Soon she spotted another eagle, and another! Soon the trees and fields all around them were filled with birds, eagles, large white snow geese, and even swans. God gave her joy through seeing such a beautiful moment as all those incredible birds flocked together in one place.

Later, at Deception Pass in Washington State, they parked the car and walked down to the beach, enjoying the warm spring sunshine. As they watched the waves of the ocean crash into the shore, they saw a big black fin far out in the water. Suddenly, a pod of orca whales surfaced! As the sun set, they watched the whales swim out toward the open ocean, surfacing and spouting every few minutes. Through the simple beauty of nature and His creation, God filled their day with joy.

God has something special for you today as well. Just take a moment to get away from all the distractions around you, and see what beauty and joy God has in store for you.

His Name Is Holy

"You shall not take the name of the LORD your God in vain,
for the LORD will not hold him guiltless who takes his name in vain."
—Exodus 20:7

The third commandment can sometimes be confusing to modern readers. What does it mean to take God's name in *vain*? Is this only talking about swearing? While it is disrespectful to use God's name as a swear word, that is not the only thing this verse is talking about. It is actually referring to something much deeper.

God's name is holy. And in His name is life. The many names that we call Him show His different character traits. Psalm 111:9 tells us, "He sent redemption to his people; he has commanded his covenant forever. Holy and awesome is his name!" So God's name is not something to be taken lightly; it holds real power!

In Old Testament times, people would sometimes take an oath or vow and make it serious and binding by including God's name or by doing it in God's name. This could be seen as similar to how in the court system people swear to tell the whole truth, and nothing but the truth, by placing their hand on the Bible as a sign of respect and binding to God because He sees the truth in our hearts and knows if we are lying. In the Old Testament, if someone promised to do something "in God's name" and did not follow through, they showed disrespect to God and might suffer consequences!

How many things do you use God's name for? While you probably do not promise to return the book you borrowed from your friend "in God's name," you have likely ended your prayer with, "In Jesus' name we pray. Amen." Every time we mention God's name, pray in His name, call ourselves by His name (Christians), or anything else and then act in a way that misrepresents or disrespects Him, we are taking His name in vain. So watch how you use His name, and be careful to accurately represent the One you follow. Speak His name with holiness and recognize the power it holds!

Second Chronicles

"Now the LORD *has fulfilled his promise that he made. For I have risen*
in the place of David my father and sit on the throne of Israel, as the LORD *promised,*
and I have built the house for the name of the LORD*, the God of Israel. And there*
I have set the ark, in which is the covenant of the LORD *that he made with the people of Israel."*
—2 Chronicles 6:10, 11

Near the beginning of 2 Chronicles, King Solomon gives a blessing over the people of Israel and the temple that had been built. He reminds them how God chose to dwell among them and traveled with them out of Egypt all the way to the Promised Land. The Lord of the universe, the Creator of everything, chose to travel by cloud and fire through the desert, leading His people. That is the kind of God we serve.

He is a God of promises, and He always fulfills His promises. He fulfilled His promise to David that his son would sit on his throne, have peace, and build the temple for the Lord. Solomon was able to complete everything God had promised! The rest of 2 Chronicles goes through the history of the kings and people of Israel. It highlights the good kings that followed God and the blessings they received as a result, as well as noting that the kings who turned against God received years of hardship as a consequence. This reminded the people of Israel—and us today—that goodness comes from following God.

After going through the entire history of the nation and all of its misguided kings, the book of 2 Chronicles ends with a good king: Josiah. His reign began when he was only eight years old! Yet he was the king God used to restore temple worship. Sadly, King Josiah is killed in battle before the end of the book. Still, the book ends with a sense of hope that God will restore His people and continue to work through them. The very last verses of 2 Chronicles relate the proclamation of King Cyrus of Persia, who allowed the Jewish captives in Babylon to return to Jerusalem and rebuild the temple. The end of the book launches us into the rest of the Bible, looking forward to when Jesus will come and truly restore God's kingdom on earth.

I Did It!

At that time the disciples came to Jesus, saying,
"Who is the greatest in the kingdom of heaven?"
And calling to him a child, he put him in the midst of them.
—Matthew 18:1, 2

Today is International Women's Day, a perfect time to celebrate the accomplishments of women around the world and stand up for the rights of women in areas of the world where they are oppressed or treated poorly. As I thought about the many women around the world who face various struggles, I was reminded of a time when I went roller-skating with students from our school and our Pathfinder and Adventurer Club members. Toward the end of the event, one little girl came up to me and asked me to skate around with her. I said yes, so she grabbed my hand, and we slowly began circling the rink at her pace. She was new to skating, so she kept stumbling as we went along—but never fell once. Each time she would look up at me when she regained her balance and exclaim, "I did it! I did it!" Then she would go back to intensely concentrating on making her way around the rink. Every time she lost her balance, instead of giving up and falling, she would work hard to straighten herself up and then exclaim, "I did it!"

I thought about her perseverance and the great example it is for how we should live our lives spiritually, never giving up even through hardship. I cannot wait for the glorious day in heaven when I will see her running toward me yelling, "Pastor Natalie, I did it!"

In Matthew 18:1, Jesus asked, "Who is the greatest in the kingdom of heaven?" Then He brought a little child before them. Follow the example of this little girl who never gave up but instead chased away her fears as she tried something new. Find women in your life to encourage you as they pursue their dreams as well. And when you accomplish something great, shout it out yourself: "I did it!"

The Female Disciple

And she had a sister called Mary, who sat at the Lord's feet and listened to his teaching.
—Luke 10:39

First-century Judaism held many customs, and understanding these traditions makes reading the Bible thousands of times more interesting! Today, sit on the floor for your devotional, because you will be entering into the world of the early disciples.

Rabbis, or the religious teachers of Judaism, often chose a group of young men to follow them as disciples. They became students of the rabbi, learning his theology, studying the Scriptures with him, and understanding God through his teachings. Jesus was a Rabbi who chose twelve disciples to follow Him, and He often taught in rabbinic ways, although what He taught usually shocked the Jewish leaders.

In Luke 10:38, Jesus entered the village where Martha, Mary, and Lazarus lived. Martha was the responsible woman of the house, providing for her guests in the traditional role of a woman at that time. Mary, however, was quite the opposite of her sister. She had a desperate thirst for the teachings Jesus shared. Luke 10:39 says that Mary "sat at the Lord's feet and listened to his teaching," while her sister served. This annoyed Martha, so she pointed it out to Jesus. His response reveals His countercultural worldview: "Martha, Martha, you are anxious and troubled about many things, but one thing is necessary. Mary has chosen the good portion, which will not be taken away from her" (Luke 10:41, 42).

Disciples would sit at the feet of their rabbi to learn. This indicated that you belonged to that rabbi as one of His chosen disciples. In this instance, Mary chose to sit at His feet, placing herself in the position of a disciple. Jesus could have rebuked her for choosing something that was not her social place to do, or He could have gently asked her to help her stressed-out sister. But that is not what He did! Jesus included her as one of His disciples by saying she had chosen something good and that He would not take it away from her. The male Gospel writers never include her name as one of the twelve, but they do mention her several times in the Gospel stories as a woman who followed Jesus. And in this verse Luke specifically mentions Jesus' response, showing us that Jesus was countercultural in His treatment of women. Not only did He talk to them and treat them with respect, He allowed them to be equals of the men around Him, something that was never done in their Jewish society. Jesus always did the unexpected and included those who were usually left out. How can you apply that to your life this week?

We Believe: God the Father

"Do you not believe that I am in the Father and the Father is in me? The words that I say to you I do not speak on my own authority, but the Father who dwells in me does his works."
—John 14:10

Here is how the Fundamental Beliefs of Seventh-day Adventists describes God the Father: "God the eternal Father is the Creator, Source, Sustainer, and Sovereign of all creation. He is just and holy, merciful and gracious, slow to anger, and abounding in steadfast love and faithfulness. The qualities and powers exhibited in the Son and the Holy Spirit are also those of the Father. (Gen. 1:1; Deut. 4:35; Ps. 110:1, 4; John 3:16; 14:9; 1 Cor. 15:28; 1 Tim. 1:17; 1 John 4:8; Rev. 4:11)."*

Adventists believe in a Triune God, meaning there is evidence of Him as three separate Persons, yet only one God. While it will always be a little bit confusing for us to understand while we are on earth, we can at least get some idea of who each part of the Godhead is and His characteristics.

Many people think that God the Father is the one with a long white beard, sitting on a throne up in heaven somewhere. God is not an old man—He does not age like we do! But He is holy and worthy of worship and praise. The Bible often describes the Father in a position of power, the authority in heaven, creating and giving life. On earth, Jesus maintained a well-developed relationship with the Father. He spent hours on end praying and communicating with God the Father. The Father gave Him strength to do His mission on earth. The Father sent the Son to save Their creation. While the Son was the physical sacrifice, the Father raised Jesus to life again so that we could have life eternal with Him.

Through Jesus and the prompting of the Holy Spirit, you can have a relationship with the Father. He will care for you as He cared for Jesus while He was on earth. He will shelter you and protect you. He will guide you, and He has given you His Word, the Bible, as a way to hear from Him. His love never ends. When Judgment Day comes, if you have accepted Christ into your heart, instead of looking at all the sinful things you have done, the Father looks to Jesus. Since Jesus paid the penalty of sin for us already, we find salvation through Him and get to be with the Father forever!

---

* Seventh-day Adventist Church, "The Father," in *28 Fundamental Beliefs* (General Conference of Seventh-day Adventists, 2015), 3, https://szu.adventist.org/wp-content/uploads/2016/04/28_Beliefs.pdf.

Ezra

"Thus says Cyrus king of Persia: The LORD, the God of heaven, has given me all the kingdoms of the earth, and he has charged me to build him a house at Jerusalem, which is in Judah. Whoever is among you of all his people, may his God be with him, and let him go up to Jerusalem, which is in Judah, and rebuild the house of the LORD, the God of Israel—he is the God who is in Jerusalem."
—Ezra 1:2, 3

Before we jump into this verse and Ezra's story, you must first understand the background. When Daniel was a young man, Babylon conquered the Israelites, and many people were taken as captives to the Babylonian kingdom. Daniel's prophetic ministry took place there. Eventually his prophecies came true, and the kingdom of Media-Persia overran Babylon. When King Cyrus came to power, God spoke to him through Daniel.

During Ezra's day, the captive Israelites had been living in Persia for some time. But God impressed Cyrus to send the Israelites home and help them build God's temple in Jerusalem. So hundreds of people moved back to Jerusalem and built the foundation for the house of the Lord. A man named Zerubbabel led the rebuilding of God's house, and prophets such as Haggai and Zechariah supported him. Finally, the temple was completed and dedicated, with much help and support from the Medo-Persian kings. Then in chapter 7 Ezra arrives in Jerusalem. He had studied God's law, and King Artaxerxes commanded him to pick magistrates and judges for the people and to instruct them in God's law. Under Ezra's faithful leadership, further reformation and revival took place in the hearts of the newly returned exiles.

A Dignified Miracle

And Jesus said, "Who was it that touched me? . . .
Someone touched me, for I perceive that power has gone out from me."
—Luke 8:45, 46

More than any other Gospel, Luke highlights the stories of underprivileged people in the Jewish society. Since women were one of the lowest groups in the social system, Luke tells several stories about women. Luke 8 shares the story of two women healed in miraculous ways by Jesus.

Do you ever treat someone differently because of a medical condition they cannot control? While Jesus was walking through a crowd on his way to heal the daughter of Jairus, the ruler of the synagogue, a woman who suffered from an untreatable medical condition came through the crowd and touched the fringe of Jesus' garment. She believed that just touching Jesus would heal her. She was quiet, not bringing attention to herself because her condition of continual bleeding for twelve years made her unclean—a rather embarrassing thing to talk about in front of all those people. For the full story, read Luke 8:40–48.

Notice how Jesus does not shame the woman or say anything about her condition. He is careful not to embarrass her in front of the crowd. His response to her is simply, "Daughter, your faith has made you well; go in peace" (verse 48).

When you encounter someone who has a medical condition you are not used to being around, be sensitive to them; this may be a condition that affects their behavior, mannerisms, or how they look. If other people point out their differences in a mean way, be kind instead. Figure out ways you can help them without making it obvious or embarrassing. Everyone deserves dignity and respect. Be like Jesus in the way you treat others today.

Loving Her Enemies

Now the Syrians on one of their raids had carried off a little girl from the land of Israel,
and she worked in the service of Naaman's wife. She said to her mistress,
"Would that my lord were with the prophet who is in Samaria! He would cure him
of his leprosy." So Naaman went in and told his lord, "Thus and so spoke the girl from the land
of Israel." And the king of Syria said, "Go now, and I will send a letter to the king of Israel."
—2 Kings 5:2–5

Never doubt God's big plans for young people. Let's take a look at one young woman who showed true compassion to her enemies long before Jesus gave the command to "love your enemies and pray for those who persecute you" (Matthew 5:44). As an Israelite captive taken to Syria, this girl with no name was given the job of attending the wife of Naaman, a commander in the Syrian army. Let's make this a little more personal. Imagine that you were this child taken captive to serve as a slave. If you were in her position, would you have compassion if your master got sick or had a terrible disease like leprosy? It would be easy for most of us to cry for justice and watch him die; however, the girl in our story did something extraordinary. She showed true love for her enemy by suggesting that he visit the prophet in Samaria who could cure him by God's power.

Naaman must have seen something in the faith of this young girl. So he set off for Israel and met Elisha the prophet. Elisha instructed him to wash in the Jordan seven times, and God healed him completely of his leprosy! He was healed because a young girl had faith in God and chose to show love and not hatred, despite everything that had happened to her.

While you may not be in the exact same situation, you have probably had moments of hatred where you wanted bad consequences to happen to someone. Instead of hating those who have hurt you, ask Jesus to give you His love for them.

Nehemiah's Walls

And I asked them concerning the Jews who escaped,
who had survived the exile, and concerning Jerusalem.
And they said to me, "The remnant there in the province
who had survived the exile is in great trouble and shame.
The wall of Jerusalem is broken down, and its gates are destroyed by fire."
—Nehemiah 1:2, 3

At one of the churches I pastored, we had a large building project to complete our school and church building. The senior pastor cleverly named it "The Nehemiah Project." While most people do not know much about Nehemiah or his role in Scripture, our church became very familiar with his story!

Nehemiah was an official in King Artaxerxes's court in Persia. He was a cup-bearer for the king, so he was in direct contact with him on a regular basis (Nehemiah 1:11). One day the king noticed that Nehemiah was sad, so he asked him what was going on. Nehemiah explained that in his homeland of Judah, the city of Jerusalem and its walls were in ruins, and he had a burden on his heart to go back and rebuild it. The king agreed to let him go back to Jerusalem, so off Nehemiah went!

After a three-day journey, he got to Jerusalem, and under the cover of night, inspected its walls. Then he went to the officials, people, priests, and nobles and said, "You see the trouble we are in, how Jerusalem lies in ruins with its gates burned. Come, let us build the wall of Jerusalem, that we may no longer suffer derision" (Nehemiah 2:17). The people agreed, so Nehemiah led the way in working to rebuild the walls of the city.

Doing big things for God can start with small actions, and often the help of a mentor or other beneficiary stepping alongside to support you is needed—just as King Artaxerxes did for Nehemiah. If you feel that God has placed a burden on you for improving something at your school or church, or if you have a humanitarian project you'd like to get involved in, put your effort into it! Find mentors and adults who will support you. Find resources to help the situation. And pray a lot about it! God will bless your efforts and help you complete it.

The Curse of Long Life

The LORD saw that the wickedness of man was great in the earth, and that every intention of the thoughts of his heart was only evil continually. And the LORD regretted that he had made man on the earth, and it grieved him to his heart. So the LORD said, "I will blot out man whom I have created from the face of the land, man and animals and creeping things and birds of the heavens, for I am sorry that I have made them."
—Genesis 6:5–7

As a pastor, I frequently get creative questions from youth about biblical concepts that are confusing. I have included some of those questions throughout this devotional as a way for you to expand your faith—maybe you have asked the same questions!

Today's question is this: Noah and all those old Bible people lived to be like 300 years old or older. Why do we not live that long today?

Great question! Adam lived 930 years, Methuselah 969 years, Noah 950 years, and Abraham 175. They lived for longer periods of time because they were closer to Creation. Since Adam and Eve were created perfect, even though they sinned, they still had incredibly resilient bodies, and those good genes were passed down from generation to generation after them. God allowed people to live for long periods of time even after the fall into sin. However, as sin got worse and corruption increased on the earth, life-spans got shorter over time. After the Flood, the majority of people lived much shorter lives than before it. God's destruction of the earth through the Flood changed many things about earth's makeup—how plants grew, how the atmosphere behaved—and humans naturally were affected by these changes. God would not allow sin to exponentially grow like it did before the Flood, so He set a limit.

Although you might wish you could live a longer life on earth, be glad that you do not have to experience sin for that long! Eternity will be *so* much better than our experiences here. God still allows us to live our lives and wants us to develop a relationship with Him, understand salvation, accept it, and invite other people to as well. But He does not make us suffer through sin eternally. Thankfully, death on this earth is not permanent. God will raise us to a perfect life one day, when we will never die again and sin will be destroyed. Praise Him for His mercy!

Job's Accuser

Then Satan answered the LORD and said, "Does Job fear God for no reason?
Have you not put a hedge around him and his house and all that he has, on every side?
You have blessed the work of his hands, and his possessions have increased in the land.
But stretch out your hand and touch all that he has, and he will curse you to your face."

—Job 1:9–11

The book of Job in the Old Testament begins with the "sons of God" (Job 1:7) meeting together with God, discussing earth. During this meeting, God points out Job's righteousness and faithfulness to Him. Then a being steps forward and questions God about this. This being is named Satan, which in Hebrew means "accuser" or "adversary." He thinks Job is righteous only because God is blessing him. So God agrees to let Satan make Job suffer in order to prove whether he will stay righteous to God or not.

Job goes through a lot of pain and suffering, even losing his own children to death. And we learn about the process of grief through his story. Almost the entire book is either Job lamenting his suffering and questioning God or his friends questioning Job's faith and character. Job even goes as far as to curse the day he was born! Yet he is righteous and faithful to God throughout it all.

The main lesson we get from Job's suffering is that *it's OK to grieve*—it's normal, natural, and needed for healing to take place. If you are going through something painful, do not stuff your emotions down and keep them hidden. Know that it is OK to feel the pain, go through the sorrow, and express it. Some people cry; others scream, go on a long run, or write music. There are many ways to express your grief, and there are various stages of grieving that you will go through. And it's all allowed; *it's OK to grieve*.

At the end of Job's story we find this hopeful verse: "And the LORD restored the fortunes of Job, when he had prayed for his friends. And the LORD gave Job twice as much as he had before" (Job 42:10). God restores and blesses. He never leaves us to suffer alone. He may not always prevent the pain, but He does bring us to a place of blessing and restoration.

The Colossians Gospel

And whatever you do, in word or deed,
do everything in the name of the Lord Jesus,
giving thanks to God the Father through him.
—Colossians 3:17

One of my favorite chapters in the Bible is Colossians 3. It begins by power-fully describing that because you have been raised with Christ, you must seek the things of God and not the things of earth. Your old life is hidden in Christ's death, and your new life is evident in His resurrection. The first four verses of the chapter describe the story of salvation, ending with a promise about heaven! Go read it now!

God has graciously given you this new life, and the next few verses talk about the earthly things you need to "put to death" in your life: sexual immorality, im-purity, passion, evil desire, covetousness, idolatry, anger, wrath, malice, slander, obscene talk, and lying (verses 5–10). But it does not end there! It talks about once you have put off the old self, you must put on the new self—then you are being renewed in the image of the Creator (verse 10). God knows you live in a sinful world, so He has provided a way out. Living in the blessings of a new life in Christ, you are remade in the image of your Creator when you accept Him!

Then, as God's chosen one, put on holiness, know you are beloved, have a compassionate heart, kindness, humility, meekness, patience with others, for-giveness, thankfulness, and love, which binds it all together. And with those gifts, go teach others in wisdom and praise God with song!

Me First!

"So the last will be first, and the first last."
—Matthew 20:16

*A*nyone who knew me as a kid would tell you I was bossy. I am a firstborn child, so I grew up always wanting my way. Whenever we went on a Sabbath hike, I always wanted to be in the front. At school I constantly competed for the top grades. During PE class, I pushed myself to be the fastest or get the most sit-ups. When my sister and I would play made-up games at home, I always told her which character I wanted her to be and how I wanted her to play, which did not always go over very well!

Being bossy negatively affected my friendships and relationships. No one likes a bossy person who thinks they are always right! Have you ever experienced something similar? Are you that person who always wants to be first, do the best, or win every game? How does it affect those around you?

My kindergarten teacher picked a new person each day to be the line leader so that everyone got a fair chance. She would then turn around and give us the symbol for "I love you" in sign language. She taught us to show one another this symbol to remind us that we were one family in that class and that we were supposed to love one another and stick up for one another, not fight about who should be first.

In Matthew 20 Jesus told His disciples about workers in a vineyard who were all paid the same amount even though some worked more hours than others. He followed this up by saying, "So the last will be first, and the first last." This phrase is a good reminder not to give in to our selfish temptation always to be number one. Try to put others first this week, and watch for ways you can give up your selfish desire to be the best and let others take a win.

Jesus Got Financial Aid

And the twelve were with him, and also some women who had been healed of evil spirits
and infirmities: Mary, called Magdalene, from whom seven demons had gone out,
and Joanna, the wife of Chuza, Herod's household manager, and Susanna,
and many others, who provided for them out of their means.
—Luke 8:1–3

Have you ever wondered how Jesus bought food, where He slept, or how He survived during His three years of ministry with His disciples? There is a little verse in Luke that gives us the answer, sharing with us something rather extraordinary about Jesus' ministry: "Soon afterward he went on through cities and villages, proclaiming and bringing the good news of the kingdom of God. And the twelve were with him, and also some women who had been healed of evil spirits and infirmities: Mary, called Magdalene, from whom seven demons had gone out, and Joanna, the wife of Chuza, Herod's household manager, and Susanna, and many others, who provided for them out of their means" (Luke 8:1–3).

Several women traveled around doing ministry with Jesus and His disciples, listening to His teachings and learning from Him. But the men were not the ones providing monetary support in this situation—Jesus and the disciples were supported financially by women! These women were probably quite wealthy, like Joanna, whose husband was the household manager for King Herod!

In accepting financial aid from these women, Jesus was doing two things. First, He was going against societal norms. Traveling with women was not a common thing for a rabbi and his disciples to do in ancient Israel, especially if some of those women had unsavory reputations like Mary Magdalene did. Second, Jesus chose not to steal their blessing. These women were financially stable and could afford to use their money to help others. By allowing them to bless Him with their funds, Jesus let them be blessed by serving Him and the disciples through financial assistance.

While letting other people help you can sometimes be embarrassing or seem like you are taking advantage of their kindness, appropriately letting others serve you can help you draw closer to one another and become humble about serving one another. Do not steal people's blessings! You know how good it feels when you do a great service project. Let other people serve you as well and receive that blessing of doing good.

Bravery and Bodies

But Queen Vashti refused to come at the king's command delivered by the eunuchs.
—Esther 1:12

Bravery is an underrated skill. True bravery can come at the most unexpected times. Being macho and trying to prove your confidence or lack of fear does not exude bravery. But being humble, protecting others, and willingly doing difficult tasks is brave. A brave story is told in the first chapter of Esther about a woman who was unwilling to bow to man's lustful desires.

King Ahasuerus of Persia gave a great feast for his officials and servants. During this feast, drinking was unrestricted, and many men got drunk. In another area of the palace, his wife, Queen Vashti, was throwing a party for the women. After a week of feasting, the king called seven of his eunuchs and told them to go get the queen and bring her before his men to put her on display. This request was clearly made with the desire to show off Vashti as if she were an object, not a queen who should be respected by her subjects. So Vashti bravely refused him and did not go before the men to show off her beauty: "But Queen Vashti refused to come at the king's command delivered by the eunuchs. At this the  king became enraged, and his anger burned within him" (Esther 1:12).

Queen Vashti was bold. She probably knew that standing up for herself against the king would have severe consequences. She was never allowed to come into the presence of the king again. Yet she sets a brave example for women, reminding women that they are not objects but people to be loved and respected. Young men: How do you treat the women in your life, and do you respect the body of the girl you like? Young women: Do you respect yourself and your body? God gives you a choice as to how you will use what He has given to you—either for His glory or for your own pleasure. You know which is the brave choice.

Heartbreak Aches

The LORD is near to the brokenhearted and saves the crushed in spirit.
—Psalm 34:18

The ache of heartbreak is not easily forgotten. Most people go through it at some point in their lives, and likely you have gone through some kind of heartbreak in high school. I remember a breakup with a boyfriend that was quite unexpected and painful for me, which was followed by lots of heartbreak. Investing my heart in someone only to have it rejected was a feeling I never forgot.

What can God or faith do during times of heartbreak? The hardest part is letting yourself feel the pain. It is easy to ask God to simply take away the pain and make your life easy and happy again. But the process of grief is far more complex than that, and we need to go through all of its stages in order to fully cope with a distressing event.

God gives us a few great promises of hope in the Bible for times when your heart feels like it's being ripped from your chest:

The LORD is near to the brokenhearted
and saves the crushed in spirit. (Psalm 34:18)

Your righteousness, O God,
reaches the high heavens.
You who have done great things,
O God, who is like you?
You who have made me see many troubles and calamities
will revive me again;
from the depths of the earth
you will bring me up again.
You will increase my greatness
and comfort me again. (Psalm 71:19–21)

"When you pass through the waters, I will be with you;
and through the rivers, they shall not overwhelm you;
when you walk through fire you shall not be burned,
and the flame shall not consume you." (Isaiah 43:2)

Hopefully, these verses will bring you comfort today if your heart is grieving. Give it all to God; He can handle your pain.

Jesus' Type of Sabbath

Now there is in Jerusalem by the Sheep Gate a pool, in Aramaic called Bethesda, which has five roofed colonnades. In these lay a multitude of invalids—blind, lame, and paralyzed. One man was there who had been an invalid for thirty-eight years. When Jesus saw him lying there and knew that he had already been there a long time, he said to him, "Do you want to be healed?"
—John 5:2–6

Jesus loved to begin a healing with that question—probing into the soul of the person in need of healing, "Do you *want* to be healed?" At the time, this man was lying near the pool where people commonly believed that an angel would stir the water, and whenever that happened, the first person that got in the pool would be healed. For an invalid, unless you had some loyal friends and family, that was impossible! Unfortunately, this man had no family or friends close enough to help him; he struggled on his own. This story took place on a Sabbath day, and because Jesus is Lord of the Sabbath, He knew that doing good was the best way to praise the Father and show His love to this man and the people witnessing his healing. So Jesus healed him on the Sabbath! Some Jews got upset at the man for carrying his bed around after this healing, and he testified about Jesus, not knowing His name. When Jesus found him, he added something to the healing. He told the man, "See, you are well! Sin no more, that nothing worse may happen to you" (John 5:14). Sin always brings consequences, and Jesus wanted this man to live a better life than he had before, not take advantage of his newfound freedom.

First, if you are the friend of someone who is disabled in some way, be a good friend and help them out when they need it. Second, follow Jesus' powerful example of what it looks like to do good on the Sabbath! The Sabbath is not meant to be a boring day of dos and don'ts. It is meant to be a day of rejoicing in God's goodness, and helping others is a perfect way to do that!

We Believe: God the Son

In the beginning was the Word, and the Word was with God, and the Word was God.
He was in the beginning with God. All things were made through him,
and without him was not any thing made that was made. In him was life, and the life
was the light of men. The light shines in the darkness, and the darkness has not overcome it.
—John 1:1–5

John 1:1–5 is one of my favorite passages of Scripture because it describes the Son in such a refreshing way. He is the Word, sent from God. He is the Creator, and His Word made life. He is the Life, and His breath of life made the first human a living soul instead of just a pile of dust. The Son came to earth and was named *Yeshua*, "Jesus" in English. He was tempted as we are, and He overcame sin by dying on the cross and being raised again, *for us*! You can have a dynamic, personal relationship with Jesus, and taking time to spend with Him will change your life! Read the Adventist belief below that talks about why we choose to trust in Jesus as the Son of God:

God the eternal Son became incarnate in Jesus Christ. Through Him all things were created, the character of God is revealed, the salvation of humanity is accomplished, and the world is judged. Forever truly God, He became also truly human, Jesus the Christ. He was conceived of the Holy Spirit and born of the virgin Mary. He lived and experienced temptation as a human being, but perfectly exemplified the righteousness and love of God. By His miracles He manifested God's power and was attested as God's promised Messiah. He suffered and died voluntarily on the cross for our sins and in our place, was raised from the dead, and ascended to heaven to minister in the heavenly sanctuary in our behalf. He will come again in glory for the final deliverance of His people and the restoration of all things. (Isa. 53:4-6; Dan. 9:25-27; Luke 1:35; John 1:1-3, 14; 5:22; 10:30; 14:1-3, 9, 13; Rom. 6:23; 1 Cor. 15:3, 4; 2 Cor. 3:18; 5:17-19; Phil. 2:5-11; Col. 1:15-19; Heb. 2:9-18; 8:1, 2.)*

---

* Seventh-day Adventist Church, "The Son," in *28 Fundamental Beliefs* (General Conference of Seventh-day Adventists, 2015), 3, https://szu.adventist.org/wp-content/uploads/2016/04/28_Beliefs.pdf.

The Roman Woman's Dream

So when they had gathered, Pilate said to them, "Whom do you want me to release for you: Barabbas, or Jesus who is called Christ?" For he knew that it was out of envy that they had delivered him up. Besides, while he was sitting on the judgment seat, his wife sent word to him, "Have nothing to do with that righteous man, for I have suffered much because of him today in a dream." Now the chief priests and the elders persuaded the crowd to ask for Barabbas and destroy Jesus. The governor again said to them, "Which of the two do you want me to release for you?" And they said, "Barabbas." Pilate said to them, "Then what shall I do with Jesus who is called Christ?" They all said, "Let him be crucified!" And he said, "Why? What evil has he done?" But they shouted all the more, "Let him be crucified!"
—Matthew 27:17–23

Pilate's decision to release Barabbas and crucify Jesus gave him more power than he admittedly wanted to have. He certainly did not like Barabbas, and Jesus seemed like a nice enough person, but Pilate's main concern was *not* having a Jewish riot on his hands in the middle of a busy time of year when many foreign visitors were in town for Passover. Jerusalem was a difficult area to rule on behalf of Rome, and the risk of a rebellion was extremely high. There were likely many people who wanted to assassinate Pilate and the other Roman officials! He was just trying to keep the peace and make the Jewish leaders happy so that they would calm the people down.

In this moment of chaos, God chose to use a woman to warn Pilate of the fateful decision he was about to make. God was showing mercy and trying to prevent him from being part of this murder. Pilate's wife had a dream sent from God that revealed to her that Jesus was a righteous man who should not be killed. She tried to warn her husband to have nothing to do with him, but because of the pressure Pilate received from the Jewish priests, he let them do what they wanted with Jesus.

Although we are not presented with the same circumstance as Pilate, understanding how Jesus got to the cross is important. We can also learn from Pilate's experience that we should pay attention when God tries to speak to us through other people who are close to us.

Praise Him

But I will sing of your strength;
I will sing aloud of your steadfast love in the morning.
For you have been to me a fortress
and a refuge in the day of my distress.
—Psalm 59:16

What is your morning routine? Maybe you wake up, hit the snooze button five times, then grumpily get out of bed. You head to the shower, maybe check Instagram first, then try to get ready for school on time. Breakfast is shoved down your throat and books are thrown in your backpack as you try not to be late. Unless you are a magical morning person, it can be a dreadful time of the day.

Praising God is not always the first thing we choose to do in the morning. Yet Psalm 59:16 says, "But I will sing of your strength; I will sing aloud of your steadfast love in the morning. For you have been to me a fortress and a refuge in the day of my distress."

Waking up and letting praise for God be the first thing on your lips will start your day on a totally different note and give you a fresh perspective. In the spring, wake up and listen to the birds singing His praises, like a chorus thanking God for the beauty of spring. Look out at the new plants poking through the soil, and praise the Creator for His creation. Praise Him for your family and friends.

Starting the day with praise may seem tedious or silly at first, but it will change your mood. When you make a conscious effort to be thankful for the good and praise Him for the beauty in life, your mind-set for the rest of the day will be more peaceful and happy. Praising Him will help de-stress you for that big test. Praising Him will give you a reason to be nice to the annoying person in class. Singing His praises will boost the production of hormones in your brain that make you happy. You will be glad you did it! What are two things you can praise God for today?

_____

_____

_____

Psalm 91

Read Psalm 91 and rest in the God who is our Safe Refuge:

> He who dwells in the shelter of the Most High
> will abide in the shadow of the Almighty.
> I will say to the LORD, "My refuge and my fortress,
> my God, in whom I trust."
> For he will deliver you from the snare of the fowler
> and from the deadly pestilence.
> He will cover you with his pinions,
> and under his wings you will find refuge;
> his faithfulness is a shield and buckler.
> You will not fear the terror of the night,
> nor the arrow that flies by day,
> nor the pestilence that stalks in darkness,
> nor the destruction that wastes at noonday.
> A thousand may fall at your side,
> ten thousand at your right hand,
> but it will not come near you.
> You will only look with your eyes
> and see the recompense of the wicked.
> Because you have made the LORD your dwelling place—
> the Most High, who is my refuge—
> no evil shall be allowed to befall you,
> no plague come near your tent.
> For he will command his angels concerning you
> to guard you in all your ways.
> On their hands they will bear you up,
> lest you strike your foot against a stone.
> You will tread on the lion and the adder;
> the young lion and the serpent you will trample underfoot.
> "Because he holds fast to me in love, I will deliver him;
> I will protect him, because he knows my name.
> When he calls to me, I will answer him;
> I will be with him in trouble;
> I will rescue him and honor him.
> With long life I will satisfy him
> and show him my salvation."

Losing to Win

For the moment all discipline seems painful rather than pleasant,
but later it yields the peaceful fruit of righteousness to those who have been trained by it.
Therefore lift your drooping hands and strengthen your weak knees, and make straight paths
for your feet, so that what is lame may not be put out of joint but rather be healed.
—Hebrews 12:11–13

Physical education classes are usually hated or loved by their participants. You can probably identify right now which people in your class love PE, and which people dread it. The competition is often fierce, the games and exercises are hard, and you are often tired at the end. But if the weather was nice out, even those who did not like PE would probably enjoy a class outside more than in a stinky gymnasium.

Physical exercise is extremely important to living a healthy life. While Jesus did not *talk* about it a whole lot, He certainly put it into practice regularly! Jesus walked everywhere. He could probably out-hike you any day! He was also a trained carpenter, so He had strong muscles, and He definitely knew how to work hard.

God has given you an incredible body—any science class will teach you that. So take care of yourself! Find time to exercise, and make it a regular habit in your life. Exercise can even be a way to connect with God. Many people enjoy going on a hike or running nature trails and spending time with God while they do it. Some people go on daily "prayer walks" with God and use it as a time to bring their requests and concerns for other people before Him. Going to a gym and joining a workout class or respectfully pushing your classmates in PE to do their best is great—God wants you to be healthy and strong.

Set some fitness goals for yourself, and remember it's not all about losing weight either. The number on the scale does not determine your worth or your fitness level. Work on a goal that is best for your body—whether that is running faster, building muscle to become stronger, or working on precise movements for your favorite sport. Lose bad health habits that are bringing you down. In doing so, you will win a healthy, stronger body that can do more amazing things! You can honor God with your body by keeping it healthy, which is a very simple step forward in your relationship with Him. Now, it's time to get out there and sweat!

Youth in the Bible: Joseph

"I am Joseph! Is my father still alive?"
—Genesis 45:3

A significant portion of the end of Genesis is dedicated to the story of another teen who followed God's call. Enter the famous Joseph! He starts as the favored child of his father, Jacob, and his brothers hate him. He has dreams and visions of his family bowing down to him, and it's possible that he was a bit of a brat as a child. The brothers end up selling him as a slave, and he is taken to Egypt and sold in the slave market to a man named Potiphar, who ends up putting him in charge of his household. Potiphar's wife gets the hots for Joseph, and when he refuses her, she gets mad, and he ends up in prison. Yet God blesses him wherever he goes because he is living righteously. He interprets the dreams of two other prisoners, which end up coming true. And finally, he is taken out of prison, interprets the Pharaoh's dream, rises to a position of second-in-command over the nation, distributes food during famine time, and lives a prosperous life.

Then his brothers show up. After talking with his brothers for a while, Joseph does not reveal his identity. On their second visit, he sees that his younger brother, Benjamin, is still alive and well. While feasting with his very confused brothers, he breaks down, finally revealing his identity to them saying: "I am Joseph! Is my father still alive?" (Genesis 45:3).

Naturally, his brothers are in shock, thinking he had died in slavery or that he would now seek revenge. So Joseph explains his story, how God had preserved and blessed him, and how God was now using him to preserve the lives of all his family members. His father, Jacob, travels to Egypt and is reunited with Joseph.

God uses this young man to do some extraordinary things for him, and I recommend reading his entire story in Genesis 37–50! God is faithful to those who trust in Him. Joseph trusted and believed, always doing what God asked of him. He followed a strict moral code that kept him out of trouble. God will bless you, and even more so when you follow the instructions He has given for living a good life! He can make you the leader of a nation if He wants to. So follow Joseph's example and be a young person completely committed to God in all you do.

The Rain Reigns

"Be glad, O children of Zion, and rejoice in the LORD your God,
for he has given the early rain for your vindication;
he has poured down for you abundant rain,
the early and the latter rain, as before."
—Joel 2:23

Do you prefer sunny, warm days? Or rainy, cloudy ones? Everyone has their own preference. Mine happens to be sunny, warm days! I enjoy going to parks and seeing the peaceful green grass, blossoms on trees, and spring flowers popping up in flower beds. Rejoicing in the beauty of God's nature in the sun is so wonderful.

Rain, on cloudy days, is needed for the beauty of the flowers and trees to grow. In the form of small water droplets, rain is condensed from the vapor in the atmosphere. As they become heavier, gravity causes the water droplets to fall to the earth. The water cycle's main component to function well is rain. It deposits fresh water onto the earth and is a necessary part of our daily lives! We need the rain to survive.

In the Bible, falling rain is often likened to the Holy Spirit. The Holy Spirit refreshes and restores us, just as the rain does for the plants. Through His power, we receive guidance and ultimately grow in our relationship with Him, learning to reflect His character more each day. Seek the Holy Spirit as He reigns in your life today.

Spirit in the Bones

As you do not know the way the spirit comes to the bones
in the womb of a woman with child,
so you do not know the work of God
who makes everything.
—Ecclesiastes 11:5

The miracle of life is an incredible thing. God gave earth a superpower the devil is incredibly jealous of: the ability to create life. Everything on this planet has the ability, from bugs to whales to humans! But even with our ability to create, God is still the one who gives us the ability. Like the verse says, it's a miracle of the Holy Spirit that enters the bones of a little fetus and helps it grow! All of God's creation was made with intense attention to detail.

King Solomon wrote Ecclesiastes when he was an old man, reflecting back on his life and what he learned from it. At the beginning of the book he says, "Vanity of vanities, says the Preacher, vanity of vanities! All is vanity" (Ecclesiastes 1:2). His major impression of life was its meaninglessness. In chapter 2, Solomon experienced every pleasure he ever wanted, gathering wealth, women, and everything his eyes desired (verse 10). But Solomon observed something God gave to humans also: "He has made everything beautiful in its time. Also, he has put eternity into man's heart, yet so that he cannot find out what God has done from the beginning to the end" (Ecclesiastes 3:11).

God gave us the ability to sense that there is something beyond this world, a heaven we were meant for. In everything, we have to trust that He is God, the ultimate Builder and Creator, who will make our meaninglessness meaningful through His power and significance.

Great-Great-Grandma Rahab

And Joshua the son of Nun sent two men secretly from Shittim as spies,
saying, "Go, view the land, especially Jericho."
And they went and came into the house
of a prostitute whose name was Rahab and lodged there.
—Joshua 2:1

Waaaaiiiiiitttt a second . . . did you read that verse? Joshua, the leader of God's people, sends two spies into Jericho, and where do they go? The house of a prostitute! That does not seem like a very appropriate thing for God's people to do! But think about it. If you were a spy going into a city, would you not plan ahead of time for the best possible places to gather information? Not only was Rahab's house on the wall (a perfect getaway point), she also was a prostitute, meaning she probably had connections with some of the most influential men in the city, and her house was likely a great place to gather information about Jericho. God clearly was already working on her heart, so the spies' intention in going to her house was not to sleep with her. And her intention with them was also innocent. Hiding in a prostitute's house makes perfect sense—if they were being watched, the least suspicious place to go would be the home of a prostitute, a very normal place for people from out of town to make a stop.

When the king's guards heard that foreign men had gone into the prostitute's home, they checked it out. And Rahab's lie was believed. Meanwhile, the men were hiding on her roof. Later, she let them down the wall and then tied a cord in her window to identify her so that when they came back, she and her family would not be destroyed. That is how God made a place for a prostitute to become a part of the children of Israel. Guess what else God did?

Rahab married an Israelite man and had a son whose name was Boaz. Recognize that name? Boaz married Ruth, and they were great-grandparents to King David! And you have already learned a bit about David and how the Messiah was to come from his lineage. One of Jesus' ancestors was a prostitute! If that is not an amazing example of God's grace, I do not know what would convince you. God is merciful, and He makes a way for every person to be a part of His family, no matter what their past is. Give your past to God, and He will make you an honored member of His family, transforming your life forever!

April Fools'!

Let there be no filthiness nor foolish talk nor crude joking,
which are out of place, but instead let there be thanksgiving.
—Ephesians 5:4

Green eggs! Blue milk! Gross! I remember loving April Fools' Day as a kid. I do not remember doing any horribly mean pranks, but I did enjoy messing with my family a little bit. Sometimes my sister and I would get up early and go make breakfast for our parents, adding a bit of food coloring to make things look less appetizing. In high school, the jokes got more intense—once we removed all the desks from our Bible classroom and put them outside, leaving the room completely empty. Our poor teacher!

Playing jokes on others can be hilarious and a great way to share humor with others. But sometimes jokes can be hurtful. I hope that you are reading this in the morning before going to school so that you can evaluate how things go today. Have fun doing silly things with your friends! But keep in mind how certain actions can hurt other people's feelings. Pay attention to what your classmates are doing. Are they planning something that will make the day a lot harder on your teacher or hurt them in some way? Are other students planning to pick on one specific student by doing a joke that will come across in a mean way? Stand up for others today, and if things are going too far, cut it off. Killing the vibe might save someone else from embarrassment and a lasting hurt from being picked on or made fun of.

God calls us to be people of integrity by standing up for others, being kind, and doing what is right. That does not mean He is a strict, mean God that hates fun or laughter. In fact, I think He is just the opposite! I am sure there is nothing God loves more than when He sees us laughing so hard we cannot stop; happy humans bring joy to His heart! So have fun today, but be kind.

She Called Me "Mom"

Train up a child in the way he should go;
even when he is old he will not depart from it.
—Proverbs 22:6

As the youngest of three girls, she was picked on the most. Yet despite a tumultuous home life, she had the brightest smile of any kid in her class. I met this little girl when I first started pastoring. She attended the local Adventist school, brought by her grandmother every day. When I went to play with the kids at recess outside or stayed after school to help with the gymnastics program, she was always one of the first to run up to me, shouting my name before throwing herself into my arms with all her might. She almost knocked me down a few times!

She had a great sense of humor, enjoyed jumping around and being silly, and did not come across as your typical "troubled child." Then one day she said something that sounded so strange to me—she started calling me "Mom." At first, I thought she was being silly, joking around and being a funny little kid. But week after week, then month after month, and eventually school year after school year, she continued to call me "Mom." When she got a little older, I asked her why she always called me that, and her response broke my heart. She explained how she did not like her mom, how her mom was not involved in her life and did not seem to care about her. Even though her mother was alive, she felt like she had no mom. So when I, an older female mentor figure in her life, started showing that I actually cared about her, she decided that, in her mind, I was her new mom because a mother should be someone who loves you, plays with you, hugs you when you are crying, and puts Band-Aids on your scraped knees.

Young children always need older people to come alongside them and show them they are cared for as a precious child of God. You are in a unique position to mentor children, whether that is by helping them with homework, playing with them at recess, leading out in their Sabbath School class, teaching them sports, helping with Vacation Bible School, praying with them, or sending them notes with Bible verses for encouragement. There are hundreds of ways to mentor children and help them see God's love firsthand. Think of a few children in your church or school that you could mentor, and talk to their parents, teachers, and your pastor about how you can be a positive force in their lives.

Pride Goes Before Destruction

Pride goes before destruction,
and a haughty spirit before a fall.
—Proverbs 16:18

Pride causes humans to do all kinds of crazy things. Some people choose to pursue a particular career because of the pride it brings them. Others participate in music to bring pride to their parents. Pride can cause the pursuit of good grades, an excellent sports season, or a stellar Christmas program performance. But if pride is what is motivating all those things, a person's heart will feel empty when it is all over.

Sadly, pride also has the ability to cause rash decisions or things that hurt other people. The wise book of Proverbs gives the famous counsel, "Pride goes before destruction." That phrase is said a lot because so many people have experienced it and know it is true!

What things are you most prideful about? Does your feeling of pride swell when you get up front and share your ideas with people? Or do you get that adrenaline rush scoring shot after shot in a basketball game, even if it means not passing the ball to other players sometimes, just to get your score number up?

Remember to release your prideful thoughts because they may just cause you to trip up and hurt someone, or yourself!

Froggy Feelings

No temptation has overtaken you that is not common to man.
God is faithful, and he will not let you be tempted beyond your ability,
but with the temptation he will also provide the way of escape,
that you may be able to endure it.
—1 Corinthians 10:13

Squish . . . squish . . . squish. I looked down in horror to see the grass covered with little frogs, all jumping quickly to escape the crushing weight of my feet! It had just rained at our vacation rental on the island of Hawaii, and the yard was covered with tiny frogs leaping in the wet grass. God created frogs to love moisture, so when it rains, they get out and enjoy it!

However, what happens in the winter when the rain turns to snow? Certain types of frogs hibernate during the winter by burying themselves in the mud. Since they are cold-blooded, their body cools down in the freezing temperatures. They do not freeze to death, however, because they naturally have chemicals that act like an antifreeze in their bodies, keeping them alive until the spring.

When the sunshine begins to warm the earth, the frogs come out into the sunshine and warm up again. God created them with the ability to get through the harshness of winter. He also has promised something similar in the Bible for people. You may have heard people say, "God will not give you more than you can handle." Here's where that idea comes from: "No temptation has overtaken you that is not common to man. God is faithful, and he will not let you be tempted beyond your ability, but with the temptation he will also provide the way of escape, that you may be able to endure it" (1 Corinthians 10:13).

When you are going through your "winter" and are not sure whether you can stay strong and faithful to God, remember that He has equipped you with the ability to endure it. God is faithful, and Jesus experienced every type of temptation possible while He was on earth. He is your way of escape, and He can keep you strong.

Resilience

For as the earth brings forth its sprouts, and as a garden causes what is sown in it to sprout up,
so the Lord GOD will cause righteousness and praise to sprout up before all the nations.
—Isaiah 61:11

Once a little tomato plant was given as a gift. Its owner was getting old and wrinkled, but the tomato plant she gave away was young and full of life. She gave the little tomato plant to a young lady who took it home and transferred it to a new pot so that it could grow bigger. She diligently watered it and put it on the porch, where it could get lots of sunshine. Soon the little tomato plant began producing its very own tomatoes!

When the winter months came and the plant started to get cold, its young owner brought it inside so that it could stay warm. She cared for it, watering it, keeping it warm, and putting it where it could catch the best sunrays. Unfortunately, the plant slowly began to turn brown. Its leaves shriveled up, its stalk began to droop, and it did not produce any more tomatoes. The owner knew the plant's days were done, so she put it back outside, waiting for a good time to get rid of the dead plant.

Months passed by, and the young owner almost forgot about her little tomato plant, now a shriveled, brown, wilted mass on the back porch. The winter was passing, and the first signs of spring began to appear. When the owner went outside to sit in the warm sunlight, she noticed something strange. On one skinny stalk of the little tomato plant was a small orange tomato! Somehow, the plant had survived the winter, with no water or care, and had produced another tomato! The owner was more excited than most people would be over a plant, and she quickly gave it some water, marveling at the new growth.

Resilience is a gift from God. Even though this little story may seem a silly thing to compare your life to, consider the times you have felt like that tomato plant—discarded, uncared for, forgotten about. God can give you the gift of resilience to make it through even those times when the people who are supposed to care for you have abandoned you. Do not doubt His power to carry you through, just like the little tomato plant!

We Believe: God the Holy Spirit

*"But you will receive power when the Holy Spirit has come upon you, and you will be
my witnesses in Jerusalem and in all Judea and Samaria, and to the end of the earth."*
—Acts 1:8

We sometimes gloss over the Holy Spirit, the most mysterious being of the Godhead, because we do not understand Him. Yet the Holy Spirit is the most personal Being of the Godhead because He dwells within you. He is just as much *God* as Jesus or God the Father. He is the Breath of Life put into humans at Creation; He is the Power that makes trees grow and babies become adults. He made Jesus' conception happen in Mary and helped the child Savior realize who He was on earth. He is the one who inspired the Bible. And He is the one who dwells in your heart and convicts you to follow Christ's example. Though Jesus returned to heaven after His time on earth, the Spirit of God has stayed with us. He was sent at Pentecost, He enters hearts at baptisms, He leads the church forward, and when we talk about "having a relationship with God," He is the one making that possible. He is the presence of God that you feel. He opens your eyes to see and understand Scripture. He has chosen to continue dwelling with us until the end, not leaving us alone to fend for ourselves here on earth. If it helps you to imagine Him as a person like you do Jesus and the Father, go for it! Above all, remember that God has chosen to dwell with you and lead you personally through this life. That is special!

This is how the Fundamental Beliefs of Seventh-day Adventists describes the Holy Spirit:

> God the eternal Spirit was active with the Father and the Son in Creation, incarnation, and redemption. He is as much a person as are the Father and the Son. He inspired the writers of Scripture. He filled Christ's life with power. He draws and convicts human beings; and those who respond He renews and transforms into the image of God. Sent by the Father and the Son to be always with His children, He extends spiritual gifts to the church, empowers it to bear witness to Christ, and in harmony with the Scriptures leads it into all truth. (Gen. 1:1, 2; 2 Sam. 23:2; Ps. 51:11; Isa. 61:1; Luke 1:35; 4:18; John 14:16-18, 26; 15:26; 16:7-13; Acts 1:8; 5:3; 10:38; Rom. 5:5; 1 Cor. 12:7-11; 2 Cor. 3:18; 2 Peter 1:21.)*

---

* Seventh-day Adventist Church, "The Holy Spirit," in *28 Fundamental Beliefs* (General Conference of Seventh-day Adventists, 2015), 4, https://szu.adventist.org/wp-content/uploads/2016/04/28_Beliefs.pdf.

Do Not Awaken Love

Let him kiss me with the kisses of his mouth! . . .
Draw me after you; let us run.
The king has brought me into his chambers.
—Song of Solomon 1:2–4

Yikes! Go take a cold shower! It is time for devotions, not sex! Ah! Song of Solomon is definitely awkward to read. I had a professor once who decided to read a whole chapter from this book to us . . . I think everyone's face was red by the end. I suggest that someday, when you get married, read through Song of Solomon with your spouse. There is some steamy stuff in there! Until then, I will not blame you if you skim over it. Why is such an explicit book included in the Bible?

This book is a poem of the love between a man and his wife. It echoes the beauty and loving expression between spouses. And it is a reminder of why waiting until marriage to have sex is important, special, and valuable.

"I adjure you, O daughters of Jerusalem, by the gazelles or the does of the field, that you not stir up or awaken love until it pleases" (Song of Solomon 2:7). Do not awaken love until you are ready for it! This book describes love in very beautiful ways, but the other side of love is that it takes work and commitment. Love is not just that butterfly feeling you get inside when you see your crush. Love is best found in a lifelong commitment to someone. And when you choose to love someone and marry them, you choose to intertwine everything in your lives, and that is when sexuality comes into play—and is an important part of a healthy marriage relationship that God wants you to enjoy!

Sadly, we live in a world that acts like love is as disposable as a tissue, not as deep and lasting as an ocean. So do not rush yourself into love, do not feel pressured to date anyone now; take your time and wait! And if you are in a relationship, do not feel pressured physically. Set up your boundaries and be patient. Love means being selfless, putting the other person first, and caring for another person's needs above your own. Do not awaken love until you are ready for it. Be patient and wait, enjoy your youth and innocence. In time, you will get to experience all the saucy things Song of Solomon talks about!

Get More From Your Bible

But he answered, "It is written, 'Man shall not live by bread alone,
but by every word that comes from the mouth of God.' "
—Matthew 4:4

Spending time in God's Word feeds my soul in ways I never anticipate. Many times when I have feared a looming problem or felt unsure of how to deal with my emotions, I feel impressed to open the Bible and start reading. Often I turn to the book of Psalms. This is a great place to start because David and the other writers of the Psalms went through some drastic life changes and their poems and songs reflect their feelings.

However, digging into God's Word is about more than just getting a warm, fuzzy feeling inside. So how can you get more from your Bible and understand it better? Here are a few ideas:

- *Make it engaging.* As you are reading, see how you can relate to the story. How does it engage your mind? How can you relate to the characters in the story and their struggles? Realizing that the Bible is relatable and engaging will make it more interesting to read.
- *Live it out.* Living what you learn from the Bible makes it practical and lets its messages have an impact on your everyday life. Take one principle from the story you read and apply it to your life, choosing to live out that character trait as best you can.
- *Make it personal.* Personalizing the Bible will help it feel less like a two-thousand-year-old book written to people long ago and more like the always applicable Book that it is. Since it is God's message to humans on earth, the messages in the Bible still apply to us today and still have an impact on our society.
- *Ask questions.* As you read, jot down questions that come to your mind. Do not be afraid to ask anything of the text. If you are confused about something, write it down! You can research it more later or ask your pastor to explain the topic to you. Asking questions is the only way you can learn and grow beyond what you already understand.

Woman at the Well

Just then his disciples came back. They marveled that he was talking with a woman,
but no one said, "What do you seek?" or, "Why are you talking with her?"
—John 4:27

Like the woman at the well I was seeking for things that could not satisfy: And then I heard my Savior speaking: 'Draw from my well that never shall run dry!'" Richard Eugene Blanchard Sr., a minister, penned these words in his hymn "Fill My Cup, Lord," about the story we find in John 4. Jesus' ministry was flourishing, but the Pharisees were getting upset. Jesus' disciples had baptized even more people than John the Baptist, and since Jesus did not want to cause an undue ruckus, he left Judea and went to Galilee. On His way north, He decided to pass through Samaria, and He stopped in the town of Sychar, located near Jacob's well.

We know the story about this woman who had been married five different times and was now living with a man who was not her husband. She came to get water from the well and found Jesus sitting there. He, a Jew, crossed over the barriers of racism and asked her, a Samaritan, for a drink of water. Then He offered her the greatest prize of all: the water of eternal life through believing in Him as the Messiah. Jesus chose to reveal Himself as the Messiah to a woman from a despised race. To the woman from Samaria, He said, "I who speak to you am he" (verse 26).

Then the disciples returned and wondered why Jesus was talking with a woman so openly, especially a *Samaritan* woman! Talking with women was prohibited in their culture. Respectable men did not talk to women in public! As they watched the curious scene, they saw the woman leave her water jar and rush back to the town, becoming one of the first missionaries for Jesus! She said to the people, "Come, see a man who told me all that I ever did. Can this be the Christ?" (verse 29).

Jesus and the disciples ended up staying there for two days, teaching the people. The people said, "It is no longer because of what you said that we believe, for we have heard for ourselves, and we know that this is indeed the Savior of the world" (verse 42). The Messiah had come, and they believed! Do you have as much faith as the Samaritans, who only spent a few days with Jesus? Will you choose to talk about Him and let Him use you even in the middle of your chaos?

Cemetery Joy

For this we say to you by the word of the Lord, that we who are alive and remain until the coming of the Lord will by no means precede those who are asleep. For the Lord Himself will descend from heaven with a shout, with the voice of an archangel, and with the trumpet of God. And the dead in Christ will rise first. Then we who are alive and remain shall be caught up together with them in the clouds to meet the Lord in the air. And thus we shall always be with the Lord. Therefore comfort one another with these words.
—1 Thessalonians 4:15–18, NKJV

*A*cross from the apartment I lived in a few years ago stood a large hill that curved gracefully down into the Puyallup Valley. On top of this hill was a cemetery. Frequently on my drive home from work, I would see the groundskeeper walking around the cemetery or the gravediggers working on a plot, and sometimes I saw a crowd gathered around a grave to say a last goodbye to their loved one.

One day I turned onto my street and noticed a hearse driving through the cemetery to a grave. At that moment, I was faced with the harsh reality of what sin does to people on this earth, but I also had another thought: Wouldn't that be a neat place to be during the resurrection?

Can you imagine it? Lying on a field of green grass, watching as Christ comes closer and closer to earth in all His glory. And while trumpets sound and angels sing, Christ calls those in their graves to rise again and meet Him in the air. Suddenly the ground around you rips open and perfect beings emerge, reunited with their loved ones in the most beautiful display of love and affection you have ever seen! Those who live until Jesus' second coming will witness a unique and special sight. I challenge you to think about the Second Coming every time you see a cemetery, and maybe even go and pray for the families who are still alive and grieving those buried in those cemeteries. Pray that they would come to know Jesus before they die. And do not be afraid of death; Jesus has conquered it once and for all!

Fear Not

For I, the LORD your God, hold your right hand; it is I who say to you,
"Fear not, I am the one who helps you."
—Isaiah 41:13

When God calls you to do something, fear is a common response. Many Bible heroes trembled at God's first call! Jeremiah said he was too young; Elisha did not want to leave his family; Samuel did not recognize God's voice at first! However, God calls young people because of their potential to change the world. He knows you have a powerful voice, and He wants you to use it!

Ask yourself these questions, and write your answers below them. Try to find a Bible verse that goes along with each question that encourages you as well.

Which scared Bible hero do you identify with most?

_____

_____

Why do you think the common response to God's call is initially fear?

_____

_____

Have you felt God's call on your heart or in your mind? What was that experience like?

_____

_____

What is a step forward God is calling you to take to draw closer to Him and make a difference for Him?

_____

_____

Loaves and Fishes

And Jesus said to them, "How many loaves do you have?" They said,
"Seven, and a few small fish." And directing the crowd to sit down on the ground,
he took the seven loaves and the fish, and having given thanks he broke them
and gave them to the disciples, and the disciples gave them to the crowds. And they all ate
and were satisfied. And they took up seven baskets full of the broken pieces left over.
—Matthew 15:34–37

This was an ordinary day. The disciples followed Jesus as He walked next to the Sea of Galilee. He found a nice spot to sit on a hill and rest, knowing that in a few moments He would be swarmed with people. Soon enough, the crowds came, bringing with them those who were sick, lame, blind, crippled, and mute. Jesus took the time to meet each one and heal their needs. As the crowd watched, the crippled ran, the mute began speaking, the lame started walking, and the blind could see! They glorified God for these miracles!

After a long day of watching Jesus, the people were tired and hungry. Jesus asked His disciples how many loaves of bread they had. They answered that seven loaves and a few small fish were available, so Jesus directed the crowd to sit and miraculously gave them food.

When we come to Jesus, we must learn to surrender to Him, watching to see what He can do and relying completely on Him. Jesus thinks outside the box, and His ministry was quite unconventional! When you feel tempted to focus on the impossible, watch God do something incredible before your eyes and choose to glorify Him as the Israelites did!

Your Creed

"Let not your hearts be troubled.
Believe in God; believe also in me."
—John 14:1

The Seventh-day Adventist Church has always upheld the importance of not holding to a particular creed. Christian denominations throughout history have developed creeds of belief, which God later showed were incorrect. At the beginning of the Fundamental Beliefs of Seventh-day Adventists is this statement: "Seventh-day Adventists accept the Bible as their only creed and hold certain fundamental beliefs to be the teaching of the Holy Scriptures. These beliefs, as set forth here, constitute the church's understanding and expression of the teaching of Scripture. Revision of these statements may be expected at a General Conference Session when the church is led by the Holy Spirit to a fuller understanding of Bible truth or finds better language in which to express the teachings of God's Holy Word."*

Our only creed is the Bible, and the teachings of the Bible influence our beliefs. Thus, our "fundamental beliefs," as recognized officially by the church, can change as the Spirit moves us! They certainly did in Ellen White's day, as she and other early Adventists learned more about Christ, the Sabbath, and other teachings in Scripture.

However, it is good to have a sort of "creed" in your mind in the sense that you are certain about what you believe. Questioning beliefs is normal, but living in a constant state of uncertainty is not healthy. If you want to grow in your relationship with God and the things you believe about Him, you have to take the time to study His Word and discern what beliefs you hold close to your heart. Take some time to write down some Scripture verses that support some of the beliefs you hold closest to your heart.

---

* Seventh-day Adventist Church, *28 Fundamental Beliefs* (General Conference of Seventh-day Adventists, 2015), 2, https://szu.adventist.org/wp-content/uploads/2016/04/28_Beliefs.pdf.

Navigating Rivers

"When you pass through the waters, I will be with you;
and through the rivers, they shall not overwhelm you."
—Isaiah 43:2

The cool air swished over my face as splashes from the river water glistened on my cheeks. I laughed, I screamed, I sweated as I paddled through the rapids. Although the river was not that dangerous or rough, I still felt like I had accomplished some huge feat when we got out.

My father loves to go white-water rafting. He has taken my family on a few trips with him down the beautiful rivers he navigates, and we have been able to see the grit and determination it takes to push through the waters and ride the currents successfully. When talking about river rafting, a pastoral mentor of mine once said, "A river rafting instructor once told me the first instinct of rookies in rapids is to pull the paddles out of the water. Bad move! The pros know this: When the river is rough, dig deep and pull hard."

Faith is not an easy journey, and you will likely have many questions for God. Why are You not showing me the clear path You want me to follow? Where is Your hope in my time of need? How can I see past this mountain in front of me? Where is Your hand when I need to cling to it? How do I get through this? It is too hard, God!

Our spiritual life is like that river—our instinct is often to just stop trying and give up on God and ourselves. Remember that the best thing to do when the rapids of life are crashing down on you is to dig in deep and pull hard. Push through, and against all odds, God will bring you out on the other side stronger for it!

Jesus Gives Me Self-Control

For God gave us a spirit not of fear
but of power and love and self-control.
—2 Timothy 1:7

How does your relationship with Jesus affect your daily actions? You are growing up in an age of spiritual depravity, where God seems harder to reach than your Wi-Fi connection and Snapchat friends. This can lead to a lack of self-control when interacting with the things you have access to in the world. It is a well-known fact that too much social media affects how you think about yourself. Many portray a false life online, and their "friends" begin questioning the importance of their own lives.

Yet because you are a child of God, you should be confident in who He made you to be. He wants you to commit to Him. Do you spend more time with Him each day than you do on Instagram or Snapchat? Giving God the most time in your life is difficult, but committing to a relationship with Him affects how you live your daily life. He can give you self-control. This concept applies to more than just your online presence. It also applies to what you eat, what you drink, what you do in your relationships, what extracurricular activities you get involved with, and so on. Self-control is a difficult skill to develop, but if you can form it in your life, you will see things start to change positively in your life.

Stay Lit for Jesus

They said to each other, "Did not our hearts burn within us
while he talked to us on the road, while he opened to us the Scriptures?"
—Luke 24:32

I was involved in my local Pathfinder club from the time I joined as a fourth grader all the way until I graduated from high school. Yes, I was that kid. But through Pathfinders I learned some of the most valuable lessons, gained lifelong friends, started my walk with Jesus, and learned to preach! If you have the chance to either be a Pathfinder or volunteer as a helper once in a while, do it. It can change not only your life but also the lives of many kids.

A key skill you learn in Pathfinders is how to build a good fire. Surviving a camping trip and getting your Camping Skills honors means you have got to build a good fire that can keep your club warm and cook your food! When you look at a fire, what shape is it generally in? Often a circle or square sort of shape, with a center and edges around it. You can sit comfortably around the edge of the fire without getting too hot. But if you were to step into the center of the fire, you would get burned! As a fire dies down, the last bits to go out are the coals that were at the center of the fire. The coals in the center are always the hottest, and as they are brought away from the fire, they get cold, and eventually, the flame in them dies.

You need to stay close to Jesus to stay "on fire" for Him. If you stay close to His heart and follow His ways, you will stay hot, and your faith and belief will not die out. But if you choose to walk away or are drawn away by the temptations of this world, slowly, your fire will die out and you will find yourself cold and lost, far away from Jesus. So keep yourself at the center of the fire with Him.

Jesus' Triumphal Entry

So they took branches of palm trees and went out to meet him, crying out,
"Hosanna! Blessed is he who comes in the name of the Lord, even the King of Israel!"
—John 12:13

The palm branches waved in the breeze. As I looked out from the Mount of Olives, across the valley to the beautiful old city of Jerusalem, I could see the gate where Jesus made His triumphal entry into the city during Passover week. All His life, Jesus had lived humbly, not drawing much attention to Himself as the Messiah, the Son of God. But now, children laughed and danced, praising Him openly. Adults stood in awe, those who had been healed or had a miraculous experience with Him unashamedly calling Him their King: "The next day the large crowd that had come to the feast heard that Jesus was coming to Jerusalem. So they took branches of palm trees and went out to meet him, crying out, 'Hosanna! Blessed is he who comes in the name of the Lord, even the King of Israel!' " (John 12:12, 13).

Jesus sent two of his disciples ahead and told them to bring him a colt that had never been ridden on, fulfilling prophecy. Then He rode down the Mount of Olives and into the city on the colt, with a multitude of people praising God and saying, "Blessed is the King who comes in the name of the Lord! Peace in heaven and glory in the highest!" (Luke 19:38).

This crowd following Jesus was about to witness the most crucial moment in earth's history. At the end of this week, Jesus would let Himself be taken to the cross and killed by the Romans, but truthfully killed by our sins. But He would also be raised to life again! Though they hardly knew whom they were praising, these believers in Jesus were about to witness the beginning of the Christian movement. Do you praise Jesus as King? You never know when He is about to do something incredible in your life! Let Him guide you.

Jesus in Gethsemane

And when he came to the place, he said to them, "Pray that you may not enter into temptation."
And he withdrew from them about a stone's throw, and knelt down and prayed, saying, "Father,
if you are willing, remove this cup from me. Nevertheless, not my will, but yours, be done."
—Luke 22:40–42

In this week leading up to Easter, we will now look at one of the most pivotal moments in the history of earth and faith. This moment determined our fate, and God's. Before Jesus was arrested, He took His disciples to the Mount of Olives to pray in a garden called Gethsemane. He drew away from them to pray on His own, asking them to pray and not sleep. Sadly, the disciples were so tired that they did not stay awake and pray for Jesus and themselves to avoid temptation. Meanwhile, Jesus prayed earnestly that He would not have to take on our sins and die on the cross, thus separating Himself from the Father. But He was still willing if there was no other way for us to be saved.

What is so incredible about this moment is that Jesus Himself was tempted in two ways. He was tempted as a man to avoid the suffering and death of the cross. But His divine side was also tempted to avoid taking on the penalty for sin. In *The Desire of Ages*, Ellen White talks about how Satan tried to convince Jesus in this moment that if He went through with the sacrifice, He would be eternally separated from God and might never come to life again. And even then, humans might still reject His sacrifice, making it all for nothing! But Jesus went forward with the sacrifice anyway. He was willing to give up His divinity for us! That is how incredible He is. Our God cares! Thankfully, He was raised from death, and because of that, we can have access to eternity with Him. Do you want to spend eternity with Him? You can! Just believe!

Healing an Ear

And one of them struck the servant of the high priest and cut off his right ear.
But Jesus said, "No more of this!" And he touched his ear and healed him.
—Luke 22:50, 51

The scene of Jesus healing someone who was part of the party come to take Him to His death is evidence enough of His divinity and goodness as the Son of God. Peter's attempt to protect an all-powerful Being proved his own lack of faith in Jesus' divinity because he thought he could protect an all-powerful Being! It is funny when you imagine it. Jesus probably felt compassion for Peter's ignorance as well as sorrow for his attempt, after three years of ministry by Jesus' side, to cut down what was coming. Jesus had warned them this would happen, but the disciples did not realize that until after Jesus' death and resurrection. So Jesus healed the servant, not just to heal him because of Peter's stupidity but also to teach his followers a lesson. Jesus is not a God of violence, and violence is not the answer.

His miracles always had a point and purpose. For the servant, he likely looked at Jesus differently after that, realizing there is more to this man than meets the eye. A criminal who blasphemed God would not be able to heal an ear that had been chopped off! Peter was humbled in an embarrassing instant, realizing his naive mind-set.

Jesus is a healer, not a breaker. He does not want us to use violence to spread any message. In light of the violence that tends to be present in our world today, do not look to more violence to solve those problems. Jesus' answer was trust God instead. Follow Him. Let Him be the all-powerful one.

We can learn from this story the lesson that we should not try to solve problems we see on our own. We should always trust God, not our own strength. What is in your path that God wants you to let go of and let Him take care of?

Simon of Cyrene

As they went out, they found a man of Cyrene, Simon by name.
They compelled this man to carry his cross.
—Matthew 27:32

Simon of Cyrene was a man who came from far away to worship at the temple during Passover in Jerusalem. Little did he know his life would be completely changed by a small experience on the crowded streets of the city. Where was he going when he encountered Jesus? We do not know. But regardless, he saw the Roman guards coming and a bloody man struggling under the weight of a wooden beam he would soon be killed on. The Romans caught sight of Simon and commanded him to carry the cross of a man named Jesus. Did they pick him because he was a foreigner or because he was tall and strong?

Who knows.

How do you think it affected this man to carry Jesus' cross and watch Him die on it? If he had not already heard the message of Jesus, he likely asked around and learned of His teachings. Those teachings of love and the kingdom likely changed his heart and made him a missionary of Jesus. All because of carrying a cross.

How would you be affected if you had carried the cross of Jesus? Would not you be curious about this man and everything the crowd was saying about Him? An experience with Jesus cannot leave you unchanged. Jesus asked us to take up our cross and follow Him. He wants you to die to yourself and your own selfishness and sinfulness, choosing to follow Him with your whole life. You never know what will happen when you have an experience with God. Ask Him for a divine experience with Him this week, and trust that He will change your life.

Jesus' Resurrection

Blessed be the God and Father of our Lord Jesus Christ!
According to his great mercy, he has caused us to be born again
to a living hope through the resurrection of Jesus Christ from the dead.
—1 Peter 1:3

*E*aster is a special time of remembrance for Christians all over the world. Every year people come together under the steeple to celebrate the resurrection of Christ and the gift He gave us that weekend. But what is Easter really all about?

Obviously, you are old enough to know that it is about more than the bunnies, eggs, and pastel colors that pop up every year. The Gospels each describe the death and resurrection of Christ from different perspectives, and we can learn something from each of them.

In Matthew, after the triumphal entry in chapter 21, Jesus tells many parables leading up to his death. Matthew 27 and 28 recount the entire story of the Crucifixion through the Resurrection, and even include His ascension to heaven—ending Matthew with a bang! The other Gospels contain similar stories, but each focuses on something different—take some time to read the accounts now.

But what is the point of this huge moment that defines Christianity today? Was it all for show? The answer is actually found in Genesis 3:15! God is telling the serpent what his consequence for bringing sin into the world is, and then He says this: "And I will put enmity between you and the woman, and between your offspring and hers; he will crush your head, and you will strike his heel" (NIV).

On the Roman torture machine, the cross, Jesus fulfilled this ancient prophecy and defeated the devil in a weekend! Though He and Satan had warred over humanity since the beginning in Eden, the moment Jesus rose from the grave, He crushed the devil eternally! Satan knew from that point on that he would not win this war. Jesus was the Victor for humanity!

Do Not Touch Me

Jesus said to her, "Woman, why are you weeping? Whom are you seeking?"
Supposing him to be the gardener, she said to him, "Sir, if you have carried him away,
tell me where you have laid him, and I will take him away." Jesus said to her, "Mary."
She turned and said to him in Aramaic, "Rabboni!" (which means Teacher). Jesus said to her,
"Do not cling to me, for I have not yet ascended to the Father; but go to my brothers
and say to them, 'I am ascending to my Father and your Father, to my God and your God.'"
—John 20:15–17

Youth question: Why did Jesus not let anyone touch Him after His resurrection?

At Jesus' resurrection, lots of powerful things happened: The angels rolled away the stone, and the Father and Spirit restored the life of the Son, bringing Jesus to life again. On Sunday, Mary Magdalene came to the tomb and found it empty! She was shocked and confused, crying, thinking Jesus' body had been stolen. She did not recognize Jesus until He said her name. Then, of course, she wanted to cling to Him, realizing He was alive. But Jesus says something interesting: "Do not cling to me, for I have not yet ascended to the Father."

In Ellen White's book *The Story of Redemption*, she explains that the reason Jesus ascended to the Father was to confirm with Him and all of heaven that His sacrifice was sufficient and had obliterated the possibility for evil to exist forever. He needed to ascend to heaven to know that His death on the cross had worked and to receive back His divine power both in heaven and on earth. Once He received that power, He returned to earth and appeared to the disciples.

Jesus wants you to be in a personal relationship with Him and know that He rose, regained power from the Father and the Spirit, and has made salvation available for you. He sent the Spirit into our hearts to dwell with us always so that we could have hope in Him and eternity as well as have His power within us. Have faith in His power today.

God Calls Teens

Before I formed you in the womb I knew you,
and before you were born I consecrated you;
I appointed you a prophet to the nations.
—Jeremiah 1:5

One of my favorite youth called by God in the Bible is Jeremiah. He was just a teenager when God called him to ministry! During this time in history, God was using young people to lead His children of Israel, because they were the only ones faithful to Him. The king on the throne was Josiah, who was only eight years old when God called him and probably in his early twenties at the time of Jeremiah's call!

God's first words to Jeremiah are very bold: "Before I formed you in the womb I knew you, and before you were born I consecrated you; I appointed you a prophet to the nations" (Jeremiah 1:5). But Jeremiah's response is, "Ah, Lord God! Behold, I do not know how to speak, for I am only a youth" (verse 6). Does God care that he hasn't taken speech class yet? Nope! God says, "Do not say, 'I am only a youth'; for to all to whom I send you, you shall go, and whatever I command you, you shall speak. Do not be afraid of them, for I am with you to deliver you, declares the Lord" (verses 7, 8).

God does not mince words when He calls you. He knows that, as a young person, you are driven and spirited, have a deep sense of justice and a slight sense of invincibility, and want desperately to make a huge impact on this world with your life. Never lose that sense of purpose! God is calling you for something big. He does not care if you are terrible at public speaking. He does not care if you are really shy and have a hard time talking to strangers. He does not care if you come from a bad home, get low grades, or struggle with depression. He can lift you out of those places, and He will call you regardless of them. He says, do not say, "I am only a youth," because He is going to use you *as a youth* to speak to adults who are blinded to Him. He will give you words when you need them, and He will deliver you from difficult situations. Believe in His call to you!

Justice

"Learn to do good; seek justice, correct oppression;
bring justice to the fatherless, plead the widow's cause."
—Isaiah 1:17

Justice and equality are problems that are not dealt with well around the world. Your generation has a burden for social justice and equality in your communities. When you or friends you know are pulled over by the cops solely because of the color of your skin, you probably have a sense of righteous justice. You know it is not right, and something needs to be done about it. Over the past year, you have seen how the voice of young people can be taken seriously. During the time when multiple school shootings took place over the past year or so, young people got on the news, used social media, and proclaimed their voices loud and clear: This is not OK!

So what are you going to do about it? How are you going to influence your community? How can you stand for justice and follow God in your community? You would be surprised at how well standing for justice works as an evangelism method. While Adventists are not typically political, you can still be justice oriented without being overtly political on one side or the other. Stand for what is right.

There are children on the other side of the world starving today. There is no justice in that. What can you do about it? There are wars being fought for selfish gain. There is no justice in that. What can you do about it? There are issues of racism everywhere you look, and there is no justice in that. What will you do about it?

You are young, but because of that, you have a powerful voice. God is a God of justice. Jesus preached justice. So can you. What do you think God wants you to do for justice today?

Youth in the Bible: Josiah

Josiah was eight years old when he began to reign, and he reigned thirty-one years in Jerusalem.
His mother's name was Jedidah the daughter of Adaiah of Bozkath. And he did what
was right in the eyes of the LORD and walked in all the way of David his father,
and he did not turn aside to the right or to the left.
—2 Kings 22:1, 2

Josiah's childhood was crazy. His life story starts when his twenty-four-year-old father abandons the Lord and is put to death in his own house by his servants. Upon the death of his father, Amon, the people decided the logical thing to do was make the king's son, Josiah, king in his place. So in the midst of mourning his father, Josiah is made the king as an eight-year-old boy. Do you know any eight-year-olds? Can you remember what you were like when you were eight? Now, can you image entrusting an entire kingdom to an eight-year-old? Yet not only did the people in Jerusalem do that, God did too.

Josiah followed God with his whole heart. When he turned eighteen, he sent his secretary to the temple and instructed him to ask the high priest to count the money in the temple. Then Josiah had that money used to repair the temple. While searching for this money, the high priest found the Book of the Law, dusty and worn. The secretary read this book before Josiah, and when he heard it, Josiah tore his clothes because he was convicted that he needed to lead the people back to God.

Do you let God's Word convict you? The Word of God is described as a double-edged sword, and when you read it, it may sometimes feel like it is cutting to your core! You can learn from the teenage King Josiah that God can convict and use the heart of a teenager to transform a nation. And if you let God transform your heart through reading His Word, maybe you will be the one that transforms a nation for Him!

Zombies in the Bible

So I prophesied as I was commanded. And as I prophesied, there was a sound,
and behold, a rattling, and the bones came together, bone to its bone.
—Ezekiel 37:7

Zombies in the Bible? No way! Despite their popularity on TV shows and during Halloween season, most people agree that zombies are not real. And as Adventists, we know zombies are impossible because death does not work like that. However, there is a chapter in the Bible that talks about bones coming to life in a way that very much resembles our modern pictures of zombies! Let's take a look.

Read chapter 37 of Ezekiel. In summary, Ezekiel is taken by the Holy Spirit to the middle of a valley full of bones. I do not know about you, but I'd be a little freaked out at this point! As Ezekiel walks around, he sees that the bones are very dry. God asks Ezekiel whether the bones can live, and his cryptic response is: "Oh Lord GOD, you know" (Ezekiel 37:3). Then God speaks to the bones, and as in Genesis, God's word brings forth life. "And as I prophesied, there was a sound, and behold, a rattling, and the bones came together, bone to its bone. And I looked, and behold, there were sinews on them, and flesh had come upon them, and skin has covered them. But there was no breath in them" (verses 7, 8). Then God tells him to prophesy again for the breath to come into them, and it does. The dry bones become living humans, standing on their feet, thousands of them in the valley.

Why did God give Ezekiel this experience? Ezekiel's job was to prophesy to Israel about rebirth, coming back to God and how the Lord would restore Israel again. Israel was like the dry bones, captives to another nation, their relationship with God dead like the bones. God wanted to bring them hope and bring Israel's future to life again.

Perhaps your life is a bit like those dry bones: your spiritual walk is almost nonexistent, or maybe you feel like a zombie just going through the motions of life without any real excitement for it in you. God wants to restore you and give you hope, just like He did for Israel. Depend on God's power to breathe life into you again.

Jesus' Symphony

"For the gate is narrow and the way is hard that leads to life, and those who find it are few."
—Matthew 7:14

Have you ever been to the symphony? I absolutely love music, so going to the symphony is always a treat! Not too long ago, I attended the symphony with my family. As the music began, we all sat on the edge of our seats with bated breath, excited to see how the musicians would perform Beethoven's Ninth Symphony. As the concert progressed, we noticed something strange. It may have been simply our perspective that caused the problem because we were at the very back in the last row on the top—farthest from the stage. We saw that at points the musicians seemed to be playing their music a bit differently than the conductor was instructing them to. They seemed offbeat or lagging behind him a bit too much. Much of this may have had to do with our distance from the stage, for the musicians certainly did a wonderful job, and it was an excellent concert. But it reminded me of how important it is for us to listen to God, as He is our Conductor. If we are not in tune with Him, our lives will quickly become offbeat. We may choose to follow the ways of the world, like the musicians following those around them, instead of following God's leading in our lives, the narrow path.

Matthew 7:13, 14 says, "Enter by the narrow gate; for wide is the gate and broad is the way that leads to destruction, and there are many who go in by it. Because narrow is the gate and difficult is the way which leads to life, and there are few who find it" (NKJV).

Keeping the commandments and following the teachings of Jesus will keep us in tune with our heavenly Conductor. Living to the beat of His music is more rewarding and fulfilling than trying to do our own thing or live our own way. Just as a symphony sounds good only if all the musicians are following the conductor together, so our lives will be rewarding and fulfilling if we as a church and as individuals follow God together. This is also a reason why corporate worship is so important. The orchestra cannot get its full sound and play the music correctly unless all the instruments are in place and all members play their parts. Worshiping together in church is important because it brings us into fellowship with one another and keeps us in tune to the needs of others and how we can help them, as well as worshiping God in a different way than we would if we were at home doing our devotions only. Find different ways you can take part in the worship service at your church. And always follow the way that the Conductor leads you.

We Believe: Creative Sabbath

"Remember the Sabbath day, to keep it holy. Six days you shall labor,
and do all your work, but the seventh day is a Sabbath to the LORD your God.
On it you shall not do any work, you, or your son, or your daughter, your male servant,
or your female servant, or your livestock, or the sojourner who is within your gates.
For in six days the LORD made heaven and earth, the sea, and all that is in them,
and rested on the seventh day. Therefore the LORD blessed the Sabbath day and made it holy."
—Exodus 20:8–11

Creative Sabbath observance is critical in today's world. When you think of keeping the Sabbath, do you think of what your parents say you are not allowed to do? Or do you think of evangelism? The Sabbath can be a day when you invite your friends to join you for a mountain hike or an evening bonfire. Sabbath is a day to worship God and find creative ways to spread His love to the world. What can you do on Sabbath that is different and special beyond every other day of the week? Pick an outreach project to do in your local community on Sabbath. Find a soup kitchen to volunteer at, or create a youth event you can invite local teens to. Have a gym night Saturday evening at your local school. Jesus is Lord of the Sabbath, and He wants you to use it both as a day of rest and worship and of evangelism and reaching out to your community for Him.

The Fundamental Beliefs of Seventh-day Adventists describes Creation and its connection to the Sabbath in this way:

God has revealed in Scripture the authentic and historical account of His creative activity. He created the universe, and in a recent six-day creation the Lord made "the heavens and the earth, the sea, and all that is in them" and rested on the seventh day. Thus He established the Sabbath as a perpetual memorial of the work He performed and completed during six literal days that together with the Sabbath constituted the same unit of time that we call a week today. The first man and woman were made in the image of God as the crowning work of Creation, given dominion over the world, and charged with responsibility to care for it. When the world was finished it was "very good," declaring the glory of God. (Gen. 1, 2; 5; 11; Exod. 20:8-11; Ps. 19:1-6; 33:6, 9; 104; Isa. 45:12, 18; Acts 17:24; Col. 1:16; Heb. 1:2; 11:3; Rev. 10:6; 14:7.)*

---

* "Seventh-day Adventist Church, "Creation," in *28 Fundamental Beliefs* (General Conference of Seventh-day Adventists, 2015), 4, https://szu.adventist.org/wp-content/uploads/2016/04/28_Beliefs.pdf.

My Heart Is Free

I will run the way of Your Law,
for You will give me a willing heart.
—Psalm 119:32, NLV

The Word of God should be a freeing force in your life, something you read that causes you to be inspired and set free! God's commands were never meant to shackle you or keep you down. They are not confining measures meant to keep you in chains. No! God's words, both in the commandments and elsewhere in the Bible, are meant to be freeing! They free you from sin and bondage on this earth. They free you from the devil's grasp. They free you to be yourself in a world that tries to define who you should be.

Today I want you to spend your devotional time *doing* something. Since God's Word frees you, what is something it inspires you to do? If you cannot go do something right now, plan a time today that you will do something with the freedom you receive in God's promises over your life. I've given you a few ideas to get you started. Then on the blank lines, journal about your time *doing* something for God and what the outcome was!

- Write a letter to your grandparents.
- Write an encouraging note to a teacher you look up to.
- Talk to your pastor about a question you have about faith, God, or the Bible.
- Text a friend you haven't seen in a while.
- Take a selfie with three things or people you see God working through.
- Write your favorite Bible verse in fancy lettering and hang it on your wall.
- Do something kind for a stranger (as long as it is safe!).
- Volunteer to play your instrument at a nursing home.
- Leave a nice card for your pastor at the church.

_____

_____

_____

127

The Dream of World History

"You saw, O king, and behold, a great image. This image, mighty and of exceeding brightness, stood before you, and its appearance was frightening. The head of this image was of fine gold, its chest and arms of silver, its middle and thighs of bronze, its legs of iron, its feet partly of iron and partly of clay. As you looked, a stone was cut out by no human hand, and it struck the image on its feet of iron and clay, and broke them in pieces. Then the iron, the clay, the bronze, the silver, and the gold, all together were broken in pieces, and became like the chaff of the summer threshing floors; and the wind carried them away, so that not a trace of them could be found. But the stone that struck the image became a great mountain and filled the whole earth."
—Daniel 2:31–35

Daniel, a young man used by God in a foreign land, spoke to kings, interpreted dreams, and saw history in a day. Verses 31–35 of Daniel 2 are Daniel's retelling of King Nebuchadnezzar's famous dream of a large statue made of different metals and clay. What was the point?

Nebuchadnezzar's kingdom of Babylon was the powerful golden head, whom God first gave power to. But soon after this, Daniel saw the next part of the prophecy come to life, when Babylon was given over to Media-Persia, represented by the torso of silver. Eventually the Persian kingdom was conquered by Greece, represented by bronze, and the Roman Empire would be last, shown by iron. The feet of iron and clay are the kingdoms that were split up after Rome, trickling down to 2019. And hopefully soon, the "stone" will come, which represents Christ's second coming! The stones smashes away all sinful, earthly kingdoms and sets up forever the eternal kingdom of God.

We know these prophecies from the Bible are accurate because you can look back in your history book and see that each of those kingdoms was overrun by the next! There are two beautiful gems in this chapter, though, that we sometimes forget when we get all excited about the prophecy. First, God used a young person, Daniel, to share this prophecy with the world's most powerful king at the time. God uses young people for big things! Second, there is a reminder that the whole Bible points to Christ and His victory over Satan. The Second Coming is represented in this chapter, giving hope that the sins of this world will not last forever. God can use you like He did Daniel, and He also gives you hope in His soon return.

Even When He Is Silent—Part 1

*When Ahithophel saw that his counsel was not followed, he saddled his donkey
and went off home to his own city. He set his house in order and hanged himself,
and he died and was buried in the tomb of his father.*
—2 Samuel 17:23

Suicide—the unexpected thief in the night that steals away a brother, sister, friend, or classmate. It is a topic we often avoid because it feels taboo. However, you or someone you know have probably lost a friend or family member to suicide. In fact, suicide is the tenth leading cause of death, according to the American Foundation for Suicide Prevention.[*]

There is a story in 2 Samuel about a man named Ahithophel who was a trusted advisor to King David. In 2 Samuel 16:23, we discover that his advice was thought to be like the word of God Himself. Ahithophel's counsel was highly esteemed; and when Absalom turned against his father, David, Ahithophel gave Absalom advice about how to overthrow the king. Another advisor, Hushai, who was loyal to David, gave Absalom opposite advice in order to thwart Ahithophel's plans. Absalom did not choose to follow Ahithophel's advice, and as a result, Ahithophel resorted to the worst possible ending to his story—he committed suicide.

The family he left behind keenly felt Ahithophel's suicide. How do we deal with unexplainable loss and the finality of death? We will discuss this more in tomorrow's devotion, but for today, I want you to take some time to think about what your knee-jerk reactions are to tragedy. How often do you try to handle your emotions yourself instead of giving them to God?

---

[*] "Suicide Statistics," American Foundation for Suicide Prevention, accessed June 19, 2018, https://afsp .org/about-suicide/suicide-statistics/.

Even When He Is Silent—Part 2

Fear not, for I am with you; be not dismayed, for I am your God;
I will strengthen you, I will help you, I will uphold you with my righteous right hand.
—Isaiah 41:10

Depression and self-harm are prevalent in today's society, even among Christians. As we learned from yesterday's story about Ahithophel, suicide can claim a life at the most unexpected times. Ahithophel was upset that his counsel was ignored; he knew that he had betrayed his king and friend David, and this drove his depression and despair. Instead of seeking forgiveness, he took his own life.

God cares about those who are hurting, and He wants to comfort the hearts of those who have thoughts of suicide. He has the ability to heal all wounds, and while the devil may work overtime in these cases, God is always stronger.

If you have a friend who is going through depression or having thoughts of suicide, be sure to talk to a trusted adult. Encourage them to seek professional help through counseling and talking to a doctor. If they are comfortable speaking to a pastor or other spiritual mentor, having a spiritual support system around them is important for getting through dark times.

If you have had thoughts of suicide yourself, do not be silent. Talk to someone about it—a friend, a teacher, a parent, a neighbor, a mentor, a pastor, a counselor—anyone you trust. There is help, and Jesus gives hope. You can get through this!

Finally, if you have lost someone to suicide, do not give up on God. You likely have questions about why He let it happen. It is normal to go through different stages of grief as you mourn the loss of a loved one and question God's goodness. God is still love, He is still good, and He will defeat sin and the devil completely one day very soon!

Faithfulness and Love

When the LORD first spoke through Hosea, the LORD said to Hosea,
"Go, take to yourself a wife of whoredom and have children of whoredom,
for the land commits great whoredom by forsaking the LORD." So he went
and took Gomer, the daughter of Diblaim, and she conceived and bore him a son.
—Hosea 1:2, 3

The story of the prophet Hosea is marked by two major traits God asks him to have, mirroring God's response to Israel: faithfulness and love. The book opens by revealing that Hosea is prophesying during the reign of King Jeroboam II in Israel, who was a very wicked king. The people of Israel followed his wicked example. During this time, Hosea is called to show God's faithfulness to them through his own life.

So God asks Hosea to marry a prostitute and have kids with her. He wants Hosea to build a family with a woman he knows will never be faithful to him, yet God asks him to love her anyway. Gomer has three kids all within the first chapter, and in chapter three, she is already sleeping around with other men. God tells him to go love her, even though she is committing adultery, and buy her back from the man she is with. And God says the whole purpose of this is to show the people of Israel their own unfaithfulness to God and His continued redemption of them. All God wants is for Israel to stop worshiping other gods and truly follow Him. He wants them to choose a relationship with Him and experience His love for them.

The point of Hosea's experience is to point us to a relationship with God. Do not be a hypocrite like the Israelites were, doing your own thing six days of the week and then turning around and devoting yourself to God on Sabbath. Do not be a Gomer. Be faithful, and experience God's love. Just like with the Israelites, He wants to redeem you, have a relationship with you, and let you experience His love. Make the choice today to give up the other "gods" you have been chasing after and devote yourself only to the true God. Choose to experience the love He has for you!

Got Milk?

Therefore, rid yourselves of all malice and all deceit, hypocrisy, envy,
and slander of every kind. Like newborn babies, crave pure spiritual milk,
so that by it you may grow up in your salvation, now that you have tasted that the Lord is good.
—1 Peter 2:1–3, NIV

One of the most successful, longest-running ad campaigns is the "Got Milk?" advertisement. It started in the 1990s, and you still see roadside billboards, magazine ads, and TV commercials of people sporting the milk mustache with the famous question, "Got Milk?" The advertisement campaign has obviously been successful!

Peter writes about how babies need their mother's milk to survive. A child thrives on it and grows because of the nutrients it provides. He then likens this to spiritual milk, something people need to grow in their salvation experience. Accepting salvation from Christ is a simple step, but the journey of salvation does not end at that choice. Making the decision to follow Jesus and be baptized is only the beginning of a walk with God, not the end!

In order to grow in your salvation experience with Christ, you must continue to be fed spiritual "milk." You would starve if you did not eat every day. Likewise, you will starve spiritually if you do not feed your walk with God every day. Peter's counsel is to *crave* pure spiritual milk. Long for it with all your heart, seek after God in every way you can, every chance you get! *Crave* time with Him. By chasing after a relationship with God every day, you will grow in your salvation experience with the Lord and become spiritually strong. Before long, you will be the one helping others taste and see that the Lord is good!

Peer Pressure

My son, if sinners entice you, do not consent.
—Proverbs 1:10

How often do you make a decision based on what your friends think? Being well-liked and doing what everyone else is doing may seem like a great decision in the moment, but in the future, it could have negative consequences for you. Learning to think for yourself and trust God's ideals instead of what your friends think is difficult, but rewarding.

When I was a teenager, the most popular brands to wear were Hollister and Abercrombie & Fitch. The most popular people at school sported brand name T-shirts, so I thought that is what I needed in order to fit in. I realized very quickly that those brands were more expensive and that even though I might have a shirt that looked cool, it did not really change much for my social status. How you dress does not determine who you are.

Peer pressure can come in far more negative ways, however. Smoking, drinking, doing drugs, and partying can get you into lots of trouble—and not just with the law. Aside from the fact that drinking and smoking are illegal at your age, they also can permanently mess up your brain. It is not worth potentially ruining the rest of your life just to fit in with a group of people you admire.

Be bold and unafraid to stand up for what is right, and be smart about how you live your life. Value what God has given you, stay away from things that will harm you, and encourage your peers to follow God's principles in those areas as well. His guidance will keep you safe and healthy throughout your life. That is worth resisting negative peer pressure for!

We Believe: Contaminated DNA

The heart is deceitful above all things,
and desperately sick; who can understand it?
—Jeremiah 17:9

You have been created in the image of God. Theologians have always struggled to pinpoint exactly what this means and how it is affected by our sinful humanity. Because Adam and Eve sinned against God, His perfect creation has been tainted.

Imagine an artist painting a beautiful piece of artwork. Then imagine a copyist coming along and painting a replica of that original painting. Then imagine a five-year-old kid duplicating it as well. Naturally, anything copied off the five-year-old's painting would be distorted from what the original image looked like. You might see some resemblance in colors and shapes, but overall, it just would not be as good as the original.

Sin's entrance into human DNA is similar—we are a distorted image of our Creator. Certain pieces of Him can still be seen in us, but because of sin, we are not perfectly portraying His image. Yet God still calls us to reflect Him on this earth as best we can, which is part of why Christ came to earth. Here is what the Fundamental Beliefs of Seventh-day Adventists says about the nature of man and God's restoration plan for us:

Man and woman were made in the image of God with individuality, the power and freedom to think and to do. Though created free beings, each is an indivisible unity of body, mind, and spirit, dependent upon God for life and breath and all else. When our first parents disobeyed God, they denied their dependence upon Him and fell from their high position. The image of God in them was marred and they became subject to death. Their descendants share this fallen nature and its consequences. They are born with weaknesses and tendencies to evil. But God in Christ reconciled the world to Himself and by His Spirit restores in penitent mortals the image of their Maker. Created for the glory of God, they are called to love Him and one another, and to care for their environment. (Gen. 1:26-28; 2:7, 15; 3; Ps. 8:4-8; 51:5, 10; 58:3; Jer. 17:9; Acts 17:24-28; Rom. 5:12-17; 2 Cor. 5:19, 20; Eph. 2:3; 1 Thess. 5:23; 1 John 3:4; 4:7, 8, 11, 20.)*

---

* Seventh-day Adventist Church, "The Nature of Humanity," in *28 Fundamental Beliefs* (General Conference of Seventh-day Adventists, 2015), 4, https://szu.adventist.org/wp-content/uploads/2016/04/28_Beliefs.pdf.

Joel

"And it shall come to pass afterward,
that I will pour out my Spirit on all flesh;
your sons and your daughters shall prophesy,
your old men shall dream dreams,
and your young men shall see visions."
—Joel 2:28

Joel is a very unique book in the Old Testament. It is short—only three chapters—so go ahead and read it! The author's primary narrative throughout the book is about a powerful "day of the Lord," one that has happened in the past and one that will happen again in the future when God saves His people from evil. In the midst of the stories about devastation from invasion, there is hope of the restoration of God's people and a very special thing that will happen in the future: "And it shall come to pass afterward, that I will pour out my Spirit on all flesh; your sons and your daughters shall prophesy, your old men shall dream dreams, and your young men shall see visions. Even on the male and female servants in those days I will pour out my Spirit" (Joel 2:28, 29).

In the Old Testament, God's Spirit was traditionally seen as residing in the temple, visibly seen through the pillars of cloud and fire in the desert, and understood as located in the sanctuary. However, this verse points forward to that moment in Acts 2:1–4 when God's Spirit enters His followers and hovers above their heads like flames of fire. Joel suggests that in the future, God's Spirit will not only reside in the temple but also reside in the hearts of His people and that His Spirit within them will prompt them to do incredible things for Him!

Part of this verse specifically mentions sons and daughters, young men and women following God. We see it fulfilled in part by Ellen White, a teenage girl to whom God gave visions and a ministry. But I think very soon we will see it fulfilled in full as God's Spirit is seen in teens like you! Be open to however He moves you and whatever He convicts you to do.

Jesus Teaches Me Patience

What is my strength, that I should wait? And what is my end, that I should be patient?
—Job 6:11

relationship with Jesus can teach you patience. But what is the purpose of having patience, anyway? Read these two verses to find out:

"For in this hope we were saved. Now hope that is seen is not hope. For who hopes for what he sees? But if we hope for what we do not see, we wait for it with *patience*. Likewise the Spirit helps us in our weakness. For we do not know what to pray for as we ought, but the Spirit himself intercedes for us with groanings too deep for words." (Romans 8:24–26; emphasis added)

"Put on then, as God's chosen ones, holy and beloved, compassionate hearts, kindness, humility, meekness, and *patience*, bearing with one another and, if one has a complaint against another, forgiving each other; as the Lord has forgiven you, so you also must forgive." (Colossians 3:12, 13; emphasis added)

The first verse tells us that our salvation through Jesus gives us a hope that is not seen. We hope for Him whom we cannot see, and we wait patiently for Him. We pray, and the Spirit helps us, so we wait for Jesus' answer with patience.

In the second verse, we learn that to be a chosen one of God, we must be patient people. We must be willing to forgive. We must be patient with one another when we disagree with others.

A relationship with Jesus teaches patience, and that patience helps us wait for answers from God about our calling. I asked God for many years where He was taking my life, and I had to choose to be patient and see what He would do with it. While patience might be hard to hold on to, try to have some today. What are the things you need patience for and can give to God today?

_____

_____

_____

My Jesus Mirror

*But the LORD said to Samuel, "Do not look on his appearance
or on the height of his stature, because I have rejected him.
For the LORD sees not as man sees: man looks on the outward appearance,
but the LORD looks on the heart."*
—1 Samuel 16:7

Often when I look at myself, I see only my imperfections. I struggled for a long time to recognize that I am a beautifully made, strong child of God. Confidence in who God made me to be took time. When you look in the mirror, what do you see? Many times when we look in the mirror, we have difficulty seeing who God really created us to be. Yet you are God's masterpiece! He wants you to see in yourself the worth He sees in you.

Do not measure your worth based on what others say or think of you. Do not listen to the lies of people who talk behind your back or say mean things about you. Their words and their opinions do not matter. Did you hear me? *It does not matter!* The only thing that matters is what God says about you! I know it is hard to let go of what people say about you or what their opinions are, especially when it is said behind your back and you find out through the grapevine of gossip. Words are very hurtful. But if you can learn to let go of what others say and not care so much about their opinions, you will be so much healthier mentally and happier!

You are unique, beautiful, handsome, and talented in God's eyes. Learn to see yourself that way—through His eyes. You hold the potential to do great things for God with your life. Allow Him to transform you. Look at who you are in Christ. Explore how He views you, and you will be amazed at the transformation that will take place! You will begin to look in the mirror and see a different person—someone stronger, bolder, more beautiful or handsome—and then you will realize, that is you! That is who God created you to be! And you can use this blessing from God to be a blessing to others and help them see themselves how God sees them as well.

Providential Pop-Tarts

"In the same way, let your light shine before others,
so that they may see your good works and give glory to your Father who is in heaven."
—Matthew 5:16

I stood in the grocery line at Safeway and stared aimlessly at the various maga-zines with celebrity's faces plastered all over them; catchy headlines about cheating spouses, baby rumors, and plastic surgery filled their covers. When my turn came, my friend and I unloaded the contents of our grocery cart for the checker to scan. Amid the healthy foods we had selected—fruits, vegetables, and nondairy supplements—we had one box of Pop-Tarts. They were a staple of grade school lunches, and we had felt nostalgic that day, so we grabbed some to try for "old times' sake."

The man in line behind us stared for a bit, then looked sheepishly at his cart. It was full of unhealthy food. He started laughing and commented, "At least you guys have some Pop-Tarts! Now I do not feel so bad about my cart!" His humor at our apparent health obsession prompted a lively discussion in line about eating food that is better for your body and the changes we have noticed when we choose to eat unhealthful foods.

Normally my witnessing radar is completely off, and it was not until we were out in the parking lot that my friend and I realized we had the perfect oppor-tunity to invite him to a series of health talks at our church, primarily related to diet! I scribbled down the information on a slip of paper, and we walked awkwardly back into the store. After inviting him to the seminar, we laughed a bit more about the Pop-Tarts in the middle of all the fruits and veggies.

Witnessing is not hard, and God puts simple opportunities to do so in our path every day. He knows what people need and what messages they may re-spond to. For this man, it was something health-related. Someone else might be interested in joining a sports league you play on or going to a music concert at your church. There are hundreds of ways to witness and share Jesus with others. Ask God to place a "divine appointment" in your path this week so that you can witness for Him.

Ethical Justice

"But let justice roll down like waters, and righteousness like an ever-flowing stream."
—Amos 5:24

Today we are going to do a word study into the Hebrew meaning behind this powerful verse smack-dab in the middle of the book of Amos, one of the Minor Prophets. Here's some context: Amos was a shepherd in Judah, near Bethlehem. He lived during the time of the divided kingdom when King Jeroboam II in Israel was leading God's people far away from Him. Amos was called by God to preach against this and share about God's coming judgment on Israel, as well as the hope for God's people to live righteous lives instead of unholy ones.

The Hebrew word translated "justice" in this verse is *mishpat*. It is used to talk about justice and judgment: doing what is right and treating others respectfully. *Mishpat* is used multiple times throughout the Bible to describe God's love of justice, how He promises never to pervert it, and it is often used in reference to treating the marginalized people of society with kindness and respect. Exodus uses it in reference to being fair to the poor and needy. It is also often paired with the word *righteousness*, meaning that when you have *mishpat*, you will do what is right to stop injustice from happening and use it to promote righteous actions instead.

The Hebrew word translated "righteousness" in this text is *tsedaqah*. This word is the result of just actions: treating people respectfully and living as God would have you live. In the Old Testament, it is used many times when God is protecting His people and administering justice to their enemies for their sinful actions against His people. *Tsedaqah* is treating people ethically. Deuteronomy uses it in the context of having an upright heart, one that is ruled by ethical justice.

In Amos, God powerfully states that He wants His people to treat others with ethical justice—being kind, fair, and righteous in your actions toward others no matter what the social differences between you are. This can be hard when all you see in someone else is the things you disagree with. But God calls you to a higher standard, asking you to be His example by treating people with ethical justice and thus living a righteous life.

Mother's Day

Hear, my son, your father's instruction, and forsake not your mother's teaching,
for they are a graceful garland for your head and pendants for your neck.
—Proverbs 1:8, 9

Mothers are special women God has blessed with patience, strength, and the ability to love no matter what. While no mother is perfect, the woman who holds that place in your life, biological or not, cares for you more than herself!

I was blessed with a mother who loves everyone around her more than herself and selflessly serves her family every day. She is consistent in her relationship with God, always dedicating the first hours of her day to spending time with Jesus. She has shown me what hard work looks like, and she loves me even when I am not the nicest.

When I was in high school, my mom and I did not always get along. I had a stubborn streak, wanted to do things my way, and was very independent in my thinking. I knew I was right, and I could prove why! Unfortunately, that got me into a lot of arguments with my mom, and we had times when we hurt each other's feelings deeply. I would seclude myself in my room, not wanting to talk about what happened anymore. Usually, my mother made the first move and would come to check on me and make sure I was OK, and we would end up hugging and talking out our differences. For a while, we never thought it would end and were worried we would never get along again. But, thankfully, I outgrew that phase, and we are super close now!

If you do not always get along with your mom or the woman who fills that role in your life, do not stress about it. You will grow out of this phase. Try to be patient, understand what your differences are, and ask God to help you respect those differences so that you do not hurt each other. Mothers are a special gift, and your mom will always love you, no matter what! Treasure every moment you have together.

Mountaintop Views

The mountains quake before him; the hills melt;
the earth heaves before him, the world and all who dwell in it.
—Nahum 1:5

I have friends who are mountain climbers. They take off on the weekends and go climb gnarly cliffs and snowy glaciers. If the weather is clear, they get to see stellar sunrises from the highest points on earth. But in order to get those incredible views, they must spend hours of hard work climbing, often in the dark, to get to the top. They must settle in and learn to enjoy the climb because the majority of their experience is hard work.

I am not a mountain climber. I have never tried it, and the idea of traversing across mountain slopes for hours on end does not sound exciting to me; it just sounds hard. I would rather someone just fly me to the top so that I can see the view. But what sort of accomplishment would that be?

We do not get the view from the mountaintop without the climb. Let me say that again, and let it sink in this time: *You do not get the view from the mountaintop without the climb.* Whatever your mountain is—bad grades, an injury, a breakup, a backstabbing friend, a job that is hard for you—you do not get the view without the climb. But that means that if you keep climbing, if you keep struggling through, at some point, you are going to overcome your mountain. You will reach the top and get to see an amazing view! You will get over that obstacle and see the amazing chances that lie ahead of you!

The best part of climbing your spiritual mountains is that God is climbing with you. Sometimes He might even carry you across a crack in the glacier, or give you extra breath in the thin air. You do not have to struggle with your mountains alone. God is with you, and He will keep climbing with you until you reach the top and see the amazing view He has ready for you.

Zambian Blessings

And he lifted up his eyes on his disciples, and said:
"Blessed are you who are poor, for yours is the kingdom of God."
—Luke 6:20

Her eyes looked up at me so innocently. I could only imagine the hardship of her life. She was a young orphan with a baby sister she carried around on her hip constantly. She was incredibly responsible for being so young. They were both dusty, with lice in their hair and bugs around their eyes and lips. Yet they smiled the most beautiful smiles I had ever seen, despite their yellow, rotting teeth.

She came to every evangelistic meeting we had and listened intently as I told the children stories from the Gospel of Luke. She always wanted to take a picture and give me a hug or hold my hand. She was probably four or five years old. I marveled at how all that responsibility was lying on the tiny shoulders of a little four-year-old girl in Zambia. Sometimes I would see her sitting with the older women in the village, and they would hold her baby sister on their laps for a bit, looking her over carefully to make sure she was healthy enough to survive. I am sure they would have taken these two girls into their homes if they could have, but even they were struggling to survive.

This was a huge wake-up call for me. I imagined my home in America, where I had all the food and clothing I could ever want or need. I never had to worry about where I would sleep at night or whether I would eat the next day. I could feel God tugging at my heart and telling me to not take what I have for granted and to dedicate my life to serving others as they were.

Those children, the ones who had tattered clothing and bugs swarming their faces, who had lice in their hair and dirt caking their skin—those children taught me a powerful lesson. True happiness and unescapable joy do not come from *things*. They can come only from God. Those children had nothing, while I had everything, by worldly comparisons. But those children had greater joy than I in leaps and bounds! They spent their days running from house to house, singing about Jesus and inviting their friends to church. They got their joy from serving God and sharing His love with others in their village—and with me.

When you are tempted to complain about what you do not have, remember those less fortunate than you. When you are lacking in joy, remember that the way to gain true happiness is through Jesus Christ!

Airport Runaround

*Because, if you confess with your mouth that Jesus is Lord
and believe in your heart that God raised him from the dead, you will be saved.*
—Romans 10:9

Gate S16," the ticket read. I stood in the security line, unpacked and re-packed my belongings, and then looked for the signs to my gate. I had about thirty minutes to find the gate before boarding, so I had no worries about getting to the plane on time. I quickly located the direction to the correct terminal, which included taking an underground tram to the other side of the airport. When I reached my gate, to my surprise, only one elderly couple stood near the ticket counter; the rest of the seats were completely empty. Confused, I looked up at the board of flight information. Oh no! My flight had been changed to a completely different terminal!

Just as I was leaving, another group of confused passengers arrived and realized the same thing, so we all began searching for the new gate together. The flight board said one thing; our tickets said another . . . which way to go? We had to make a decision. After running as fast as we could to the correct terminal, with only a few minutes to spare before boarding would be closed, we finally found the gate, with most of the people already loaded onto the plane.

Thankfully, getting to heaven is not that complicated! I am so thankful for a God of grace and mercy who gives salvation as a free gift, not as a reward for earthly achievements. Getting to heaven is simple: all you have to do is believe! Jesus is the way, the truth, and the life, and through Him, you are welcomed in as a child of God.

Obadiah

For the day of the LORD is near upon all the nations. As you have done,
it shall be done to you; your deeds shall return on your own head.
—Obadiah 1:15

Obadiah is one of the tiny Minor Prophet books that you probably have not paid much attention to before. Since it is only one chapter long, I suggest that you read it now!

Whew! It is quite a chapter! Battle, pride, deceptive hearts, thieves, slaughter, violence—it is a busy chapter full of intensity! But what is the background for this book? Obadiah was a prophet who received a vision about the relatives of the Israelites: Edomites. The nation of Edom sat right next to Israel, and they were also descendants of Abraham and Isaac, but not Jacob. They descended from Isaac's other son, Esau—the hairy man who sold his birthright to his brother Jacob for some stew. Esau became a powerful man, and his descendants followed in his footsteps. Unfortunately, as we see in Obadiah, they did not always treat their Israelite relatives kindly.

When Israel was beaten down by the Babylonians, Edom stepped in and plundered them. Through Obadiah, God promises to punish Edom for their actions against Israel. "Because of the violence done to your brother Jacob, shame shall cover you, and you shall be cut off forever" (Obadiah 1:10).

Although this chapter seems dismal and destructive, there is a message of hope embedded in it: "Saviors shall go up to Mount Zion to rule Mount Esau, and the kingdom shall be the LORD's" (Obadiah 1:21). There is hope in this chapter, like in many of the prophets' books, for the restoration of God's people and the spreading of His kingdom through Israel to all nations.

This book is a good reminder that God expects us to act kindly toward our brothers, sisters, and relatives. Sadly, we tend to hurt those closest to us the most, just like Edom and Israel. We are reminded here that God wants us to love one another, and that when we do that, His kingdom is spread and His love is shown to the world.

Growing Like Crazy

"You did not choose me, but I chose you and appointed you
that you should go and bear fruit and that your fruit should abide,
so that whatever you ask the Father in my name, he may give it to you."
—John 15:16

Confession time: I am a crazy plant mom. I love getting cute little plants and potting them. Watching how much they grow brightens up my life. But confession number two: I do not have a green thumb, and I frequently kill plants by overwatering them, giving them too much or too little sun, or who knows what else. I have not had good luck with plants, so I buy plants—not seeds to start myself.

In 2017, however, I decided to try to tackle some seeds. I got a pot, put in some Miracle-Gro, and carefully planted a bunch of seeds according to the directions. After a few weeks of watering and waiting, I was sad to see no change in the pot. I gave up hope and thought they would not grow.

Then one morning when I was getting ready for work, I went to open the blinds and was surprised to see lots of tiny little plants had sprouted in the pot! Over the next few months, I watched them grow into flourishing plants, eventually producing vegetables I could eat and share with my friends!

Do not give up hope. Personal growth takes time and lots of patience. Forgive yourself when you do not grow in the ways you thought you would, or when you do not complete a goal in the amount of time you thought you would. God will produce good fruit from your efforts in His time. Just wait and see! I had to wait weeks to see the sprouts, and months to see their vegetables. In the same way, God will produce good fruit in your life if you are patient and let Him work.

Pity the Plant or the People

But God said to Jonah, "Do you do well to be angry for the plant?" And he said,
"Yes, I do well to be angry, angry enough to die." And the LORD said, "You pity the plant,
for which you did not labor, nor did you make it grow, which came into being in a night
and perished in a night. And should not I pity Nineveh, that great city, in which there are more
than 120,000 persons who do not know their right hand from their left, and also much cattle?"
—Jonah 4:9–11

Jonah's story starts with a prophet whom God calls to minister to Nineveh, a Gentile city completely against God. Jonah runs away from God by getting on a ship headed for Tarshish, in Spain! God intervenes by causing a storm, then Jonah volunteers to be thrown overboard; God lets him get swallowed by a whale, where he hung out for three days and nights. Finally, the whale threw him up on dry ground. So off Jonah went to warn Nineveh of the coming consequences for its sins. When the king of Nineveh heard Jonah's prophecy, he actually listened, to Jonah's surprise. He commanded all the people to turn from their evil ways, and God decided to save them and not destroy the city because of their repentance.

At the end of the book, we find Jonah sitting angrily outside the city, where he could watch God destroy the city. God, in His mercy, made a plant grow up quickly and cover Jonah so that he would not faint in the heat of the sun. When God later let it wilt, Jonah got mad and wanted to die from the heat. The story ends with God questioning His prophet about his lack of compassion for the people of Nineveh. What?

I think one reason this book is included in the Bible is to remind us of our own hypocrisy. It is so easy for us to get comfortable ministering to only certain people. Frequently God calls us out of our comfort zone! How often do we grumble about it without watching for God's good work, focusing instead on how those miserable people will ruin themselves? God reminds us that 120,000 persons, and even cattle, are more important than our annoyance at and resistance to His grace. Ask God to help you always accept His way instead of your own.

We Believe: The Great Controversy

*"And if it is evil in your eyes to serve the L*ORD*, choose this day whom you will serve,*
whether the gods your fathers served in the region beyond the River, or the gods of the Amorites
*in whose land you dwell. But as for me and my house, we will serve the L*ORD*."*
—Joshua 24:15

Once a student asked me what the great controversy meant. I explained that in the context of the Bible, it means a war that is going on right now between God and Satan. It began when Satan sinned against God, convinced one-third of the angels in heaven to follow him, and was kicked out of heaven for rebelling against God. From the moment humans gave in to the devil's temptation to sin, we have been central characters in this war. Battles are fought over our minds and the decisions we make every day. Ultimately, Christ's death on the cross won the war, but there are still many battles that will be waged until His second coming. Until then, we must choose who to follow: God or the enemy.

The Fundamental Beliefs of Seventh-day Adventists explains the great controversy in this way:

All humanity is now involved in a great controversy between Christ and Satan regarding the character of God, His law, and His sovereignty over the universe. This conflict originated in heaven when a created being, endowed with freedom of choice, in self-exaltation became Satan, God's adversary, and led into rebellion a portion of the angels. He introduced the spirit of rebellion into this world when he led Adam and Eve into sin. This human sin resulted in the distortion of the image of God in humanity, the disordering of the created world, and its eventual devastation at the time of the global flood, as presented in the historical account of Genesis 1–11. Observed by the whole creation, this world became the arena of the universal conflict, out of which the God of love will ultimately be vindicated. To assist His people in this controversy, Christ sends the Holy Spirit and the loyal angels to guide, protect, and sustain them in the way of salvation. (Gen. 3; 6-8; Job 1:6-12; Isa. 14:12-14; Ezek. 28:12-18; Rom. 1:19-32; 3:4; 5:12-21; 8:19-22; 1 Cor. 4:9; Heb. 1:14; 1 Peter 5:8; 2 Peter 3:6; Rev. 12:4-9.)*

---

* Seventh-day Adventist Church, "The Great Controversy," in *28 Fundamental Beliefs* (General Conference of Seventh-day Adventists, 2015), 5, https://szu.adventist.org/wp-content/uploads/2016/04/28_Beliefs.pdf.

Wind Chimes

*Do not be anxious about anything, but in everything by prayer
and supplication with thanksgiving let your requests be made known to God.*
—Philippians 4:6

Outside my grandparents' living room window is a beautiful set of large wind chimes. When the wind blows, their soothing melody chimes out across the garden. On a stressful day, the sound of the wind chimes can be so relaxing to the tired mind!

As I watched the wind chimes move in the wind, I realized something interesting about them: to make that beautiful sound, they must be hit. They go through a "stressor" in order to create that glorious noise. Without that initial hit, they will not sound at all but just blow silently in the wind.

When you are hit by something stressful in life, you get to choose how you respond. The wind chimes have one choice because of how they were made: to make a beautiful noise. God made you to also make a beautiful noise with your life, but when stressful moments hit you, He gives you a choice as to how you will respond. You can stress out and blow in the wind, but with no purpose. Or you can choose to make something good out of it and redirect your stress into productivity or creating something beautiful instead. And better yet, when you let the Holy Spirit work in your heart during stressful times, He can transform you and change your response to being hit by stress. His presence in you can give you a calm assurance of peace and His love for you. And through you, the Holy Spirit can work to be a blessing to others as well.

Happy Hormones

You make known to me the path of life;
in your presence there is fullness of joy;
at your right hand are pleasures forevermore.
—Psalm 16:11

Hormones! I know you hate that word. Teachers talk about it. Parents talk about it. Sometimes adults use it as the reason why they think you are acting in a way you should not be. Or they say, "Hormones are normal, your body is going through changes!"

"Blah, blah, blah, please, can we not talk about this, Mom?" Do not worry, you are not alone.

So let's talk about hormones that make you happy. Serotonin, dopamine, oxytocin, and endorphins are all hormones secreted in your brain that make you feel things like joy and love . . . and goosebumps when you see your crush. God created us with these hormones so that we would be able to bond with one another in a loving marriage or feel good when we meet a goal we have been working toward. He wanted us to have a way to measure love and joy in life in our emotions and feelings, and that is the job of hormones!

Dopamine is the hormone that makes you feel happy when you meet a goal; it is the feeling of excited joy that goes off in your brain when something good happens. Oxytocin is a bonding hormone that lets you feel love and trust toward another person, like when you hug your mom, or it may be why you might really like a shoulder massage! Serotonin is important for keeping your mood happy on a regular basis. The vitamin D you get when you go for a walk in the sunshine will help your body produce serotonin. Believe it or not, carbs are actually good for you because they help with the production of serotonin as well! Endorphins are the hormones that rush through your body when you exercise. They prevent the feeling of pain and can help you push yourself during an intense basketball game or soccer match.*

Thank God for these hormones, because they help you live a happy and healthy life. Do some activities that will produce more healthy hormones in your system and contribute to a better mental state as you face the stresses in your path this week. Your Creator made you well!

---

* "The Four 'Happy Hormones,'" Joyful Days, accessed June 19, 2018, http://www.joyfuldays.com /happy-hormones/.

Seek Justice and Love Mercy

"He has told you, O man, what is good;
and what does the LORD require of you but to do justice,
and to love kindness, and to walk humbly with your God?"
—Micah 6:8

This verse from the prophet Micah is one of my favorite verses in the entire Bible. I remember walking to class when I was in college and seeing it on the outside wall of one of the buildings, a beautiful reminder of the three pillars of living a God-led life. Let's discuss those three pillars:

1. Seek justice

God has called you to live a life of social justice. Jesus was the perfect example of this. He cared for the poor, He loved the widows and orphans, He helped those in need, He healed and preached and taught. He forgave and loved the most unlovable in society. He touched people with disgusting diseases covering their skin. He looked into the eyes of prostitutes, eyes only filthy men had ever looked into. He asked tax collectors and Zealots to work together, people on complete opposite ends of the political spectrum in Israelite society. He worked hard for justice, and as He taught about the kingdom of God on earth, one of its primary pillars was justice for the underprivileged.

2. Love mercy

Depending on the version you read, either *mercy* or *kindness* is used here. God asks you to forgive. He wants you to love those around you, to show kindness to people who are not kind to you, and to have a merciful attitude toward people who let you down. Be an example of what His grace looks like.

3. Walk humbly with your God

Most importantly of all, walk with Him. Have a relationship with Him. Do not flaunt it like some prize you won because you are better than everyone else. Use that relationship as the source of your strength. Let Him fill you and ooze out of your heart! Let Him drive your work for social justice, loving-kindness, and merciful grace toward those around you. That is what God requires of you.

Empathy

If one member suffers, all suffer together;
if one member is honored, all rejoice together.
—1 Corinthians 12:26

Empathy has incredible power. Being empathetic means you do not just sympathize with someone and what they are going through but actually listen and feel their stories in your heart. I remember one day when I was going around after school to say hi to the kids, and out of the corner of my eye I saw a student on the other side of the gym shrink into the corner, put her head down, and start shaking a little bit. I finished my conversation and went over to sit down right next to her. I put my head down too and asked her what was wrong. She cried quietly for a little bit and then began to open up to me about her life. At home, her parents were arguing. At school, students were bullying her. There was no church connection in her life. I comforted her, listened and prayed with her, and continued to check up on her following that event. Eventually she started asking questions about God and wanted to read the Bible together. So I gave her a Bible, and she read that Bible nonstop for the next few hours after school!

Empathy for her meant having me listen and care. I was her safe place to share her story, and I felt her pain with her. And because I felt that pain empathetically, she trusted me and began pursuing God because of that first conversation. Be empathetic, and God can use you to reach people you would never expect need help.

Salvation and Honor

*"Honor your father and your mother,
that your days may be long in the land
that the LORD your God is giving you."*
—Exodus 20:12

While playing a game called Things with my family, one question asked us to name things that were the most hassle for teenagers. Everyone secretly wrote down their answers and passed them to the person who would read them aloud. Almost every answer had something to do with parents! We all laughed at the similarity of our answers, noting that every teen goes through some kind of aggravation with the people raising them.

When I was a teen, my mom and I did not always get along. I was the typical stubborn, strong-willed eldest child, constantly questioning my mother's wisdom and authority. Unfortunately, it was not until college that I started to realize that everything she said and did was in my best interest. Your parents love you more than you know, and they will do anything to protect and guide you in the right way—even if it means disciplining you.

Respecting and honoring your father and mother is not something God just said to be ornery to teens. He instructed it both to help people remember to take care of their parents in their old age and so that we would respect their wisdom and learn from them. God is like a parent to us: He loves us, always has our best interest in mind, and gave up His life for us, yet He lets us deal with the consequences of our actions so that we learn right from wrong. Your parents are doing their best to follow His example—loving you, raising you, guiding you through life, giving you opportunities, and letting you deal with your actions. They also would probably give up their life to save you if it came to that. A parent's love is one of the most intense connections between humans! It is worth honoring.

God even says He will bless us if we honor our parents! Try writing a note of encouragement to your parents and leaving it somewhere they can find it while you are away at school or with friends. Let them know you are thankful for all they do for you and the sacrifices they have made so that you can have a better life.

Nahum

The LORD is good, a stronghold in the day of trouble;
he knows those who take refuge in him.
But with an overflowing flood
he will make a complete end of the adversaries,
and will pursue his enemies into darkness.
—Nahum 1:7

In our series about the Minor Prophets of the Old Testament, we come upon the book of Nahum. It begins as an "oracle concerning Nineveh." If you've got the time, read it! I bet you did not learn these stories in Sabbath School class growing up!

One of Israel's most annoying neighbors was Assyria. The Assyrians were constantly plundering God's people, attacking cities, and destroying all in their path in a violent wave of oppression. This book is about the fall of Assyria and its destruction by God because of the way they treated His people. Nineveh was the center of Assyria, the seat of power, so its destruction would be the downfall of the entire nation.

In this book, Nahum reveals God's glory in magnificent ways, similar to how Job talks about God's power. God is seen as the Creator who brings justice to those who have inflicted pain on His chosen people. And Nahum 1:7 is the hopeful reminder that God is the safe place for His people to seek refuge. The book promises destruction to Israel's enemies and victory and safety in God.

You can learn from Nahum how God is always in control. No matter what, He cares about His people, and He will do what is necessary to save them. Because He is just, He will not let destructive earthly political powers continue in their evil forever. He will use their arrogance against them. This book also reminds us of how seriously God views violence toward your fellow man. He does not want you to use it as your source of strength, He needs to be in that place in your life. Let Him be the one who fixes the problems of the oppressors, and take refuge in His protection. He always defends the innocent, and He will take care of you in any circumstance.

Be Yourself

For everything created by God is good,
and nothing is to be rejected if it is received with thanksgiving.
—1 Timothy 4:4

Individuality is not something most people are conditioned to appreciate. The social atmospheres you circulate in tell you to be a certain kind of person, act in certain ways that are seen as acceptable, attract attention through specific means, and surround yourself with like-minded people who agree with you and get along with you.

During high school, I loved playing on our school's basketball team. But when I was an underclassman, I was easily intimidated by the girls who were a few grades above me on the team. I figured they knew exactly what they were doing, they had it all together, and that if I wanted to be popular, I needed to be like them. One day one of the older girls made fun of me and said I looked stupid when I was running. Now, I am a fast runner, and it has been my one area of pride in sports my whole life, so her taking a jab at that hurt me more than getting made fun of normally would. Her words tore me down, and comments like that throughout high school caused me to try and be a person I was not. I tried to please others, and I thought I needed to be accepted and approved of by the popular crowd.

In college, I discovered how freeing it was to just be myself and have the personality God gave me instead of trying to be somebody else. I was much happier not trying to be like other people or please those I thought were popular. Knowing I am God's child made a world of difference in my outlook on life and my own self-esteem!

Be proud of who you are. Be yourself. Be who God made you to be. Never try to be someone you are not. Do not do things just to please others. Be your own unique individual. That is the most beautiful thing of all. And if you are worried about attracting a guy or girl based on these things, trust me, one of my very attractive male friends once told me that what makes someone attractive is when they are unapologetically themselves, not trying to be something they are not. Your uniqueness is attractive, so express it!

Sexual Purity

Put to death therefore what is earthly in you:
sexual immorality, impurity, passion, evil desire, and covetousness, which is idolatry.
—Colossians 3:5

Cue the awkward cringes, immature giggles, and grossed out faces that spread across the classroom whenever this topic comes up in class. Sexual purity is something you need to think seriously about in high school, however. You have likely encountered sexual content of some kind at least once in your life. From the racy photos in your Snapchat news to the Instagram photos that pop up and the advertising photos in the mall or on TV, sexual content is everywhere—and what you see affects you.

If you feel tempted to get involved sexually with someone you like, slow yourself down and wait. Giving yourself away now will be something you regret later and may lead to unexpected consequences, like becoming a parent far too young or harming someone else physically. Here are a few ways you can guard yourself and protect your sexual purity:

- *Be careful what you watch.* Protect your eyes from porn, and choose not to view it.
- *Walk away from compromising situations.* If you feel tempted sexually, physically remove yourself from the situation. Walk away.
- *Get a mentor.* If you do not feel comfortable confiding in your parents about things you may have already done, talk to a pastor, teacher, or another adult you trust. If you have a school counselor, that person may be a great resource for you. Stay accountable to them.
- *Date your values.* When you choose to date someone, make sure they have the same values as you do. Do not be shy in talking about your moral convictions and sticking to them.
- *Stay casual.* If you choose to date in high school, do it in groups or casual settings. Do not be alone with the other person, or you may be tempted more heavily.

Even though it is an awkward topic, committing yourself spiritually to God and choosing to save your sexuality for marriage will be so much more rewarding. If you already have done things that you feel guilty for, God is a God of second chances, and He can forgive you and help you stick to new moral convictions.

God's Wondrous Works

"Look among the nations, and see; wonder and be astounded.
For I am doing a work in your days that you would not believe if told."
—Habakkuk 1:5

Too often I find myself reading the latest news headlines or listening to the most recent radio broadcast about wars and the terrible things happening all over the world, and my first response is: God, where are You? What are You doing? What is Your plan here? How long are You going to let this last?

It is easy to see only the negative things happening in the world; yet God is Lord of all, and He is still doing a good work on this sinful planet. Habakkuk serves as a reminder of His power, an answer to my questions: *Look and see what I am doing. Be amazed at the miracles that are being performed in nations all over the world! See all the lives that are being changed and the hearts that are turning to Me? I am doing a good work here still; trust that I have everything under My control.*

In Habakkuk's day, God amazed the people by using a Gentile nation, pagans who did not worship Him, to complete His task. He used the Chaldeans, better known as Babylonians, to mark out history. And as we know from the prophet Daniel's experience, God even spoke to Babylonian kings, turning their hearts to Him!

God gives us grace when we doubt, and He keeps working and moving despite our doubts. Instead of getting all caught up in the depression of the headlines, look for the good that He is doing. Read mission stories; be amazed at the work God is doing around the world! Be encouraged. And look in wonder as He does ministry through unexpected people.

He Will Make You New

Having purified your souls by your obedience to the truth for a sincere brotherly love,
love one another earnestly from a pure heart, since you have been born again, not of perishable
seed but of imperishable, through the living and abiding word of God; for

"All flesh is like grass
and all its glory like the flower of grass.
The grass withers, and the flower falls,
but the word of the Lord remains forever."

And this word is the good news that was preached to you.
—1 Peter 1:22–25

I love spring. There is something profoundly spiritual about this season: What has been hidden beneath the cold, hard ground of winter is not dead; it is just waiting for the right time to emerge and grow. Flowers such as the crocus, tulips, and daffodils poke up through the dirt as the ground thaws in the warmth of spring. They grow, withstanding the rain showers that come unexpectedly. They wait patiently for the warmth of the sun to give them strength to grow into their full beauty. Soon the beautiful bloom of the flower emerges with bright color and joy into the world again.

You may feel a bit like a bulb in the winter—hidden beneath the cold, hard reality of life. The social circle at school never seems to have room for you. You do not feel like you are measuring up to your parent's expectations. The pressure to compete against classmates and do better than them weighs you down. The standards for beauty and strength that the world sets seem unattainable.

Yet you are like those flowers. God is waiting for your springtime when He can bring you into your moment of full beauty and strength. Be patient and wait on Him; His timing is perfect. The teenage years are awkward for everyone. Almost every adult will tell you they look back and cringe, thankful for where God has taken them! I know I have certainly changed since high school, and God has given me the confidence to be myself and everything He made me to be. He will give you that strength and confidence as well. Be patient, wait for His Son to shine on you, wait for your spring moment, and He will grow you into exactly what He has made you to be.

We Believe: Jesus Is Everything

And [He] was declared to be the Son of God in power according to the Spirit of holiness by his resurrection from the dead, Jesus Christ our Lord, through whom we have received grace and apostleship to bring about the obedience of faith for the sake of his name among all the nations.
—Romans 1:4, 5

The Adventist doctrine of Jesus' life, death, and resurrection is one of our most pivotal beliefs. Without it, we would have no reason for our faith! Our name is *Seventh-day Adventists*—worshiping on the Sabbath and looking forward to the soon return of Jesus Christ! If Jesus was just a man, we would have no foundation for our beliefs. Because He was not just a man but was actually the Son of God, we have an eternal hope in His soon return! His death wipes our sins clean, and His resurrection guarantees that our place in heaven is reserved. Jesus is our everything! Believe in Him, and live with an eternal hope.

Here's how the Fundamental Beliefs of Seventh-day Adventists describes the importance of Jesus' life, death, and resurrection:

In Christ's life of perfect obedience to God's will, His suffering, death, and resurrection, God provided the only means of atonement for human sin, so that those who by faith accept this atonement may have eternal life, and the whole creation may better understand the infinite and holy love of the Creator. This perfect atonement vindicates the righteousness of God's law and the graciousness of His character; for it both condemns our sin and provides for our forgiveness. The death of Christ is substitutionary and expiatory, reconciling and transforming. The bodily resurrection of Christ proclaims God's triumph over the forces of evil, and for those who accept the atonement assures their final victory over sin and death. It declares the Lordship of Jesus Christ, before whom every knee in heaven and on earth will bow. (Gen. 3:15; Ps. 22:1; Isa. 53; John 3:16; 14:30; Rom. 1:4; 3:25; 4:25; 8:3, 4; 1 Cor. 15:3, 4, 20-22; 2 Cor. 5:14, 15, 19-21; Phil. 2:6-11; Col. 2:15; 1 Peter 2:21, 22; 1 John 2:2; 4:10.)*

---

* Seventh-day Adventist Church, "The Life, Death, and Resurrection of Christ," in *28 Fundamental Beliefs* (General Conference of Seventh-day Adventists, 2015), 5, https://szu.adventist.org/wp-content/uploads/2016/04/28_Beliefs.pdf.

Zephaniah

"For at that time I will change the speech of the peoples to a pure speech"
—Zephaniah 3:9

The book of Zephaniah is intense! It is only three chapters long, but it begins with a very harsh-sounding judgment from God on the Israelites, who have turned away from Him. The prophet Zephaniah, who lived during the reign of King Josiah, wrote this book. Josiah was a good king who in his youth worked hard to bring God's people back to worshiping Him. He restored the temple and had the Scriptures read aloud for the first time in ages! Sadly, the Israelites did not all turn 180 degrees from their evil to follow God in goodness again. Instead, many of them continued in their old ways. So Zephaniah was one of the many prophets in this time period who tried to warn God's people of their coming captivity and destruction at the hands of the Babylonians.

While most of this book is about the harsh judgment of God and the consequences of choosing sin instead of following Him, the last part of the book gives us a sense of hope—finally! The prophet writes:

> For at that time I will change the speech of the peoples to a pure speech, that all of them may call upon the name of the LORD and serve him with one accord. . . . On that day you shall not be put to shame because of the deeds by which you have rebelled against me; for then I will remove from your midst your proudly exultant ones, and you shall no longer be haughty in my holy mountain. But I will leave in your midst a people humble and lowly. They shall seek refuge in the name of the LORD. (Zephaniah 3:9–12)

This gives hope for God's people! He is pointing forward and letting His people know that He will restore them and fulfill that promise. He will heal their wounds and transform their sinful lives into a testimony about Him. How have you seen this fulfilled in your own life?

Walmart Woes

Children, obey your parents in the Lord, for this is right.
"Honor your father and mother" (this is the first commandment with a promise),
"that it may go well with you and that you may live long in the land."
—Ephesians 6:1–3

One day while perusing the endless aisles of Walmart, I overheard an inter-esting conversation between a father and his adult daughter. The father was obviously a successful man, wearing a nice dress shirt, slacks, a tie, and some fancy shoes. He was very well put together and appeared to be wealthy from all outside appearances. In contrast, his daughter, an adult probably in her thirties, appeared disheveled. She was dressed in sagging, dirty sweatpants, a too-tight tank top, and an oversized sweatshirt. Scuffed sneakers and a messy hair bun finished her look. Her face and mannerisms sadly revealed her addiction to drugs.

In the cart, the father was pushing a sad young girl, soon revealed to be his granddaughter. She was surrounded by a few toys, and her grandfather was asking her questions about what she wanted from the store. Then the arguing started. The father and daughter began a heated debate over what to get the girl. The father obviously had money that he wanted to spend on higher quality items for his granddaughter. But her mom wanted him to buy things for her because she did not have enough of her own money. From repeated, loud state-ments, it was clear the father was the financial support for his granddaughter but had cut off his daughter due to her poor behavior and bad spending habits.

The daughter disrespected her father's advice and counsel on how to improve her life and habits as they argued back and forth down the aisles around me. I was sad listening to it; sad to hear a family that was already broken falling apart even more. What would become of them? How would the little girl grow up?

It reminded me of the importance of respecting our elders and those who have more experience than we do. If we do not, this family's story could turn out to be our own sad reality. Do you respect your parents and their wisdom and experience?

Powerful Words

A man who is kind benefits himself,
but a cruel man hurts himself.
—Proverbs 11:17

Words are one of our most powerful tools. They can slice people open like a knife or sew them back together like a suture. Think of a time someone's words cut you to the heart. What did they say that hurt you so badly?

_____

_____

Now, think of a time someone was able to heal your pain with words. What did that person say that soothed your heart and helped you heal?

_____

_____

When you look at these two examples from your life, you can probably remember the tremendous impact both events had on you. Because words are so powerful, we must think carefully about how we use them. But what is really special is that you can change people's whole outlook on life simply by speaking kindly to them or encouraging them in a time of crisis. Think of a student at your school or a member of your youth group who is frequently left out or made fun of. Write a short note of encouragement to this person. If you feel brave enough to speak those words to him or her, go for it, and encourage this person the next time you see each other! If you are too shy, that is OK; you can give him or her the note of encouragement instead. Being able to encourage people well is a spiritual gift. Ask God today whether He has given you this gift and how you can use it to help others.

What Is Tithe?

"Every tithe of the land . . . is the LORD's; it is holy to the LORD."
—Leviticus 27:30

Every Sabbath in churches around the world, someone will get up front and talk about the importance of giving money to help keep the church running. You have no doubt heard countless offering calls in your lifetime. Maybe at your church the kids bring up the offering, or maybe the deacons do. When I was young, my parents would slip me a dollar bill to place in the offering plate at church.

What are offerings anyway, and why do we give them? There are two main types of offerings, or money that you give to God. The first kind is called tithe, which is 10 percent of the money you make that you give back to God. The second kind is whatever "offering" beyond that 10 percent that you feel convicted to give to the church to help with its various ministries.

So tithe—what is it, and where did this 10 percent tradition come from? Giving 10 percent to God started early on. The first time the giving of tithe is recorded is from Abram, after he defeats Chedorlaomer and rescues his nephew Lot. Genesis 14:19, 20 relates, "And he blessed him and said,

'Blessed be Abram by God Most High,
     Possessor of heaven and earth;
and blessed be God Most High,
     who has delivered your enemies into your hand!'

And Abram gave him a tenth of everything."

The man blessing Abram was Melchizedek, who was both the king of Salem (the future location of Jeru*salem*) and a priest of God. Abram gave him 10 percent of everything he had as a tithe, money for God.

In Leviticus 27:30, tithe was made a requirement for the people of Israel: "Every tithe of the land, whether of the seed of the land or of the fruit of the trees, is the LORD's; it is holy to the LORD." Today your tithe goes to help pay pastors, teachers, evangelists, conference workers, Bible workers, and missionaries around the world. All the ministries in your local church are funded by the offerings beyond what you give in tithe. Reevaluate how much you give to God, and ask Him to guide your giving and budgeting.

Driving Like Jesus

Whoever walks in integrity walks securely,
but he who makes his ways crooked will be found out.
—Proverbs 10:9

"In memory of . . ." the sign listed the names of four people, two of them presumably a married couple, because they had the same last name. This blue sign was next to a busy road where people whizzed by every day, probably never noticing the sign asking them to drive safely, "in memory of."

You have probably seen many "in memory of" signs in your lifetime beside busy streets, on park benches, or next to freeways. They remind us of those who have been killed by a reckless driver who was too tired, too busy texting, drinking, doing drugs, or too distracted to pay attention to their surroundings. Life is precious, so we should take care to protect it.

Likely you and many of your friends have begun learning to drive. If you have the opportunity to go to a driving school and take classes on motor vehicle safety, do it! The knowledge you gain may save a life someday. Learning new things such as driving gives you a chance to give something huge in your life to God. When you are learning to drive, develop habits such as praying when you get in the car for safety on your drive. Pray for the people you see on the road. Be patient with drivers who are impatient, and send up a prayer for them too.

Believe it or not, you can be a great witness on the road just by driving how Jesus would drive—safely and kindly. Show other people Jesus' love by being smart out on the roads. It might not be the first place you would think about being a good Christian example, but people can tell a lot about you based on how you drive! I remember times when I have seen families praying at stop signs or heard people listening to a Christian radio station and singing along with the windows down or someone in traffic slowed down to let me in their lane, and I wondered whether their kindness came from a Christian heart. God can use you even as you learn to drive.

The Encouragement of Haggai

"Work, for I am with you, declares the LORD of hosts, according to the covenant that I made with you when you came out of Egypt. My Spirit remains in your midst. Fear not."
—Haggai 2:4, 5

The book of Haggai is all about rebuilding God's temple in Jerusalem after the Israelites had been in captivity from Babylon for a long time. At the time of Haggai's prophetic ministry, the Babylonians had been conquered by Media-Persia, and Darius is king. You might remember him from the book of Daniel! Haggai shares God's Word with the people of Israel, bringing their attention to their actions. They are more concerned with their own selfish desires, building houses to live in, while God's temple is in ruins. The people listened to Haggai, and they obeyed God's voice. God promised to be with them, and they began to rebuild the temple. In chapter two, God encourages the leaders, Zerubbabel and Joshua, to fear not, continue building, and be strong because God is with them.

This book is like the final joyous hurrah for God's people. They have gone through terrible captivity, they have strayed from His ways, but finally, they are coming back to worship Him, and God is pouring out His blessings upon them.

Haggai is encouraging because it reminds us of God's faithfulness. God did not give up on the people of Israel though they treated Him horribly. And God does not give up on you. Even if you come from a rough past and have a family history that is terrible, that does not need to define your future. God asks you to turn away from those things and focus on Him instead. He will bless you and transform your life into a powerful testimony of Him. Let His blessings rain down on your life. Be strong and do not fear. God is with you, and He will help you in all you do!

School's Out!

"The flowers appear on the earth, the time of singing has come,
and the voice of the turtledove is heard in our land."
—Song of Solomon 2:12

chool is ending, and the summer is beginning. While you are going to miss
the friends you cannot see during the summer, it is also a great time to grow
in your relationship with Christ. Usually there is an Adventist camp meeting
or two that you will attend with your family. Go to the Youth class and really
soak in what the speaker talks to you about. If your family enjoys camping and
summer road trips, enjoy the time in the outdoors and try to find creative ways
to connect with God while hiking or sightseeing; just remember your mosquito
repellant!

Here's a summer challenge: Pick three ways you want to grow with God and
make a plan of how to accomplish them. Write them here:

1. _____

_____

2. _____

_____

3. _____

_____

Do you want to grow with God through Christian music? Take this summer
free time to discover new artists, write some lyrics of your own, and try putting
together a song for Him. Do you want to grow in your prayer life? Begin a
prayer journal or list, and add new things to it every day. Do you want to read
interesting theological books? Talk to your pastor and parents to get some ideas,
and check out some at a local library.

Community

Live in harmony with one another.
Do not be haughty, but associate with the lowly.
Never be wise in your own sight.
—Romans 12:16

One of the most important Christian principles demonstrated by Jesus' ministry was His effort to create and encourage a sense of community among His believers. Jesus believed community was important. He attended the synagogues on Sabbath to worship with the believers. He traveled with a group of people who took care of one another. He encouraged participation in faith. He taught about caring for those in your community—the poor, disabled, widowed, and all who were marginalized in the Jewish community.

Yet His words infused truth into the lives of the people He touched, and out of His push for community was born a movement of Christian believers who truly followed His principles for a thriving community. How can you let His model of community infuse your sphere of influence? In your church, do believers truly take care of one another and care about the needs of the people around them? Think of ways you can expand the sense of community in your local church or school! You do not need to be in student government to create a sense of community. You can start simply by saying hi to people in the hallway, or high-fiving more than just your friends as you walk past them on the way to class. Talk to the people who share the lockers around you—find out how their day is going, and use more phrases than the typical:

"How are you?"

"Good."

"Good! See you later."

Community starts with the initiation of one person, so be that one person that begins it! Trust that God has got your back on this, and the Holy Spirit will inspire those you talk to so that they also will spread the sense of community. Soon you will see the results—more people loving, caring, and truly taking the time to nurture relationships with those around them!

Sometimes Life Is Just Hard

Jesus looked at them and said, "With man it is impossible,
but not with God. For all things are possible with God."
—Mark 10:27

Being a teenager is tough. It is an exciting time of life but also a time when you are trying to figure out who you are and make sense of the painful world you live in. You develop some of your deepest friendships, experience some of your worst heartaches, and figure out what things you are most passionate about in life. But sometimes the hard moments do not pass, and you discover you are suffering under a cloud that will not go away. If you or someone you know is suffering from depression, here are some ways you can spot it and deal with it:

Do you have any friends who are not interested in sports anymore like they once were? Do your friends complain about always being sleepy and feeling worthless about themselves? Do you notice that your friends have started hanging out with people who are a bad influence on them, or perhaps they have started using drugs or alcohol? Have any of your friends ever talked about death, self-harm, or suicide? Are you the one going through this?

If so, **get help:** check out **suicide.org** or call **1-800-273-8255** or **1-800-852-8336**; these are both suicide hotlines with trained, professional counselors on the other end to help you through what you are feeling.

I have friends who have unsuccessfully tried to commit suicide, and they have ended up coming out the other side of their depression much happier people who are now living successful lives and helping others who are going through depression. Their number one message is, do not give up—there is help, and you will get through this! Open up about how you are feeling to someone you trust, and ask them to help you take the steps to get professional help. In the meantime, here are a few tips: spend time with friends, do not play video games or check social media as often, exercise, get involved in extracurricular activities you enjoy, eat healthfully, and find a place to volunteer and help other people. If you are an animal person, interacting with a pet or volunteering at an animal shelter are some of the best ways to help deal with depression! Most importantly, pray. Focus on your relationship with God. Read your Bible—especially from the book of Psalms. Let God be a part of this healing process; He really will get you through it!

Children's Day

And they said to him, "Do you hear what these are saying?"
And Jesus said to them, "Yes; have you never read,
'Out of the mouth of infants and nursing babies you have prepared praise'?"
—Matthew 21:16

Today is Children's Day! Kids are annoying, kids are sweet, kids are messy, kids are adorable. Kids. If you are one of the older siblings in your household, you know how precious and annoying younger siblings can be. Even in seventh and eighth grades, being the older ones in the school, the younger grades can be quite annoying to deal with. Kids look up to teens, however, and they watch you—what you do, how you act, what you say, what you wear—and they want to be just like you.

I was reminded of this recently when a young girl, after listening to me preach one Sabbath, asked her mom if she could get an outfit like mine. I was wearing a simple pantsuit—black slacks and a black blazer, nothing fancy. But because she looked up to me, she wanted to be like me and dress like me. I felt very honored. It was a special moment—but also a realization that kids are always watching—and they may copy you!

Can you think of kids in your church or school who always seem to want to talk to you, play with you, give you hugs, or seek to find approval in your eyes? These kids are looking to you as a mentor, a big sister or brother, and they need you to support them. Even though sometimes it can be annoying, the rewards of loving those kids and paying attention to them will pay off later in life. You never know how you could change their life just by caring about them! Write down the names of a few kids whom you want to be more intentional about mentoring, and spend some time praying for them today:

_____

_____

_____

We Believe: We Are Justified

He has delivered us from the domain of darkness and transferred us to the kingdom
of his beloved Son, in whom we have redemption, the forgiveness of sins.
—Colossians 1:13, 14

*J*ustification is a big word. It means to show something as right or reasonable. Religiously, that means righteousness in God's eyes. Since we are sinful, we are not righteous because sin is rebellion against God. However, when Jesus died on the cross and rose again, He took our place completely. He delivered us from sin's power. Through Him we are justified and worthy of receiving eternal life. This gift is given because Jesus paid the price for you. He was the sacrifice in your place. And because He took that on, you are given the opportunity to have not just an earthly relationship with Him but an eternal one as well! The deepest longings of your heart on earth are nothing compared to how God will fill you up with joy, peace, and happiness in heaven with Him!

The Fundamental Beliefs of Seventh-day Adventists describes Jesus' redemptive act to give us salvation like this:

In infinite love and mercy God made Christ, who knew no sin, to be sin for us, so that in Him we might be made the righteousness of God. Led by the Holy Spirit we sense our need, acknowledge our sinfulness, repent of our transgressions, and exercise faith in Jesus as Savior and Lord, Substitute and Example. This saving faith comes through the divine power of the Word and is the gift of God's grace. Through Christ we are justified, adopted as God's sons and daughters, and delivered from the lordship of sin. Through the Spirit we are born again and sanctified; the Spirit renews our minds, writes God's law of love in our hearts, and we are given the power to live a holy life. Abiding in Him we become partakers of the divine nature and have the assurance of salvation now and in the judgment. (Gen. 3:15; Isa. 45:22; 53; Jer. 31:31-34; Ezek. 33:11; 36:25-27; Hab. 2:4; Mark 9:23, 24; John 3:3-8, 16; 16:8; Rom. 3:21-26; 8:1-4, 14-17; 5:6-10; 10:17; 12:2; 2 Cor. 5:17-21; Gal. 1:4; 3:13, 14, 26; 4:4-7; Eph. 2:4-10; Col. 1:13, 14; Titus 3:3-7; Heb. 8:7-12; 1 Peter 1:23; 2:21, 22; 2 Peter 1:3, 4; Rev. 13:8.)*

---

* Seventh-day Adventist Church, "The Experience of Salvation," in *28 Fundamental Beliefs* (General Conference of Seventh-day Adventists, 2015), 5, https://szu.adventist.org/wp-content/uploads/2016/04/28 _Beliefs.pdf.

Generation Z

"Thus says the LORD of hosts, Render true judgments, show kindness and mercy to one another, do not oppress the widow, the fatherless, the sojourner, or the poor, and let none of you devise evil against another in your heart."
—Zechariah 7:9, 10

ne of the most beautiful and powerful things about your generation, labeled Generation Z, is that you are not afraid to speak up about injustices that you see in the world. A defining character trait present in your generation is acceptance and love. In a similar way, the prophet Zechariah lived during the time after the Israelite people who had been living as exiles in Babylon finally returned to Jerusalem to rebuild the city and God's temple.

"Thus says the LORD of hosts, Render true judgments, show kindness and mercy to one another, do not oppress the widow, the fatherless, the sojourner, or the poor, and let none of you devise evil against another in your heart" (Zechariah 7:9, 10). During Zechariah's day, God used this prophet to try to call His returned people to continue working toward these principles in their city. Throughout the book, Zechariah has a series of dreams that are prophetic and symbolic in their nature, representing both the things that have happened between Babylon and Media-Persia and the promise of the coming Messiah. And in it is a promise of hope and a return to a peaceful state where God will bless His people tremendously. But the blessings are available only if that generation of Israelites stays faithful in their relationship with God (see Zechariah 6:15).

You are the next wave of leadership to rise up in the church, and you are already using your voice in powerful ways. Keep these verses from Zechariah 7 close to your heart. Form fair opinions about people. Be kind to everyone. When you meet someone who comes from a rough past, help them and care for them; do not put them down or bully them. Care for the poor. Befriend the new student who moves to your school or church. Keep evil away from your heart. Follow God with everything you have, and be a kind example of Him.

Inside Your House

"And I will give you a new heart, and a new spirit I will put within you.
And I will remove the heart of stone from your flesh and give you a heart of flesh."
—Ezekiel 36:26

Imagine this scene with me: You are walking down a residential street on a beautiful day. Both sides of the street are lined with houses of all shapes and sizes. Some have large windows, perfectly manicured lawns, and fancy trimmings. Some are small and humble, with white picket fences around the yard and a tree with a swing in front. Some are drab, with grey paint chipping away from the walls. As you walk down the street, you inspect the numbers carefully, glancing down at the paper in your hand, until you finally reach the house with the address on the paper. You have been told that this is your house, a perfect representation of you, inside and out. Imagine with me—what does it look like on the outside?

You turn the doorknob and swing the door open wide. Imagine that the inside of your house is like the inside of your heart. What does it look like? Is it clean, or a complete mess? Walk through the house in your mind, and look at every room. What do you see? What state is your heart in?

One of my chaplains in college had a group of us do an exercise similar to this at a leadership retreat. I remember sitting there with my eyes closed, thinking of my house—a representation of everything that I am, both good and bad. On the outside, my house was perfect. There were flowers everywhere, and it was very inviting. But on the inside, it was bare, empty, with hardly any furniture, charred as if it had been burned. There was a painting on the wall that showed what the house used to look like on the inside—beautiful, lavish, and pure. I realized at that point in my life that I was drifting away from God. Sure, I was involved in ministry, so the outside looked perfect. But on the inside, I was broken and discouraged. I was not where I wanted to be in my relationship with God. The next part of this imagination story is what helped change everything for me.

Now imagine that you find another door. You open it slowly and walk into a bright room. In the center sits Jesus. He holds a hammer in one hand and nails in the other. He says, "Let's go fix this place." No matter what state your heart is in right now, Jesus is always there to help fix you up and get you back on the right path. He does not care what has happened in your life, He still wants to clean you up and give you a new heart. Why not take a few moments right now to ask Him to fix your heart today?

Jesus Gives Me Faithfulness

"I will betroth you to me in faithfulness.
And you shall know the Lord.*"*
—Hosea 2:20

Peter is the disciple we are embarrassed to relate to so easily. His moments of lack of faith remind us of our humanity and distrust of God. His anger reminds us of our own impulsive reactions. But his fierce love of Jesus eventually turned him into one of the most powerful preachers and apostles for Jesus after He returned to heaven.

Sometimes Peter failed Jesus, though. He let Jesus down because he let his emotions and impulsive behavior get in the way of his connection to the Savior. While Jesus was on trial, Peter infamously denied Jesus three different times out in the courtyard. When he realized his own mistake, his heart sank and he realized his need of Jesus.

Jesus never gave up on Peter. He patiently showed compassion toward Peter and loved him despite his unfaithfulness. Jesus forgave Peter and built his faith through miraculous moments such as walking on the waters of the Sea of Galilee, healing the servant's ear that Peter cut off, and forgiving Peter for denying Him!

Like Peter, you have probably made plenty of your own mistakes that have hurt Jesus' heart. But He forgives you over and over again, extending His hand and inviting you to walk on the waters with Him. Being faithful to Jesus may not always be easy, but if you trust in Him, He will help you stay faithful. Forgive yourself for the times you mess up, and accept Jesus' forgiveness as well as you learn to walk faithfully with Him each day.

Geronimo!

And let us run with endurance the race that is set before us.
— Hebrews 12:1

"Geronimo!" It is a term that was popularized in the 1940s by the US Army when paratroopers began yelling it as they jumped out of planes. Supposedly, the night before their first jump they saw the movie *Geronimo*, which was about an Apache leader called Geronimo. This Native American was given the name Geronimo by Mexican soldiers after he attacked them with only a knife while being shot at. The soldiers would call out to their Saint Jerome, pleading for mercy as they faced the Apache they called Geronimo, who charged forward and risked his own life to protect his people. The paratroopers adopted the term and used it as their own battle cry, yelling it while they leaped out of an airplane! Since then, the term has been popularized by the media, and people today still might be heard shouting it as they jump.*

God desires that we live boldly for Him. The early Christians and apostles did not fear for their lives but charged forward into the face of danger and death to spread God's message at all costs. Read through the book of Acts, and you will quickly get a sense of the urgency and power with which the gospel message was spread.

Hebrews 12:1–3 says, "Therefore, since we are surrounded by such a great cloud of witnesses, let us throw off everything that hinders and the sin that so easily entangles. And let us run with perseverance the race marked out for us, fixing our eyes on Jesus, the pioneer and perfecter of faith. For the joy set before him he endured the cross, scorning its shame, and sat down at the right hand of the throne of God. Consider him who endured such opposition from sinners, so that you will not grow weary and lose heart" (NIV).

God asks us to be Geronimo-style Christians. We must charge forward in faith and run with perseverance, throwing off sin and living a life of example for those watching us. Being a Christian takes courage and perseverance. It is time for you to decide to follow God for yourself. It is time for you to shout "Geronimo!" at the top of your lungs and jump into the adventure God has in store for you!

---

* "Geronimo," History.com, accessed Jan. 2, 2016, https://www.history.com/topics/native-american-history/geronimo; Daven Hiskey, "Where the Tradition of Yelling 'Geronimo' When Jumping Out of a Plane Came From," Today I Found Out, updated Jan. 20, 2011, http://www.todayifoundout.com/index.php/2011/01/where-the-tradition-of-yelling-geronimo-when-jumping-out-of-a-plane-came-from/.

Persevering Amputee

Blessed is the man who remains steadfast under trial, for when he has stood the test
he will receive the crown of life, which God has promised to those who love him.
—James 1:12

Every Monday, Wednesday, and Friday morning, I try to go work out at a favorite free class at my local YMCA. Afterward, I take some time to stretch so that my muscles do not get sore. The place where people stretch has a window overlooking the entrance to the YMCA. Every week, without fail, a man is pushed into the YMCA in a wheelchair. He is elderly; his wrinkled hands grip the handles of his wheelchair.

Sometimes when I leave, I see this man in the area with lots of weight machines where you usually see the serious weight lifters. Now, this man is different from the rest—he is an amputee. I do not know why his leg was amputated, but because of his age, I imagine it could be the result of fighting in a war as a soldier. What stands out to me about this man is his incredible perseverance. Rain or shine, he shows up at the YMCA and works out as much as he physically can! He has not given up over all these years, even though he has a physical handicap.

This persevering amputee has inspired me to continue exercising on a regular basis to stay healthy. But he has also inspired me spiritually: never let your physical or spiritual "handicaps" define you or hold you back. No disability or spiritual downfall can keep you from God, even though the devil may try to convince you of that. Persevere no matter what and stand up during the trials, and you will receive the crown of life!

Little Children Sleep

Answer me when I call, O God of my righteousness!
You have given me relief when I was in distress.
Be gracious to me and hear my prayer.!

. . . But know that the LORD has set apart the godly for himself;
the LORD hears when I call to him. . . .

In peace I will both lie down and sleep;
for you alone, O LORD, make me dwell in safety.
—Psalm 4:1–8

June is the month when we celebrate Father's Day. I remember the comforting feeling of my dad's arms picking me up from the back seat of the car, cradling me carefully as he walked through the front door and took me upstairs to my bedroom. He would lay me down softly in my bed and gently place the covers over me, making sure I was all tucked in. Then he would kiss my forehead, turn out the lights, and close the door, leaving just a crack open so that I would not be too scared of the dark.

Little children often fall asleep while riding in the car. When they get home, a loving parent carries them to their bed, safe, sound, and cozy. Your heavenly Father can see when you are tired from the journeys life takes you on. He knows when you need rest. That is part of the reason that He gave us the Sabbath, a time to rest and relax from the busy week.

In moments when you are most tired, feel His loving arms wrap around you and carry you, keeping you safe and secure. Now, since it is Father's Day, go tell your dad you love him! If you do not have a good relationship with your father, spend some extra time with your heavenly Father today and be secure in His care for you. If you have another good father figure in your life, thank him for being there for you. May the Father of all give you peace and rest today!

Malachi

"I have loved you," says the LORD. But you say, "How have you loved us?"
—Malachi 1:2

Malachi is the last book in the Old Testament. It closes the history of the Old Testament and begins the four hundred years of biblical silence before Jesus, the promised Messiah, comes to earth in the New Testament. Malachi lived with Israelites who had been living in Jerusalem once again—Babylon had fallen, they were no longer exiles, and they had been freed to live at home after the Medo-Persian rule. Unfortunately, the Israelites at this time in history

were just like their ancestors, straying from God. God loves them, but they do not love Him back. They have not changed or learned anything in all the hardships they have gone through.

As you read the first chapter of Malachi, you will notice a pattern in the book. God tells them something, and they question Him. Malachi 1:2 says, " 'I have loved you,' says the LORD. But you say, 'How have you loved us?' " Sadly, God's people question Him and continue living in rebellion against Him even though they have seen how mightily He has worked for them in the past.

In your relationship with God, think about how you relate to Him. Write down a few examples of how He has worked in the past of your life. Every one of us is at risk of falling into the same pattern the Israelites did, questioning and rebelling against God even though we have seen clear evidence of Him in our lives. Take some devotional time today to talk with Him about where you are at in your relationship; think about how you want to grow, and express the questions you have so He can help you discover the answers.

Your Own Experience With God

And he said, "My presence will go with you,
and I will give you rest."
—Exodus 33:14

Today I want you to create your own devotional experience with God. Relying on someone else's words makes it easy to forget that spending time with God is about more than just reading a devotional; it is about having a living, breathing experience with Him. Below are some questions for you to ponder, and there is space for you to write your answers as you pray with God about them.

What has God placed on your heart recently?

_____

_____

Where is an area God is calling you to improve in?

_____

_____

Who are some people you need to forgive?

_____

_____

What is holding you back from going deeper with God right now?

_____

_____

How do you plan to improve that this summer?

_____

_____

We Believe: Transformation

Rejoice always, pray without ceasing, give thanks in all circumstances;
for this is the will of God in Christ Jesus for you.
—1 Thessalonians 5:16–18

When I was in high school, I thought I had learned everything there was to know and had my relationship with Jesus down. Then I discovered I was letting go of my relationship with God and replacing it with pride. God certainly humbled me.

Here is how the Fundamental Beliefs of Seventh-day Adventists describes growing in your relationship with Jesus:

By His death on the cross Jesus triumphed over the forces of evil. He who subjugated the demonic spirits during His earthly ministry has broken their power and made certain their ultimate doom. Jesus' victory gives us victory over the evil forces that still seek to control us, as we walk with Him in peace, joy, and assurance of His love. Now the Holy Spirit dwells within us and empowers us. Continually committed to Jesus as our Savior and Lord, we are set free from the burden of our past deeds. No longer do we live in the darkness, fear of evil powers, ignorance, and meaninglessness of our former way of life. In this new freedom in Jesus, we are called to grow into the likeness of His character, communing with Him daily in prayer, feeding on His Word, meditating on it and on His providence, singing His praises, gathering together for worship, and participating in the mission of the Church. We are also called to follow Christ's example by compassionately ministering to the physical, mental, social, emotional, and spiritual needs of humanity. As we give ourselves in loving service to those around us and in witnessing to His salvation, His constant presence with us through the Spirit transforms every moment and every task into a spiritual experience. (1 Chron. 29:11; Ps. 1:1, 2; 23:4; 77:11, 12; Matt. 20:25-28; 25:31-46; Luke 10:17-20; John 20:21; Rom. 8:38, 39; 2 Cor. 3:17, 18; Gal. 5:22-25; Eph. 5:19, 20; 6:12-18; Phil. 3:7-14; Col. 1:13, 14; 2:6, 14, 15; 1 Thess. 5:16-18, 23; Heb. 10:25; James 1:27; 2 Peter 2:9; 3:18; 1 John 4:4.)*

---

* Seventh-day Adventist Church, "Growing in Christ," in *28 Fundamental Beliefs* (General Conference of Seventh-day Adventists, 2015), 6, https://szu.adventist.org/wp-content/uploads/2016/04/28_Beliefs.pdf.

Online Responsibility

For each will have to bear his own load.
—Galatians 6:5

The world of the internet is a beautiful place. You can log on and surf the waves to any place you choose. One moment you can be reading a novel, the next you are in Bangladesh, exploring the city streets. You can order clothing and have it delivered to your front door, or learn about any subject. You can take classes, email your local politician, watch the news or a TV show, or use social media sites. And not only that, you do not even need a computer to do it. The whole world is accessible through your fingertips as you tap and swipe your phone screen.

Online responsibility is something we must consider. So sit for a minute and think seriously about how you use the internet, what you search for on it, how you use social media, and who your comments affect. Be responsible.

My father always counseled me wisely in regard to online content. He reminded me that once I put something out there on the internet, it is there forever. I did not want to believe him, but his words ring true, and I have seen their power firsthand.

What language do you use? What pictures do you send on Snapchat? What messages do you send? What comments do you make on other people's Instagram posts? How do your words and actions online affect those around you?

Do not believe the lie that the screen can protect you from the real-world results of cyberbullying or sending things you should not. Protect yourself and others while you are online by censoring the content you search, by being safe about who you talk to, and by thinking twice before you post something. God needs your generation to come up with new and responsible ways to use the internet and social media to further His message. So figure out how to use it for good and prevent its use for evil. The power is at your fingertips; use it wisely.

God the Lion

Seek the LORD and his strength;
seek his presence continually!
—1 Chronicles 16:11

My hand gently gripped the tail of the creature in front of me. I stepped carefully onto the dirt path, following its lead as we walked down the path through the brush. Every second felt like a dream, the sun filtering through the trees with a more magical glow than usual. But it was not a dream. My hand held the tail of a lion, and its paws padded quietly along; it seemed to not have a care in the world. Eventually we came to a large tree, and the lion climbed gingerly into the branches, its tail sliding softly out of my fingers.

During my senior year of high school, I went on a mission trip to Zambia, which afforded me this extraordinary experience with the lion. The power and grace of these large beasts gave me a picture of God I never understood before. He is full of power, with the ability to obliterate anything in His path if need be. He is also a protector, doing everything He can for the humans He created. But He has the fortitude of the lion to hold back His power and walk with grace next to us though we are immeasurably less in every way than Him.

Portraying Himself as a fiercely powerful yet gentle and kind lion was a clever move, showing both His soft, loving side and the mysterious, strong side of God. He is loving and protecting of His own, like the lion. He is fierce against anyone who hurts His children, like the lion. But He is tenderhearted, and lions do have that quality! His loyalty to you as His child goes beyond what you could imagine. But trust that loyalty to see you through anything you encounter and to protect you from the evil one.

Fighting the Current

But Jesus looked at them and said, "With man this is impossible,
but with God all things are possible."
—Matthew 19:26

Stand up! Reach out for my hand and stand up!"

I heard the words, but my mind could not seem to get my legs to do what they were supposed to do. The ocean waves crashed over my head, and I could feel them pulling me back away from the shore. It felt like a silly moment. I could see people not far away laughing and splashing in the waves, having a grand time at the beach. But for me, it was a moment of panic, not being able to find my footing in the shifting sand, not strong enough to swim against the current to calmer waters, and not being able to reach out to the hand that was right in front of me. I thought I might drown.

Then I felt the reaching hand grab my wrist and pull me out of the crashing waves, half dragging my tired body forward to the beach. I coughed, shook from my anxious nerves, and thanked the chaperone who pulled me from the waves. She smiled and comforted me, knowing I felt embarrassed—a high schooler should be able to get out of the ocean on her own, after all. I was afraid my crush had seen it, or worse, that the popular girls would laugh at my inability to find my balance and get out of the waves. I was thankful for the hand that reached out to save me that day.

Jesus is reaching out His hand toward you today. His voice is calling to you: "Stand up! Reach out for My hand and stand up!" He wants to save you from the waves crashing on your soul, to pull you from the unstable shifting of your situation. If you have the strength, today is the day to stand up and take His hand, walking forward in your relationship with Him. But if you are not strong enough and do not know what to do, just have faith in His godliness. He is strong enough to grab your wrist and pull you out. If that wrist has scars from blades you hope no one sees, His touch can heal them. If that wrist has bruises from the beatings you receive, He can sooth them. If that wrist is weak from the diagnosis the doctors gave, He can strengthen you. Let Him do the work and create a clear path for you to follow.

Preserve Life

"You shall not murder."
—Exodus 20:13

As you read through the Ten Commandments, do you ever find yourself treating them like a checklist? "I respected and obeyed my parents today. Check! I did praise team last Sabbath, check! I have not told any lies or been jealous of anyone this week. Double check! Murder? Nope, definitely have not done that! Check! I am all good."

The point of the Ten Commandments is not supposed to be a measuring stick or checklist that you go through every week to show how good you are. Following them is about forming new patterns of living so that your life is transformed by God's Spirit residing in you. I am assuming that none of you has murdered anyone, so it feels like we could just skip this commandment. But let's dive a little deeper into the thought process behind this commandment.

Yes, the sixth commandment is a moral imperative to refrain from the un-justified killing of another human being. In Hebrew, the word translated as "murder" is *ratsakh*, and it refers to killing someone as a manslayer, a murderer, putting people to death, dashing them to pieces—a really violent form of kill-ing. The Israelites went to war against other nations as they invaded Canaan, the Promised Land, but this word is never used in that context. The context it is used in is something that can actually apply to you and me; any thoughts of hatred or animosity toward another person fall under this word's broad spiritual meaning.

"Everyone who hates his brother is a murderer, and you know that no mur-derer has eternal life abiding in him" (1 John 3:15). Clearly, this commandment does apply to you! Keep thoughts of hatred out of your heart. When you are annoyed at someone or are mad at them for their actions, ask Jesus to give you a heart of forgiveness and love so that you can move on and not end up in a cycle of hatred.

Take the Church!

"Commit your way to the LORD;
trust in him, and he will act."
—Psalm 37:5

How often have you heard people tell you, "You youth are the future of the church!"? What goes through your mind when you hear that phrase? I am in my mid twenties and have been serving as a pastor for a little while now, and I still hear people tell me that I am the "future of the church." What about the church at present? When I was a teen, I wanted to be a part of the current church, and I still do. Thankfully, I think the tide is turning, and young people are being given more opportunities to use their voice and make a difference in their local congregations.

However, I recognize that this is not the case everywhere in Adventism. If you are in a local congregation where people tell you this phrase a lot, try responding by asking how you can be a part of the church at present, and even suggest some of the ideas that you have for your local church. Find ways to be involved. Ask if you can be a youth elder or deacon, or teach a Sabbath School class, or lead a praise team. Find the area of ministry you are most passionate about, and get involved! Do not wait for "someday" when you are an adult. Take advantage of the youthfulness that you have now, and do something!

Work with your local pastor and elders, express interest, look for where there is a need in your community, and find creative ways to fill that need. Do not wait for people to come to you, asking you to be involved. Take initiative, and go do things yourself! God has blessed you with passion and the power of a young voice. Let Him use you!

Hands On

So I will bless you as long as I live; in your name I will lift up my hands.
—Psalm 63:4

Today your devotional time is meant to grow your relationship with Jesus by going out and doing something. I have a challenge for you for this activity: Start by praying in a posture you do not usually pray in, and listen to a Christian song while you pray. Then go outside and go on a prayer walk with God, talking aloud to Him as you walk through a favorite space near where you live. (Be safe, obviously.)

Here are a few verses to give you some ideas of postures you could pray in:

- "Then King David went in and sat before the LORD and said, 'Who am I, O LORD God, and what is my house, that you have brought me thus far?' " (1 Chronicles 17:16).
- "Stand up and bless the LORD your God from everlasting to everlasting. Blessed be your glorious name, which is exalted above all blessing and praise" (Nehemiah 9:5).
- "And Moses quickly bowed his head toward the earth and worshiped" (Exodus 34:8).
- "While Ezra prayed and made confession, weeping and casting himself down before the house of God, a very great assembly of men, women, and children, gathered to him out of Israel, for the people wept bitterly" (Ezra 10:1).
- "So I will bless you as long as I live; in your name I will lift up my hands" (Psalm 63:4).

Healing Begins With a Cut

He heals the brokenhearted and binds up their wounds.
—Psalm 147:3

When someone has a medical problem for which they need surgery, they must go to the hospital and trust a surgeon to cut them open, get inside, and fix the problem. Surgery is an incredible thing that humans have learned how to do in order to save lives. But there is something rather incredible about the process of recovery: healing begins with a cut.

When people get spiritually "cut" in life—when something goes wrong or an event happens that hurts deeply—believing that healing will come seems impossible. Healing seems far off in the future or something that only happens to other people. During the middle of the pain, when it is most severe, hope is distant, and healing does not exist. For people who do not believe in God, this is the reality.

But for those who do believe in His healing power as the Master Surgeon, God can sometimes heal you to a better state when you have been "cut open." Getting "cut" may reveal a piece of your life patterns that need to be changed, habits that need to be fixed, or character flaws that only He can rectify. Because God is the Surgeon, you can trust Him to fix what is broken and mend what has been torn to pieces. Sometimes healing begins with a "cut," and sometimes the road to recovery is long and difficult. The pain will not go away instantly, but your Surgeon is the most experienced, and His goal is to heal your brokenness and give you freedom from what oppresses your heart. Trust the process; trust the Surgeon. He will stitch you back together again.

Relevant Faith

*He said to them, "Because of your little faith. For truly, I say to you,
if you have faith like a grain of mustard seed, you will say to this mountain,
'Move from here to there' and it will move, and nothing will be impossible for you."*
—Matthew 17:20

One of the greatest questions Christians must ask themselves is this: Is our faith still relevant? In other words, is what we believe enough to carry us through all that life throws at us? Being a Christian in a primarily secular world is hard. Strong faith takes guts, determination, and lots of conviction.

However, is the conviction you have about your faith enough? Christ told us in Matthew 17:20 that even faith as small as a mustard seed was enough to move a mountain. Did Jesus want His disciples to go find a mustard seed

and see whether it would move a mountain? No, of course not! His point was that it does not take much faith for God to do amazing things in your life. You can rely on Him to take care of the things that seem insurmountable to you.

So what makes that kind of faith relevant in today's world? On the radio, I heard a woman say: "He or she who chooses comfort over the good of those you disagree with who are around you has become irrelevant." Choosing comfort and an easy life makes you irrelevant to the people around you who are dealing with much deeper issues!

Do not be afraid of having a radical faith. Christ wants a deepening relationship with you as your faith grows and your convictions solidify. If you feel like your faith is not as strong as it should be, do not be discouraged. God has a plan, and He will help strengthen your faith day by day if you ask Him to.

Live It Up

For am I now seeking the approval of man, or of God? Or am I trying to please man?
If I were still trying to please man, I would not be a servant of Christ.
—Galatians 1:10

How old are you? Do your parents still feed you? Most likely, they do not! Only babies need to be spoon-fed, not most well-functioning adults. Yet spiritually, many people enter church expecting to be spoon-fed their Christianity, wanting only to sit in the seat and not participate in the Christian community in a major way. Do you find yourself approaching church this way? Are you a seat warmer or an active participant?

Church and Christianity are meant to be a lifestyle, not a nice program you attend once a week. Just as you do not need to be fed your meals since you are a teenager—you know how to do that yourself and you have been doing it for a long time—do the same with your spiritual life! Do not expect to be fed; learn how to feed others!

Now is the time for you to grow in your own personal relationship with God. This experience with Jesus will affect how you live your life and how you participate in church because it is no longer you leading, but the Holy Spirit. Church is a way of life, and in order to have a thriving life, you need to act! What gets you most excited in ministry, volunteering, or helping out at church? If you enjoy outreach projects, get in contact with your local outreach coordinator and plan a project to serve your community. Do you enjoy music? Offer to lead a praise team or be involved with one in a larger way. If you like challenges, take on some responsibility in a leadership role in your local congregation. Do not let the fear of what others think get in your way. Other people's opinions do not matter because, again, church is not meant to be just a nice program but rather a lifestyle. Live your life for Jesus, and you will not have any regrets!

Petra's Water

The soul of the sluggard craves and gets nothing,
while the soul of the diligent is richly supplied.
—Proverbs 13:4

While on a few Holy Lands tours I have taken, I was able to visit one of the most magnificent places on earth: Petra, in Jordan. The engineering feats accomplished there are incredible! Petra lies in the middle of the desert and was home to the Nabataeans. Living in the middle of the desert would be extremely difficult without water, so the Nabataean engineers thought up incredible systems to gather and retain water. They formed a system of pipes to guide water from springs and dams into the city and then stored the water in cisterns and reservoirs throughout the area. Petra was along a major trade route a few hundred years before Jesus lived on earth, so maintaining a civilization for the exchange of commerce was essential for the Nabataean kingdom to thrive. In their city set among the desert cliffs, they created hydraulic technology and a complex water supply system that rivals technology discovered in western society in just the past few centuries!*

God has blessed us with incredible brains. He gave us the ability to accomplish amazing things and make beautiful structures while on this earth, and He wants us to use the abilities He has given us to make greatness. The Nabataeans used their God-given skills to build a thriving society in a place where hardly anything survives. God has given you skills to do things you never dreamed possible. Classes such as math, science, and history might seem difficult, boring, or pointless at times, but just check out what took place in Petra when people used the brains God gave them! Let God influence the way you use your brain, and see what new things you can come up with!

---

* Charles R. Ortloff, "The Water Supply and Distribution System of the Nabataean City of Petra (Jordan), 300 BC–AD 300," *Cambridge Archaeological Journal* 15, no. 1 (April 2005): 93–109.

God's Voice

And he said, "Go out and stand on the mount before the LORD."
—1 Kings 19:11

God's voice has been described in many different ways throughout history. Some think of Mount Sinai and the Israelites, imagining His voice as a thundering noise booming through the heavens. Some think of Revelation, where His voice is described as sounding like trumpets or rushing waters. Some think of the still, small voice often used to describe how God speaks to the heart.

A famous story you have probably heard is that of Elijah, which we read in 1 Kings 19:11–13:

> And he said, "Go out and stand on the mount before the LORD." And behold, the LORD passed by, and a great and strong wind tore the mountains and broke in pieces the rocks before the LORD, but the LORD was not in the wind. And after the wind an earthquake, but the LORD was not in the earthquake. And after the earthquake a fire, but the LORD was not in the fire. And after the fire the sound of a low whisper. And when Elijah heard it, he wrapped his face in his cloak and went out and stood at the entrance of the cave. And behold, there came a voice to him and said, "What are you doing here, Elijah?"

After this, we know that Elijah was called to go back to the Israelites and serve as God directed instead of hiding away in a cave. God's voice did not come breaking through the heavens to Elijah. Instead, it was a low whisper. The Hebrew words used here refer to a silence, a thin sound, something we probably can imagine as very quiet, soft, gentle, and mysterious in its quality. God does not always get our attention with miraculous signs or loud noises. More often than not, He is subtle and quiet, like a gentle tugging at the heart or a soft whisper in the ear.

I have heard God speak, but it was never an audible voice. I hear God in the words of the Bible or the gentle breeze as I am praying while walking through nature. Sometimes His voice is a quiet but clear voice in my mind or a thought in my heart, where I feel compelled to do or say something.

Have you heard God's voice in your life? Maybe you have not seen a grandiose miracle or handwriting in the sky. But have you heard His quiet voice in your heart? Do not ignore that soft whisper. Follow wherever His voice leads you.

The Theology of Coffee Shops

Therefore welcome one another as Christ has welcomed you, for the glory of God.
—Romans 15:7

Coffee shops are great places to hang out if you want to understand the underlying current of thought in a particular area. People use coffee shops as a place to discuss ideas, a meeting place for dates, and the perfect place for Instagram photos that will rack up followers. They are known as places of hipster ideas and free conversation, where anything is accepted, and progressiveness is encouraged.

As I was sitting in a coffee shop working on this devotional book (sipping on a warm salted caramel chocolate-flavored drink), I decided to do some people watching. To my left were two men discussing Jewish theology in comparison to other Middle Eastern religious ideas. In front of me were two women who, after a long conversation, revealed one was in Alcoholics Anonymous, and the other was checking in with her to see how she was doing and whether she was following through with the program.

I was struck by a thought as I sat there: Coffee shops have a "theology" in the way they operate and relate to people. Their theology welcomes all, promotes new ideas, allows free conversation on any topic, and encourages progressiveness. People do not usually fear to enter a coffee shop—unless they have not decided on their order yet!

So I thought, How do we create these kinds of spaces in the church? I am not suggesting starting up your own church coffee shop is necessarily the answer, but rather, let's look at the principles of their theology. How do we challenge our social circles, school, and church to be like the coffee shop—serving something wonderfully tasty and encouraging an environment of conversation and friendliness? How do you think we can promote the message of Jesus' love, abide by His biblical principles, and have an environment where it is OK to ask big questions? I challenge you to write down your top three ideas and go talk to your pastor about them.

_____

_____

_____

The Guts to Be Honest

"You shall not bear false witness against your neighbor."
—Exodus 20:16

Have you ever done something on accident and then lied about it to cover your tracks and not get in trouble? Have you ever broken a toy belonging to your sibling, or lied to your friend, or cheated on a test, or hid something from your parents? I can certainly remember quite a few times in my childhood when I broke my sister's toy and lied about what happened or blamed a friend for something that I did wrong. We can all relate to doing those types of things when we were "kids that did not know any better." But what about now? You are at the age where you are learning to be a responsible person and to take ownership of your own actions and intentions. How honest are you? The Bible has a lot to say about being an honest, truthful person of integrity. Proverbs 19 has a few verses I think we can learn from, so I will let them speak for themselves:

- "Better is a poor person who walks in his integrity than one who is crooked in speech and is a fool" (verse 1).
- "A false witness will not go unpunished, and he who breathes out lies will not escape" (verse 5).
- "A false witness will not go unpunished, and he who breathes out lies will perish" (verse 9).

This is serious business! Check out what the Ten Commandments say in Exodus 20:16: "You shall not bear false witness against your neighbor."

Do you have a friend whom you stab in the back sometimes? Or have you ever spread gossip or things that might not actually be true about someone in your school or your class? Our words go a whole lot further than we think they will. It's like when you drop a pebble into a lake; the ripples end up going all the way to the other side.

Telling lies and being dishonest are also this way. Eventually your secrets will find you out, and it will come back to bite you. I encourage you to work on being honest in everything that you do. Work hard on your homework so that you will not be tempted to cheat because you already know the answers from your studies! Be kind in your interactions with others, and do not continue spreading things that are not true. When you make a mistake, own up to it and take responsibility for your actions. People will respect you for it! It takes guts to be honest, but it is well worth the effort, and God will reward your truthfulness.

Solar System

Again Jesus spoke to them, saying, "I am the light of the world.
Whoever follows me will not walk in darkness, but will have the light of life."
—John 8:12

The solar system Earth rotates in is incredible. God created this place in the universe to be perfectly conditioned for human life to thrive. At the center of the solar system is a large star that we call the sun, and all the planets move around it in very specific paths. Earth is the perfect distance from the sun to receive warmth and light, making plants grow. Earth takes about 365 days (plus a little smidge of time we fix through leap years) to go around the sun, while other planets take other amounts of time. Everything about this solar system is perfectly designed for you to enjoy life here.

Jesus' ministry to humans is mirrored in the solar system He created. Just as the sun is the center of the solar system, so He must be at the center of your life. And He should be a part of all 365 days of your year! Jesus wants to bless us and grow us, increasing our strength and power by our proximity to Him, just as the sun's energy grows life on Earth. Jesus is also the light of the world! And through His death, Jesus showed us His love and gave us an opportunity for eternal life with Him, just as the sun's warmth grows all living things.

Whenever you look to the skies and see the planets and stars God created in the solar system and beyond, marvel at His creative power, as well as His individual love for you. Let His love grow you into who He has made you to be. Bask in the light of His presence, and feel the warmth of His love surround you today.

Freedom

The Spirit of the Lord GOD is upon me, because the LORD has anointed me
to bring good news to the poor; he has sent me to bind up the brokenhearted,
to proclaim liberty to the captives, and the opening of the prison to those who are bound.
—Isaiah 61:1

In my third year of pastoral ministry, I got to know a young person who struggled greatly. He was imprisoned, metaphorically, by the forces around him that he could not control: a chaotic family life where he bore much of the responsibility, a dangerous public school experience where standing up for your faith was not safe or popular, and a neighborhood where guns and drugs were rampant. This young man needed a way out; he needed freedom.

For him, that freedom came in the form of an opportunity to attend an Adventist school. I remember praying fervently as I filled out the recommendation letter for him, hoping that his experience there would be life-changing and that his relationship with God would flourish.

Each one of us is imprisoned by something in our lives that is holding us back from truly committing to God. It could be the names you are called behind your back. It could be the grades that keep creeping lower and lower. It could be the coach who does not invest in training you. It could be the parent who is too self-absorbed to notice when you are hurting. It could be the best friend that betrayed you or the mean notes you find in your locker. There are hundreds of things the devil tries to use to keep you imprisoned in a negative life.

But we serve a God of freedom who has the ability to set us free from all our burdens! What do you need freedom from the most today? What is chaining you down and keeping you from truly giving your heart to God? Write it here, and give it to Jesus today:

_____

_____

_____

We Believe: You Are the Church

And above all these put on love, which binds everything together in perfect harmony. And let the peace of Christ rule in your hearts, to which indeed you were called in one body. And be thankful. Let the word of Christ dwell in you richly, teaching and admonishing one another in all wisdom, singing psalms and hymns and spiritual songs, with thankfulness in your hearts to God.
—Colossians 3:14–16

What do you think it means to be a part of the body of Christ? In the Seventh-day Adventist Church, when someone gets baptized, they are automatically voted into membership in the church. The reason for this is because when we are baptized into Christ, we also join His family! The church is the body of Christ, believers who gather together in worship, who support and care for one another, and who pray with one another. Work together with those in your church family to make your church one of love and care—just like Jesus did, and just as the early Christians did!

Here is how the importance of the church is explained in the Fundamental Beliefs of Seventh-day Adventists:

> The church is the community of believers who confess Jesus Christ as Lord and Savior. In continuity with the people of God in Old Testament times, we are called out from the world; and we join together for worship, for fellowship, for instruction in the Word, for the celebration of the Lord's Supper, for service to humanity, and for the worldwide proclamation of the gospel. The church derives its authority from Christ, who is the incarnate Word revealed in the Scriptures. The church is God's family; adopted by Him as children, its members live on the basis of the new covenant. The church is the body of Christ, a community of faith of which Christ Himself is the Head. The church is the bride for whom Christ died that He might sanctify and cleanse her. At His return in triumph, He will present her to Himself a glorious church, the faithful of all the ages, the purchase of His blood, not having spot or wrinkle, but holy and without blemish. (Gen. 12:1-3; Exod. 19:3-7; Matt. 16:13-20; 18:18; 28:19, 20; Acts 2:38-42; 7:38; 1 Cor. 1:2; Eph. 1:22, 23; 2:19-22; 3:8-11; 5:23-27; Col. 1:17, 18; 1 Peter 2:9.)*

---

* Seventh-day Adventist Church, "The Church," in *28 Fundamental Beliefs* (General Conference of Seventh-day Adventists, 2015), 6, https://szu.adventist.org/wp-content/uploads/2016/04/28_Beliefs.pdf.

How Would You Respond?

"By this all people will know that you are my disciples,
if you have love for one another."
—John 13:35

Once while I was out to eat with some church members, we had an interesting encounter at a restaurant. When we first entered, we were the only people there, so we were given a large table at the back of the restaurant and had fun catching up, talking about life and laughing with one another. While we were eating, another couple came into the restaurant. They sat down a few tables away, but since it was a small restaurant, everyone was within earshot of one another. As we were laughing with one another, the woman at the other table mocked us by fake laughing loudly, and her husband made some passive-aggressive, unkind comments toward us.

At that moment, we each had a choice of how to respond. Would we respond similarly, saying something unkind back to the couple? Would we stop talking and laughing completely? Would we be a little quieter and more respectful to the other guests? Would we let them ruin our experience? Would we do something Christlike in response to them?

It was hard to know exactly how to respond, but we apologized for being too loud and continued eating and talking together. But it definitely cast a sour mood over the experience, and our table felt hurt by these other people's actions. If we were bothering them, the appropriate thing to do would be to kindly ask us to not laugh as loudly. Instead, they chose to respond to our joyous moment by being unkind and doing something rude.

As Christians, when we face moments like this when other people are outright rude to us, we have a few options as to how we respond. Sometimes it is necessary to call out injustice and not tolerate unkind behavior. Other times, it is important to be respectful and kind even though they were rude to us. Hopefully, you would not choose to be mean in response. Today ask God to help you pick a wise way of standing up for yourself and show a Christlike character.

Video Game Evangelist

Oh give thanks to the Lord; call upon his name;
make known his deeds among the peoples!
—Psalm 105:1

Evangelism is a tough game in today's world. While some areas of the world respond in huge ways to traditional evangelistic "tent" meetings, many secular areas show no interest in a traditional evangelistic campaign. They are wary of "those crazy Christians" and their Bible-thumping. Evangelism needs to be reformatted to fit the culture it operates in. I have seen a large campaign work near a big city and bring many people to Christ, but I have also seen it fail. Young people especially question the motives of Christian evangelism and do not tend to respond to its efforts.

The problem of how to evangelize in a postmodern world has stumped many church leaders. While your pastor might have some clever ideas, they too have probably wrestled with this issue, unsure of the best response! Christianity needs youth like you to revamp evangelism and reach people for Christ in new ways. How would you do it? How would you choose to evangelize?

One sincere student I did baptismal studies with was very excited about sharing God's Word but also very excited about his video games at home. I wondered whether we should study not having modern-day idols or the importance of doing other kinds of activities. But ultimately, I decided that was up to his parents. Instead, I learned some gaming lingo and used video game-like words to help him study Revelation, the second coming of Christ, the great controversy, and other major Bible themes.

One day during our Bible study, I asked the student how he would choose to tell other people about Jesus or whether he had any great evangelistic ideas. His response was that he would start a YouTube channel where he would talk about both video games and Jesus! He would use his video game platform to get to know people and then use that as a chance to share with them his passion for Christ. I was blown away by his ingenuity!

If a grade school kid can come up with that evangelistic idea, I bet you can come up with something even more incredible. God's got a plan for how He can use you evangelistically. Ask Him about it in your prayer time today.

Pentecost Spirit

When the day of Pentecost arrived, they were all together in one place. And suddenly there came from heaven a sound like a mighty rushing wind, and it filled the entire house where they were sitting. And divided tongues as of fire appeared to them and rested on each one of them. And they were all filled with the Holy Spirit and began to speak in other tongues as the Spirit gave them utterance.
—Acts 2:1–4

For ancient Jewish believers, Pentecost was a harvest festival that brought Jewish believers from all over the world to Jerusalem to worship and sacrifice at the temple. After Jesus had left earth and returned to heaven, He instructed His followers to wait for the coming of the Holy Spirit. So, in Acts we find the believers gathered together in Jerusalem, praying for this "Holy Spirit" to come. They had no idea exactly what Jesus meant by that or what God's Spirit would do when He arrived. So they waited.

The Spirit came like a rushing wind and tongues of fire resting on them. He gave them the power to preach in every language. In Acts 2:9–11 you can read a list of some of the nations represented: people from Asia, Greek regions, Italy, Arabia, and others! Each believer preached powerfully, and those listening heard the gospel in their own language.

God's Spirit has continued to dwell with humans on earth. Our bodies are the temple of the Spirit. And He lives inside us, helping us make decisions and guiding us through life. When you have a feeling of conviction in you about something you believe or something that is right to do, that is the Spirit in you! Asking for His guidance daily will help you grow in your relationship with Him and help you learn to hear His voice more clearly in your heart.

Park Benches

Know this, my beloved brothers:
let every person be quick to hear, slow to speak, slow to anger.
—James 1:19

Here's a summer challenge for you: Go to a park, find a bench in a comfortable place, sit, and just listen. Maybe close your eyes and focus on what your ears can sense around you. What can you observe about the world around you by just listening?

While writing today's entry, I sat on a park bench in San Diego, California, basking happily in the sunshine. As I listened, I heard lots of birds singing ballads in the trees to one another. I heard the clashing sounds of a sharp ambulance siren and the revving of engines on the nearby freeway. Closer by were the footsteps of joggers and the heavy breaths of an experienced runner pacing himself as he glided through the park. Farther away were the noises of large trucks, cars driving into the parking lot, and honking horns. The laughs of a couple lying on a blanket and the smooth sound of a saxophone being played live drifted my way. I also heard the swishes of critters in the bushes and the soft voices of people talking while children played.

What do all these sounds tell you about the lives of the people living them? If our mission is to evangelize the world and tell people about Jesus, what can we learn about how to reach them if we just listen? Though this exercise might seem silly, it can teach you an important lesson about taking the time to listen to other people's stories and observe more than just what they are telling you.

How do you feel when you are opening up to a friend, but all they can do is talk about themselves? Being talked over is not a great feeling. When other people open up to you, pretend you are sitting on that park bench, listening attentively to their needs and thinking about how you can be a spiritual support to them.

God of the Hurts and Worries

"And those who are wise shall shine like the brightness of the sky above; and those who turn many to righteousness, like the stars forever and ever."
—Daniel 12:3

A relationship with Jesus seems like it should be easy, right? You may have heard people say that with Jesus, everything will be all right, and as long as you are close to Him, you will be free from worry or hardship. However, as you get older, you have probably started to experience things that hurt you and worry you, even making you question God and His goodness.

Thankfully, you are not alone in your feelings. It's completely normal to question God when bad things are happening and we do not understand why. If you have lost a loved one or watched your parents argue or had a friend struggle with suicidal thoughts, you probably have questioned God a time or two. *Where are You when I am going through this mess?*

A relationship with Jesus might not make this sinful planet a perfect place to live, but He can give you an incredibly important tool for dealing with it: hope. The devil tries to steal hope from us, but Jesus gives it as a gift. During those moments of hardship when you do not understand why bad things are happening, ask Jesus for hope. The Holy Spirit will enter your heart and inspire your mind, leading you to think hopefully about the future instead of with fear or worry. Here are a few verses about hope to encourage you:

- "And those who are wise shall shine like the brightness of the sky above; and those who turn many to righteousness, like the stars forever and ever" (Daniel 12:3).
- "He will wipe away every tear from their eyes, and death shall be no more, neither shall there be mourning, nor crying, nor pain anymore, for the former things have passed away" (Revelation 21:4).
- "So the poor have hope, and injustice shuts her mouth" (Job 5:16).

The Way of Love

If I speak in the tongues of men and of angels, but have not love, I am a noisy gong or a clanging cymbal. And if I have prophetic powers, and understand all mysteries and all knowledge, and if I have all faith, so as to remove mountains, but have not love, I am nothing. If I give away all I have, and if I deliver up my body to be burned, but have not love, I gain nothing. Love is patient and kind; love does not envy or boast; it is not arrogant or rude. It does not insist on its own way; it is not irritable or resentful; it does not rejoice at wrongdoing, but rejoices with the truth. Love bears all things, believes all things, hopes all things, endures all things. Love never ends. As for prophecies, they will pass away; as for tongues, they will cease; as for knowledge, it will pass away. For we know in part and we prophesy in part, but when the perfect comes, the partial will pass away. When I was a child, I spoke like a child, I thought like a child, I reasoned like a child. When I became a man, I gave up childish ways. For now we see in a mirror dimly, but then face to face. Now I know in part; then I shall know fully, even as I have been fully known. So now faith, hope, and love abide, these three; but the greatest of these is love.
—1 Corinthians 13

The way of Jesus is the way of love. Without His love in your life, you will be empty. Having a life-transforming relationship with Him must be centered in love. But how can you experience love from Someone you cannot see, hear, or touch? While it is difficult, it simply takes a paradigm shift. You have learned to communicate on this earth with other humans through very specific means: your senses. Things like voice, touch, or someone spending time with you show you that you are loved, and they are ways you show love to other people. But God can communicate with you outside of these human senses. He can speak internally to your heart and mind. He can inspire you and influence your thoughts. He can create a rainbow in the sky and music among the birds. He can give you the gift of making your own music, creating your own art piece, writing your own thoughts, and preaching your own sermons. He communicates with you in hundreds of ways, and they all boil down to His incredible love for you.

No matter where you have been, no matter whom you have become, no matter what has troubled you in this life—His love never fails. And He wants His relationship with you to be defined by love, directed by love, and displayed to others through love. Share that love you receive from Him with the world around you, and you will discover just how transforming the gospel message of love can be in your life!

Observations on Queen Anne Hill

"This is my commandment,
that you love one another as I have loved you."
—John 15:12

One beautiful summer evening I sat in Seattle near a Starbucks on Queen Anne Hill, listening to the conversations of the passersby. It was the end of a workday, so families were out and about, couples were going for food, and people were walking their dogs. But it was obvious the pace of life is much quicker in the city. Everyone was looking at their phones or rushing somewhere with stressed looks on their faces. They were either dressed to the nines in their fancy suits or dressed in expensive workout gear—everyone wanting to be somebody, to achieve something in this busy life.

Two giggling little girls ran past me, the first screaming, "Run, run! Mom's going to tag us!" I looked back down the sidewalk for "mom"—she was a few yards back, head buried in her phone, brows furrowed. She was not paying attention, and definitely was not playing with her daughters. Instead, she was caught up with something on a screen. Watching them made me sad. All they wanted was their mother's love and attention in an innocent little game, but she was too distracted to notice.

Do not get caught in the trap of living life through your screens. You will miss the most important moments. Our devices and tablets are useful, but they often distract us from the real world and what is happening around us. We will miss moments with our siblings or parents. Stay in the moment today, and pay attention to who and what is around you. Listen to God as He laughs and smiles through the little children or cute dogs passing by.

Junia the Apostle

Greet Andronicus and Junia,* my fellow Jews who have been in prison with me. They are
outstanding among the apostles, and they were in Christ before I was.
—Romans 16:7, NIV

Though she is mentioned only once in the New Testament, Junia was clearly an influential woman. She did ministry alongside Paul and a man named Andronicus. Paul's mention of her shows his support of her ministry and reveals a bit about what that ministry may have been like. Since she was apparently thrown into prison with Paul and Andronicus, she must have been a serious Christian leader! As a female apostle, she must have been doing some incredibly powerful ministry for local officials to want her in prison.

Sometimes God calls people to ministry that we least expect. It is import-

ant that we do not judge others—only God knows their motives. God wants us to find ways to support and help one another in ministry, just as Paul, Andronicus, and Junia did. He prefers that we walk alongside one another, lifting one another up, encouraging one another in the faith, doing ministry together. Maybe the popular kid at your school who never seemed interested in spiritual things suddenly wants to talk for chapel, or the guy with a lisp, or the person who is too talkative in class, or the bully, or the person who is socially awkward and gets picked on—God can use them all. And you should support everyone who wants to do big things for God, step in with them, and get your hands dirty too!

---

* There is some question as to whether this should be translated Junias, a male, or Junia, a female. For the purposes of today's devotional we will assume this is Junia, a female.

Dealing With Pain

*Blessed be the God and Father of our Lord Jesus Christ, the Father of mercies
and God of all comfort, who comforts us in all our affliction, so that we may be able to comfort
those who are in any affliction, with the comfort with which we ourselves are comforted by God.*
—2 Corinthians 1:3, 4

When I was going through a very difficult breakup, my mom told me, "God does not waste our pain." He may not always stop the pain from happening, but He never wastes it. Knowing what to expect while grieving can help you recover. There are five major stages of grief that people usually go through when they have experienced the loss of a loved one, a hard breakup or divorce, or another type of difficult pain.

The first is denial. When in denial, people see everything as too overwhelming to handle, so the mind copes by making you feel numb. You are in shock from what has happened and trying to make sense of everything.

However, when the feelings start to surface after the denial phase, anger can set in. This is where people often blame God for what happened and question why He would allow such suffering.

After this, bargaining takes place. Because people naturally want life to go back to the way it was, they make promises by looking back at the "what if" moments and try to bargain their way out of the pain.

Next is depression, when the emptiness sets in. This state is hard but normal and necessary to realize the truth of what has happened and feel the pain from it.

Ultimately healing comes from going through this phase into the next one: acceptance. This is when you finally accept the loss and choose to live on. A new normal sets in, and while you still miss whoever you have lost or remember whatever heartache you went through, you also learn to move on and invest in your future again.

Each of these stages of grief is fluid—you can go through them in a matter of minutes or over a period of months. And they can occur in any order. But most people will experience each of them in some way while grieving. God gave us the ability to grieve because we need a way to deal with the trauma of sin on earth. God does not waste our pain. He knows what you have been through because He feels it too! One day He may help you use that experience to minister to someone else who is grieving.*

---

* David Kessler, "The Five Stages of Grief," Grief.com, accessed June 19, 2018, https://grief.com/the-five-stages-of-grief/.

Driver's Ed

Guard me, O LORD, from the hands of the wicked;
preserve me from violent men,
who have planned to trip up my feet.
—Psalm 140:4

I took driver's ed during the summer when I was in high school. It was taught at a local public high school where we got to practice in the school parking lot before going out on the real roads to drive. In the afternoon, my dad would take me to big parking lots and even set up garbage cans like cones for me to practice driving around and parking between. There might have been some times I knocked them over! By the time I got to the end of my driving school course, I was pretty confident in my abilities and thought I had this driving thing all figured out.

After the classes ended, there was an opportunity for what they called a defensive driving course, where we would have a series of obstacles to drive through and practice avoiding crashes or unexpected events on the road, like when a deer jumps out in front of you or someone gets into a crash ahead of you. On one of the tracks, the instructor would throw a plastic sign shaped like a child that read "Children at Play" and yell, "Do not hit Jimmy!" We had to pretend a child had run out into the road after a ball and slam on our brakes, engaging the antilock braking system to avoid hitting the plastic road sign. While the course was fun and entertaining, it also taught some serious lessons about how you handle your car in unexpected situations!

How do you handle your faith in unexpected situations? Humans do not have an antilock braking system that engages when we realize we are about to crash and burn. But we do have the Holy Spirit's guidance. He can be like that brake system, speaking to your heart and influencing you to make good decisions. Listen to His guidance. He will help you avoid some big crashes!

We Believe: Communion

And when the hour came, he reclined at table, and the apostles with him.
And he said to them, "I have earnestly desired to eat this Passover with you before I suffer.
For I tell you I will not eat it until it is fulfilled in the kingdom of God."
—Luke 22:14–16

While there are not very many religious rituals in the Adventist Church, a staple of any Christian denomination is the Lord's Supper, or Communion, as it is commonly called in Adventism. This is when we eat bread and drink grape juice together in memory of Jesus' death on the cross for our sins. This ritual comes from an instruction that Jesus gave to His disciples before He was betrayed by Judas and sentenced to death. The Lord's Supper comes out of the tradition of the Passover meal that Jews ate in remembrance of when the angel of death passed over their homes in Egypt and did not kill their firstborns as long as they had the blood of a lamb on the doorposts. The Lamb Himself, before giving His blood, ate this meal, creating a new tradition and meaning for it in Christianity, which is why we still do it today.

The Fundamental Beliefs of Seventh-day Adventists describes Communion like this:

The Lord's Supper is a participation in the emblems of the body and blood of Jesus as an expression of faith in Him, our Lord and Savior. In this experience of communion Christ is present to meet and strengthen His people. As we partake, we joyfully proclaim the Lord's death until He comes again. Preparation for the Supper includes self-examination, repentance, and confession. The Master ordained the service of foot-washing to signify renewed cleansing, to express a willingness to serve one another in Christlike humility, and to unite our hearts in love. The communion service is open to all believing Christians. (Matt. 26:17-30; John 6:48-63; 13:1-17; 1 Cor. 10:16, 17; 11:23-30; Rev. 3:20.)*

---

* Seventh-day Adventist Church, "The Lord's Supper," in *28 Fundamental Beliefs* (General Conference of Seventh-day Adventists, 2015), 7, https://szu.adventist.org/wp-content/uploads/2016/04/28_Beliefs.pdf.

Lessons From the Galatians

I have been crucified with Christ. It is no longer I who live,
but Christ who lives in me. And the life I now live in the flesh
I live by faith in the Son of God, who loved me and gave himself for me.
—Galatians 2:20

The book of Galatians brings up a very crucial topic for Christians to address. When people choose to believe in Jesus, do you often find that they are told they must follow an intense set of rules before they can be a part of God's family? While behavioral and lifestyle issues are important to correct, it is best to let God do the correcting and instructing and not try to take that job on for Him. The Holy Spirit convicts people's hearts, not the words of an angry Christian.

In Galatia, many non-Jewish people, or Gentiles, were being converted to Jesus' message, and a church was started there. Paul wrote to the Galatians because some Judeo-Christian believers from Israel had told them they needed to follow all the old Jewish laws before they could be a part of the Christian church. However, following these laws was not necessary in this new faith. God was not calling only one culture, Jewish culture, to His church—He was calling all cultures! Racism was a problem in the early church, and the apostles had to work hard to overcome it.

Do cultural differences affect the church today? Does the church sometimes expect people to conform to certain cultural expectations before they can become a part of it? Or do we have the ability to be a worldwide church that recognizes the differences in culture and celebrates our diversity in Christ? Try to be the kind of Christian that celebrates racial and cultural diversity within Adventism. When someone turns to God, walk with them as the Holy Spirit prompts changes in their life. Do not expect everything to change instantly! Be welcoming of others, and help them grow in their personal relationship with Him as you have in yours.

When Jesus Talked About Poop

Keep your heart with all vigilance,
for from it flow the springs of life.
—Proverbs 4:23

In Matthew 15:11, Jesus told the Pharisees, "It is not what goes into the mouth that defiles a person, but what comes out of the mouth; this defiles a person." The disciples told Jesus that the Pharisees were offended by this saying, so He answered and told them that the Pharisees were blind guides. Harsh!

Peter asked Jesus to explain the parable, so Jesus responded, "Are you also still without understanding? Do you not see that whatever goes into the mouth passes into the stomach and is expelled? But what comes out of the mouth proceeds from the heart, and this defiles a person. For out of the heart come evil thoughts, murder, adultery, sexual immorality, theft, false witness, slander. These are what defile a person. But to eat with unwashed hands does not defile anyone" (verses 16–20).

Jesus just did a mic drop. He says whatever you put in your mouth is pooped out. What is the significance of mentioning that? The Pharisees believed that you had to follow strict rules about washing hands, utensils, and containers in very specific ways before eating anything. But at the same time, those people would turn around and be rude, prideful people, criticizing everyone around them! Jesus' point was that the more important issue is what comes out of the mouth, not what goes into it. Sure, what you put in your body is important health-wise. But if unkind, foul, "poop-like" things are coming out of your mouth, that is evidence of a deeper heart issue that needs to be fixed!

So while you pay attention to what you ingest, also pay attention to what is coming out of your mouth and the condition of your heart! Inspect your thoughts and feelings, and if you discover a problem, ask Jesus to help you resolve it.

Spiritual Morality

But Peter and the apostles answered,
"We must obey God rather than men."
—Acts 5:29

What is a *conviction*? No, not the kind that a judge gives to a criminal in a court of law. I am referring to a very different type of conviction. Our handy Google dictionary would describe it as "a firmly held belief or opinion." A conviction is something that happens within your mind. It is when you decide for yourself that a belief you hold is absolutely vital. Convictions lead to the formation of values and morals.

Sometimes when we talk about values and morals, we make them sound so stingy, as if they are rules that must be kept or we will be considered terrible people. I would like to look at them differently. Your values and morals are the promises you make to yourself and to God in your beliefs, which you choose to keep and not break. They are your "must-haves" in life. For example, maybe you value loyalty in a friend. When you are developing new friendships, this means that you will act on your value by being loyal to your friends, not sharing their secrets, not talking behind their backs, always being there for them, and so on. And you would expect the same kind of treatment from your friends.

Spiritual morals and values can be viewed in the same way. These are things in life and in your beliefs that are important at the core of who you are and affect how you see the world. If you choose to keep the Sabbath as one of your values, then you plan to orient your life around keeping the Sabbath. You will make other plans change so that you can set aside that special day to spend with God. Do not be afraid to stand up for what you believe in. God always has your back! Also, do not be afraid to stick to your morals and values. Do not let peer pressure influence you to try things such as drugs, alcohol, smoking, or sex. It might look fun at first, or it might sound enjoyable and seem harmless, but compromising your values in these areas will change your life completely and affect it in a very negative way. I am not saying you need to sign a pledge of abstinence because a piece of paper cannot stop you from doing something. Instead, I would encourage you to spend time praying about the situations you might be in where you are pressured or tempted to let go of your morals and values. Standing up for what is right is always the best thing to do, even if it seems unpopular at the time. Trust it to God. He will convict your heart of what is right and lead you where you need to go.

The Value of Stories

It has seemed good to me to show the signs and wonders
that the Most High God has done for me.
—Daniel 4:2

Stories are powerful tools of engagement. Through oral tradition, stories were passed down from generation to generation, and they have led to some of our most famous worldwide stories today. True stories, like the ones found in the Bible, and fairytales, like Cinderella, started out in the oral tradition—stories told by elders to the younger generation, kept fresh by gifted storytellers whose primary role was to keep a record of those oral stories for other generations to hear.

God even revealed Himself to us through a story. The Creation account in Genesis reads somewhat like a poem, a carefully told story about the beginning of the world. Do your research, and you will find that every ancient culture has a creation story that echoes pieces of God's story.

Eventually humans began writing down our stories, which is how we have books like your history book and the Bible today. One of the negative things that has followed writing down our stories is that we no longer have as many public spaces for storytelling in our communities like the generations before us did.

But sharing our testimonies, or personal life stories, is so powerful! We need to hear those stories to grow in our faith and encourage one another in our walk with God. How often when someone is brave enough to get up and share their testimony do you find yourself criticizing them, or thinking of how you would tell the story better, or even of how your own story is more powerful than theirs? I know I am guilty of it! Do not discredit the impact of other people's stories. You may think they do not measure up to your expectations, but remember that no one's testimony is complete. The story continues to grow and change even after their initial conversion. So listen and learn from the stories of others. Be inspired by the journey they have gone through. And be brave enough, when the moment is right, to get up and share your own story. Give a testimony of how God has moved in your life and brought you to where you are today.

Do Not Cheat

"You shall not commit adultery."
—Exodus 20:14

Children of divorce can attest to how heartbreaking the split of a family is. In many cases, when adultery is committed, families do split because of the unfaithfulness of one marriage partner. If you have suffered from a split between your parents, talk to a counselor or your pastor about that pain. Dealing with those feelings while you are young is important so that they will not hinder your ability to connect and have meaningful relationships later in life.

God made marriage sacred—something special between a man and a woman. And sex, as a part of that, should be kept as a commitment between those two people. Because God loves His people and does not want them to experience heartache and pain, He set up this commandment to show people how to live happy lives. Adultery leads to pain, heartache, betrayal, confusion, and destruction of a relationship.

If you have started dating, you can apply this principle to your dating relationship as well. Do not cheat. Stay faithful. Your job in that relationship is to guard the other person's heart and show that you care about them by not looking around at other options. If you are tempted to do that, then you need to break up and be single until you can figure out how to be in a committed relationship with another person. Cheating hurts everyone involved, and it's not worth the moment of fun you might have.

Lastly, this can also be applied to your relationship with God. Do not let anything else on earth cause you to cheat on God. Stay faithful to Him. Do not let anything else come before your relationship with Him. He loves you, and He will bless you. So give Him that love in return, and keep Him first in your heart.

Breaking the Wall of Hostility

But now in Christ Jesus you who once were far off have been brought near by the blood of Christ. For he himself is our peace, who has made us both one and has broken down in his flesh the dividing wall of hostility by abolishing the law of commandments expressed in ordinances, that he might create in himself one new man in place of the two, so making peace, and might reconcile us both to God in one body through the cross, thereby killing the hostility. And he came and preached peace to you who were far off and peace to those who were near. For through him we both have access in one Spirit to the Father. So then you are no longer strangers and aliens, but you are fellow citizens with the saints and members of the household of God, built on the foundation of the apostles and prophets, Christ Jesus himself being the cornerstone, in whom the whole structure, being joined together, grows into a holy temple in the Lord. In him you also are being built together into a dwelling place for God by the Spirit.
—Ephesians 2:13–22

Part of growing in your relationship with God is being willing to ask yourself hard questions. So today let's do that for a bit. Ephesians 2:13–22 is powerful, so read it and try to understand the meaning behind it. Write your thoughts in the spaces below or in a prayer journal.

Do you truly allow Jesus' peace to dwell in you?

_____

Are there any walls of hostility in your heart?

_____

What does this verse mean when it says that the "law of commandments expressed in ordinances" was abolished? Does that mean they do not matter anymore?

_____

Is Christ Jesus the cornerstone of your church and personal relationship with God?

_____

The Woman With the Spiked Club

The LORD will keep you from all evil;
he will keep your life.
The LORD will keep
your going out and your coming in
from this time forth and forevermore.
—Psalm 121:7, 8

While I was on a mission trip to Zambia, Africa, I met a very brave woman. Every evening we would drive up the highway for an hour or so until we reached the border of Zambia, then we turned off onto a dirt road and drove a few miles into the brush until we reached the Adventist church. We would set up for evangelistic meetings and hold them late into the evenings. This meant that all the people who attended would have to go home in the dark. For most of them, it was not a problem because they lived very close to where we held the meetings.

However, for one woman, it was not this way. She was probably the age of your grandparents. She walked with a slight limp, and her back hunched over. We found out that she lived many miles from the church. But she sincerely wanted to learn more about Jesus and the Bible, so she came faithfully to every meeting. She would leave her house hours before the meetings would start so that she could get there in time, and she would spend another few hours walking home after the meetings—alone in the dark! This woman carried a large stick. It was really more like a club because it had one large rounded end with spikes sticking out of it. When we asked her why she brought it, she explained that she lived so far away that she had to carry it with her so she could fight off wild animals if they tried to attack her. We offered to drive her home, just to make sure she was safe!

This woman's incredible faith that God would keep her safe inspired me. She reminded me how important it is to trust God with our lives in everything we do. She placed God as a top priority in her life and risked her own life in order to learn more about Him when the opportunity arose. God rewarded her by keeping her safe. She was baptized at the end of the series of meetings! If you are questioning whether or not it is worth it to go to church, chapel, or vespers, remember how lucky you are to have the safe opportunity to do so! Take full advantage of those moments to worship God with others and learn more about Him. He will give you the faith you need to keep on going.

God Can Use You

There is therefore now no condemnation for those who are in Christ Jesus. For the law of the Spirit of life has set you free in Christ Jesus from the law of sin and death.
—Romans 8:1, 2

I once saw a poster in a Youth room with a long list of Bible characters and their negative attributes on it. Normally we do not point out all the negatives about our heroes from the Bible in church, but I found this poster especially meaningful. It was a reminder that every person in the Bible was just as human as you and I, and sometimes they had a lot worse problems than we do. Sprawled across the top of the poster was this question: Do you seriously think God can't use you?

It sounds rather unbelievable! But after reading the list, the phrase made sense. Here's a reminder of some of the defining things about our popular Bible heroes that will remind you how human they were, and how powerful our God is that used them!

- Abraham and Sarah were old
- Rahab was a prostitute
- Noah got drunk
- Leah was ugly
- Jonah ran from God
- Lazarus was dead
- David committed adultery and murder
- Paul was a persecutor
- Joseph was abused and falsely accused
- Moses had a temper
- Samson was a ladies man
- Elijah was discouraged
- Ruth was a foreigner
- Mary was demon possessed
- Peter was impulsive

Ever think God cannot use you because of all the sinful issues you have going on in your life? Lucky for you, God can transform your life, and those things do not scare Him. He can use you no matter what you have been through or how rough your life is. He can take you out of that dark place and lead you into the light, surprising you with all He can do through you!

Receive the Good

*As far as evil extends, the voice of our Father is heard, bidding His children see in its results
the nature of sin, warning them to forsake the evil, and inviting them to receive the good.*
—Ellen G. White, *Education*

Have you ever seen the face of evil in a dramatic and obvious way? I have, and it is ugly and terrifying. When I was in my senior year of high school, I was able to go on a mission trip to the Dominican Republic and preach a series of evangelistic meetings in a local church there. One evening before our meeting, the local elder told me about a man in the village who wanted to come to the meetings but was not able to because he was being tormented by an evil spirit within him. We prayed diligently for the man to be freed, and I believe he was! But on that island, I saw for the first time how prevalent the presence of demonic forces can sometimes be.

One evening we had to drive through a sketchy section of downtown during a holiday of one of the local devil-worshiping religions. There were people dancing through the streets, people shouting unintelligibly, crazed men running around, and women screaming in high-pitched tones. We heard strange music and sensed an odd feeling in the air. At first, we did not know what was going on until the local pastor explained to us about this demonic festival. So we all prayed that God would get us through safely. The streets were backed up with people everywhere, so our car was blocked, people were running past, some banging on our windows and looking at us with deranged eyes. It was scary. But we found peace and safety through trusting in God to get us through, and He did.

That experience was a real reminder that the devil has many footholds in this world. Some are obvious, like that experience. Others are sneakier, like through the electronic devices you use every day. Ellen White, in *Education*, page 27, gives courage to the worried heart. God's voice extends further than evil ever can. And God invites you to turn away from evil and receive the good things He has in store for you instead. Make that choice to renew your walk with Him again today.

"But our citizenship is in heaven, and from it we await a Savior, the Lord Jesus Christ, who will transform our lowly body to be like his glorious body, by the power that enables him even to subject all things to himself" (Philippians 3:20, 21).

Angry Old Testament God?

"The steadfast love of the LORD never ceases."
—Lamentations 3:22

Have you ever asked any the following questions or had one of your friends ask these questions about God?

- Why does God seem so angry and harsh in the Old Testament?
- How can the God of the Old Testament and Jesus of the New Testament be the same God?
- Why does Jesus seem so loving and caring, while the Old Testament God is distant and angry?

When you read about all the bloodshed in the Old Testament, especially times when God commanded the Israelites to destroy foreign nations, it makes Him seem like a God of chaos and death, not love and compassion. But without reading the entire Old Testament, this is an unfair portrayal of God's character. It's only a partial picture, like looking at one puzzle piece and trying to determine what the whole puzzle picture looks like.

God has a huge sense of righteous justice. The Old Testament was a chaotic time in earth's history, filled with wars and bloodshed, as well as many pagan religions where children were sacrificed and people did detestable things to one another in the name of "religion." God is passionate about His creation, and even though He has allowed sin to exist for a while, He sometimes has to put a stop to it. Because of His passion to rescue this broken world, He does not have tolerance for the terrible things that humans do to one another. And it is out of this sense of passionate justice and love for His creation that He wants to create a world of safety where people can live peaceably with one another. And the way He chose to do that was supposed to be through the Israelites. He promised them that if they would just follow Him, He would use them to bless all nations. Part of that process meant cleansing the world of evil forces and societies that would cause destruction. God was not an angry God in the Old Testament; He was a fiercely loving God, trying to protect His people as much as possible and sadly having to destroy some in the process. So do not be afraid of this image of God; just read more widely in the Old Testament to get a truer sense of God's character during those times. And remember these verses from Lamentations: "The steadfast love of the LORD never ceases; his mercies never come to an end; they are new every morning; great is your faithfulness" (Lamentations 3:22, 23).

Drawing Nearer

Draw near to God, and he will draw near to you.
—James 4:8

Youth question: What are ways to keep your relationship with God strong besides prayer?

Building a relationship with God is just like building a relationship with anyone on earth—you have to put in time, effort, and genuine care. God wants a real relationship with you where you actually open up your heart to Him. Prayer is a huge part of that because it's the way you talk to God—prayer is how you communicate with Him. *But what else can I do besides praying to have a strong relationship with God?*

When you have a big chemistry test coming up, you eat, sleep, and breathe chemistry, right? You study your brains out and saturate yourself in the information. Maintaining your spiritual life is similar, except it produces less stress and helps you relax and stay happy.

First, realize that your life has a purpose. There is a reason God put you here on this planet, and that means you need to train for the mission He wants you to do. Then, prioritize time with Him. Spend time alone with God. What you do in that time is flexible: read the Bible, listen to an audio Bible in the car, keep a prayer journal of requests and answers, or journal about what you have seen God doing in your life. Memorize Scripture. Go to church on a regular basis, and get involved! Join a small group outside of Sabbath School class, spend time studying the Bible, and then learn theology and discuss it with other people. Read a spiritual book, like something written by Ellen White, or pick up a new book from the Adventist Book Center, or find Christian books written for youth to grow in their relationship with God. Watch documentaries about missionaries and what other people are doing to grow the kingdom of God. Volunteer and help people in your community. Preach the gospel to yourself by reminding yourself of Christ's love and redeeming power in your life! Listen to Christian music, and sing your favorites in the shower. Find an accountability partner whom you can talk to about your relationship with God and the time you are spending with Him.

There are hundreds of ways to grow in your relationship with Jesus outside of just prayer, even though that is a very important and necessary part of your walk with Him. Try a few of the ways listed above, and come up with some of your own!

Jesus' Teachings

Being asked by the Pharisees when the kingdom of God would come, he answered them,
"The kingdom of God is not coming in ways that can be observed, nor will they say,
'Look, here it is!' or 'There!' for behold, the kingdom of God is in the midst of you."
—Luke 17:20, 21

Jesus became a well-known teacher during His ministry on earth. The kingdom concept He taught was the idea that God's kingdom was not going to be brought by Him conquering the Romans and overthrowing their oppressive government, but rather, it would be a spiritual kingdom that lives in the hearts of God's people and would continue throughout time from one generation to the next. Jesus meant to pass on His teachings about the kingdom of God to His disciples and those who would come after them. Thankfully, they have been preserved through the New Testament, and we still learn about these teachings and share them with others today! As you ponder the questions below, think about how you are participating in the kingdom Jesus started and spreading it on earth:

What do you feel is a big lesson God has been trying to teach you lately?

_____

Where does God want you to grow, and where is He trying to "prune" you?

_____

How do you think you best reflect God's kingdom?

_____

How would God like you to reflect His kingdom?

_____

Where do you see the kingdom mind-set in other people?

_____

Cliffs

"Everyone then who hears these words of mine
and does them will be like a wise man who built his house on the rock."
—Matthew 7:24

Have you ever been out camping or hiking and seen a sign next to a cliff or drop-off that says, "Falling can be deadly"? I laugh every time I see these signs because they state what seems so obvious. Yes, if you step off that cliff you will fall, and when you hit the bottom of the ravine, you might die. Falling can be deadly, obviously! Even though it seems like a dumb saying to have on a sign, it is there for a reason: to warn people not to fall off the cliff face! Sometimes we need these obvious reminders in order to realize how bad the choices are that we are making.

God's instructions to us in the Bible probably look a little like that sign to Him. In His eyes, it's obvious why He would instruct us to do certain things and stay away from others. However, we need the signs in order to see clearly what is right and wrong on earth and what the consequences of making certain choices will be!

There is only One we can rely on to be a firm foundation for us when we cannot seem to make the right choices or are ignoring the signs by a cliff face. Jesus is our Rock, our safe and stable place to stand. With Him holding us, we can see over the edge of the cliff and know the consequences of stepping over that cliff. He holds us steady and helps us read the signs. So even though those "Falling can be deadly" signs seem obvious, pay attention when God puts one in your path, and listen to His instructions, even when it seems silly.

We Believe: Church Body

"I do not ask for these only, but also for those who will believe in me through their word,
that they may all be one, just as you, Father, are in me, and I in you,
that they also may be in us, so that the world may believe that you have sent me."
—John 17:20, 21

*L*et's read how the Fundamental Beliefs of Seventh-day Adventists describes the church body:

The church is one body with many members, called from every nation, kindred, tongue, and people. In Christ we are a new creation; distinctions of race, culture, learning, and nationality, and differences between high and low, rich and poor, male and female, must not be divisive among us. We are all equal in Christ, who by one Spirit has bonded us into one fellowship with Him and with one another; we are to serve and be served without partiality or reservation. Through the revelation of Jesus Christ in the Scriptures we share the same faith and hope, and reach out in one witness to all. This unity has its source in the oneness of the triune God, who has adopted us as His children. (Ps. 133:1; Matt. 28:19, 20; John 17:20, 23; Acts 17:26, 27; Rom. 12:4, 5; 1 Cor. 12:12-14; 2 Cor. 5:16, 17; Gal. 3:27-29; Eph. 2:13-16; 4:3-6, 11-16; Col. 3:10-15.)*

One of the most unique things about the Seventh-day Adventist Church is that we have churches in almost every nation around the world. And in the areas where there are no churches, we send missionaries to help people learn about Jesus. Many of these areas have outlawed Christianity and made it illegal to worship Jesus, but Seventh-day Adventists tactfully enter these areas, risking persecution, to teach people about their Savior!

The church is diverse, with people from every nationality, language, and location. We also are diverse in our economic demographics. The message of the gospel is for rich and poor, and people of every social status. Consider how you can help transform your church into a place that is truly the body of Christ, where all people can worship together and find forgiveness in Jesus.

---

* Seventh-day Adventist Church, "Unity in the Body of Christ," in *28 Fundamental Beliefs* (General Conference of Seventh-day Adventists, 2015), 7, https://szu.adventist.org/wp-content/uploads/2016/04/28 _Beliefs.pdf.

Ask Yourself . . .

"The LORD your God is in your midst, a mighty one who will save; he will rejoice over you with gladness; he will quiet you by his love; he will exult over you with loud singing."
—Zephaniah 3:17

Today, have another spiritual check-in with God. Ask yourself the following questions, find a Bible verse that relates to them, and challenge yourself as you write down your answers. Journal about them for a bit, and pray over your responses. Your relationship with God is the most powerful relationship you will ever have in your entire life! Trust Jesus as He shows you the way. Ask yourself these questions, and grow a bit more with God today.

What have you learned recently that has changed your mind about something you once believed since growing in your relationship with Jesus?

_____

When was the last time you got down on your knees and sincerely prayed?

_____

In what settings do you become most aware of God's presence?

_____

In what moments or settings do you feel furthest away from God?

_____

Why do you choose to worship Jesus?

_____

What is your biggest prayer request currently?

_____

Revelation Studies 1:
Alpha and Omega

"Fear not, I am the first and the last, and the living one. I died,
and behold I am alive forevermore, and I have the keys of Death and Hades."
—Revelation 1:17, 18

When I taught a Bible class at Northwest Christian School in Puyallup, Washington, the students frequently asked to study the book of Revelation. At the time, I was terrified to tackle the topic, but I have decided to go through each chapter of Revelation in this devotional book. It will be a very brief summary, but hopefully, you will learn a bit more about the Revelation of Jesus Christ through the process. Buckle up!

I recommend that you read Revelation 1 before we begin. This book was written by John while he was a prisoner on the island of Patmos in the Mediterranean Sea. I once spent seven hours wandering around that island, and trust me, there is not much to do. While John was on this island, on a Sabbath day, God gave him a vision.

The picture of God in Revelation 1 is powerful and majestic, and we already see some important patterns that will show up throughout the book. First, the pattern of seven will repeat throughout the book; it is a number clearly associated with God and perfection. The seven churches John describes were both literal churches with actual problems and symbols of things to come later. Key verses to remember are Revelation 1:17, 18, where God asks us not to fear because He is the first and last, and though He died, now He is alive forever.

In chapter 1, we see a few things that are important to remember when reading Revelation: (1) It is all about Jesus, since it is His revelation; (2) those who read and hear the words of Revelation are blessed; (3) God is all-powerful, and He is in control; His goodness will be revealed through the prophecies of this book; (4) God cares for His people on earth that follow Him, and He will take care of us. We do not need to be afraid of the book of Revelation because God is in control.

For further study
Nichol, Francis D. *The Seventh-day Adventist Bible Commentary*. Vol. 7, *Philippians to Revelation*. Washington, DC: Review and Herald*, 1980.

Pierce, Seth J. *What We Believe: Prophecies of Revelation for Teens*. Nampa, ID: Pacific Press*, 2013.

Stefanovic, Ranko. *Revelation of Jesus Christ*. Berrien Springs, MI: Andrews University Press, 2009.

Thessalonica

For you, brothers, became imitators of the churches of God in Christ Jesus that are in Judea.
For you suffered the same things from your own countrymen as they did from the Jews.
—1 Thessalonians 2:14

The book of 1 Thessalonians was written by Paul from him, Silvanus, and Timothy to the Christians meeting together in Thessalonica. You can read about the conversion of the Thessalonian people in Acts 17. For three Sabbaths, Paul reasoned with the people and taught them the Scriptures, explaining and proving how it was necessary for Jesus to die and be raised again. Many devout Greeks, women with prominent positions, and other people from Thessalonica were persuaded by their words and believed in Jesus. Unfortunately, the church that formed in Thessalonica was persecuted heavily by their Greek neighbors and Roman leaders. The people of the city did not like their new beliefs, and they struggled. However, in Paul's first letter to the Thessalonians, we learn that this persecution did not turn them away from God but actually made them grow stronger!

What made the Thessalonians so strong was their ability to prioritize Christ in their lives and truly live in Christian brotherhood. They took care of one another, strengthened and encouraged one another in faith, and relied on one another during hard times. They teach modern Christians that prioritizing good relationships with the people in your local church is what helps a church grow and stay strong in faith.

What is your relationship with your church family like? Do people at your church truly love and care for one another, or is there a spirit of bitterness and gossip and an unkind attitude that permeates the church? Christian fellowship should be the safe place people can go to be loved and protected from a persecuting world. If your church is unhealthy, work hard to foster good relationships and build kindness into your church family. If your church is healthy, work to grow the church and make a larger family that welcomes those who are not already a part of it. Having that strong bond is what will keep your church alive and thriving in Christ.

God's Fire Hydrants

"But whoever drinks the water I give them will never thirst. Indeed,
the water I give them will become in them a spring of water welling up to eternal life."
—John 4:14, NIV

Once when I was a young Pathfinder, we attended a camporee with clubs from lots of different states. Some firemen came to teach us about the fire engine and what firefighters' jobs are like as part of the daily activities. One of the fun things the firemen let us kids do was suit up in a fireman's outfit, grab the fire hose, and drag it while running as fast as we could to a "fire hydrant" to get water. Of course, my spindly little arms and legs did not help me get very far with all that gear on, but it was fun to feel like you were a part of something as big as firefighting!

The most important part of that activity was getting to the fire hydrant. It is the connection point where firefighters tap into the local water supply and a key component in active fire protection. Without that powerful flow of water from the hydrant, it would be very hard to put out any fire! As you drive around town, count how many fire hydrants you see. They are everywhere! But are they any use just sitting there by the street? Nope. You have to physically connect the hose to the hydrant for them to have any purpose.

We have access to an unlimited power supply through Christ. But we have to make the choice to pursue a relationship with Him. It's like connecting the hose to the hydrant. God is ready and willing to provide all that we need to live an abundant life, but He does not force us to have a relationship with Him. He has given us the choice. Yet if we choose to accept His living water into our life, we will be protected from all the "fires" that may happen in our life! Yes, it sounds cheesy, but it is true—He is the only one that can protect us. Make that choice today to connect to your Source of living water.

Church History: James White

Then the LORD God said, "It is not good that the man should be alone;
I will make him a helper fit for him."
—Genesis 2:18

oday marks the birthday of James White, one of the founders of the Seventh-day Adventist Church, along with his wife Ellen White and friend Joseph Bates. James White was born on August 4, 1821, and was raised with his nine siblings in Maine. He was not able to go to school until he was nineteen because he had bad eyesight. But when he did go to school, he worked extremely hard, and he got his certificate to teach.

After hearing William Miller's message about Jesus' soon return to earth, James felt convicted to preach the message himself. After the Great Disappointment, when Jesus did not come back to earth as expected, he returned to studying the Bible and became closely acquainted with Ellen Gould Harmon, whom he married a few years later. God loves power couples who are both willing to follow His will!

Later in life, after the establishment of the Seventh-day Adventist Church, he became the second General Conference president. He used his life to serve by his wife's side as they led thousands of people to Jesus.*

When you are young, you do not know whom God will have for you to marry. James probably had to reprogram his thinking a bit when he decided to pursue a marriage relationship with a prophet! But God knew that if both Ellen and James were willing to commit their lives to Him, He could use them in powerful ways and truly change the world through them.

God has a plan for your life too, and if you trust Him to make it happen, He will do it in His time. God used Ellen and James when they were teenagers to start a movement that has become a worldwide church. He uses teens to do big things! What do you think He has in store for you?

---

* "Pathways of the Pioneers: James White, 1821–1881," The Ellen G. White Estate, accessed June 19, 2018, http://www.whiteestate.org/pathways/jwhite.asp.

Why Religion?

"And let us consider how to stir up one another to love and good works,
not neglecting to meet together, as is the habit of some, but encouraging one another,
and all the more as you see the Day drawing near."
—Hebrews 10:24, 25

Youth question: Can you believe in God but not ascribe to a specific religion? This is a hard question to answer because you need to have a fundamental understanding of how religions come into existence in the first place to really even begin your quest. But technically, no. Technically no specific religion is needed to worship God. Was Abraham a part of a specific religion with a name and organization of beliefs? Nope. Was Noah part of a religion that had rituals of worship? Nope. But did each of these famous patriarchs worship God faithfully and follow His calling in their lives? Yes. And what happened as a result of following God was . . . religion!

Religion is essentially the organization of your beliefs and thoughts about this God you have faith in, and sometimes it includes spiritual practices and rituals as a part of expressing that faith or religious belief. So, no, you do not *have* to be a part of a specific church to believe in God. But you will eventually create your own religion, in a sense, once you develop your relationship with God.

However, the other side to this question is that, yes, you do need to be a part of a specific religion to have a belief in God. What I mean is, as you go deep into your relationship with God and your study of the Bible, you need to know what you believe. You need to be certain of those beliefs and be able to understand and defend them on a philosophical level. This is where religion steps in. I am a part of the Seventh-day Adventist Church, a denomination in the Christian religion, because I believe the same things this church teaches. It is biblically based, and while no church is perfect, this church, I think, best represents what God teaches in the Bible. So, no, you do not have to be a part of a specific religion to believe in God. But your experience with Him will be very shallow without it. You need community, and organized religion brings that to the table. So believe first, then find a community of believers to surround yourself with.

We Believe: Double Dunked

Baptism, which corresponds to this, now saves you, not as a removal of dirt from the body but as an appeal to God for a good conscience, through the resurrection of Jesus Christ.
—1 Peter 3:21

The Fundamental Beliefs of Seventh-day Adventists describes the importance of baptism like this:

By baptism we confess our faith in the death and resurrection of Jesus Christ, and testify of our death to sin and of our purpose to walk in newness of life. Thus we acknowledge Christ as Lord and Savior, become His people, and are received as members by His church. Baptism is a symbol of our union with Christ, the forgiveness of our sins, and our reception of the Holy Spirit. It is by immersion in water and is contingent on an affirmation of faith in Jesus and evidence of repentance of sin. It follows instruction in the Holy Scriptures and acceptance of their teachings. (Matt. 28:19, 20; Acts 2:38; 16:30-33; 22:16; Rom. 6:1-6; Gal. 3:27; Col. 2:12, 13.)*

The first baptism I ever performed was exciting, terrifying, and hilarious, from my perspective! After raising my hand and saying the typical, "I now baptize you in the name of the Father, Son, and Holy Spirit," I quietly instructed him to plug his nose and bend his knees, and then I dipped him into the water. Only, he did not go under. There he was, just floating right at the surface, his eyes squeezed shut, but his face out of the water! I quickly decided I better dunk him again, so I pushed him down under the water—a double dunk!

Thankfully, God does not have to double dunk us. When we choose to follow Him and accept Jesus into our hearts, we are washed completely clean in His blood! We get baptized as a sign of that initial step in our relationship with Him. After that, we simply ask for forgiveness for our sins and continue walking toward Jesus more and more every day. Have you made the choice to dedicate your life to Him in baptism yet? If not, talk to your pastor about starting baptismal studies and beginning your new life with Jesus!

---

* Seventh-day Adventist Church, "Baptism," in *28 Fundamental Beliefs* (General Conference of Seventh-day Adventists, 2015), 7, https://szu.adventist.org/wp-content/uploads/2016/04/28_Beliefs.pdf.

Revelation Studies 2: To the Churches

"I know you are enduring patiently and bearing up for my name's sake,
and you have not grown weary."
—Revelation 2:3

Revelation chapter 2 opens the messages of God to seven churches in the area of Asia Minor. These churches were real places where early believers worshiped, but they also stand for periods in Christian church history. Ephesus represents the early church that formed after Jesus was on earth. Smyrna represents the church that was persecuted by Rome from A.D. 100 to about A.D. 300. Pergamum represents the time when Christianity was finally accepted and then made the official religion of some areas of Europe, ending in A.D. 538. Thyatira represents about a thousand years of Christian history, from approximately A.D. 500 to A.D. 1500. During this time, Christianity became the well-established Catholic Church, which became a political power in the West during the Middle Ages and the Renaissance.

To Ephesus, God says: "I know you are enduring patiently and bearing up for my name's sake, and you have not grown weary. But I have this against you, that you have abandoned the love you had at first" (Revelation 2:3, 4). This is a solemn reminder not to abandon your early love for God. God asks you to endure patiently; let your love for Him stand the test of time.

Smyrna is poor in worldly wealth but rich in the Lord and their faith in Him. You may face persecution or be ridiculed because of your beliefs, but do not let go of them just because other people put you down.

The residents of Pergamum lived in the middle of a society led by Satan. God calls for you to keep your heart pure and committed to Him even though people in your school or the society around you live lives that go against what you have been called to.

Thyatira tolerated Jezebel, meaning they allowed immorality to exist among them. When you see something that goes against God, do not be afraid to call it what it is. Stay faithful to God's Spirit in your heart and to the conviction He has placed in you.

For further study

Nichol, Francis D. *The Seventh-day Adventist Bible Commentary*. Vol. 7, *Philippians to Revelation*. Washington, DC: Review and Herald®, 1980.

Pierce, Seth J. *What We Believe: Prophecies of Revelation for Teens*. Nampa, ID: Pacific Press®, 2013.

Stefanovic, Ranko. *Revelation of Jesus Christ*. Berrien Springs, MI: Andrews University Press, 2009.

You Matter

Blessed be the God and Father of our Lord Jesus Christ, who has blessed us in Christ with every spiritual blessing in the heavenly places, even as he chose us in him before the foundation of the world, that we should be holy and blameless before him.
—Ephesians 1:3, 4

When people around you tell you negative things, after a while, you will start to believe them. I once had someone very close to me tell me horrible things about myself on a regular basis when they were upset, and after a while, I realized that I believed every word they said even though those things were not true. I let myself fall into believing what that person was saying about me. I did not have confidence in myself or the gifts I knew God had given me anymore. It tore me down, and it took a long time to build myself back up into seeing myself as worthy in God's eyes.

You probably can think of that one person in your life who tries to tear you down or whose opinion matters to you so much that you believe everything they tell you about yourself. But remember that they are just as human as you are. Choose to believe in yourself and what God says about you. He says you are His child and worthy of love and respect. And you matter to Him. You matter so much that He has a special mission for you on this earth. He has something for you to do that only you can do. And He will reveal it to you in His time. So know that you are important and that your life is valuable to Him.

Going Deeper

"Whoever believes in me, as the Scripture has said,
'Out of his heart will flow rivers of living water.'"
—John 7:38

Twenty tiny toes crept over the edge of the pool. Five toes slowly dipped into the water, then quickly came back out again. A little boy wearing deep blue goggles was shy about getting in the pool. Next to him was his sister in a bright pink swimsuit, wearing blue flotation devices securely around her arms. They stood tentatively at the edge of the pool as their mother entered the water alongside them. Her arms gently lowered them into the pool, holding them up as they swam around her.

Blue goggles gained confidence and began ducking quickly under the water, his feet splashing madly behind him. The mother patiently taught her children what to do, giving examples of kicking and swimming strokes. The two children copied her example to the best of their ability. But every so often, their faces would dip unexpectedly into the water, startling them and making them cling to her side.

As they gained confidence, they swam farther and farther from their mother's grasp. At one point, the little boy ducked his head under the rope separating the deep and shallow sides of the pool. His mother quickly pulled him back, knowing he was not ready to swim in the deep end yet.

God in His constant care for us is a bit like this mother. He knows exactly what we can handle and when we are ready for the next step. Sometimes He pushes us deeper into the pool, and other times He pulls us back when we have gone too far. His strong arms are always ready to pull us up when we think we are drowning. And His example shows us how to swim in the deep waters of life.

Revelation Studies 3:
Hear What the Spirit Says

"He who has an ear, let him hear what the Spirit says to the churches."
—Revelation 3:6

Today, our Revelation studies continue on the seven churches of Revelation 3 and how their messages apply to you. Each of these churches represents a time period of Christian history as well as a literal church when John was alive. Sardis represents the Protestant Reformation church, when God's truth in the Bible was rediscovered and the Catholic Church was called out for hypocrisy and false teachings between the mid 1500s and the end of the 1700s. Philadelphia represents a time when Christianity again transformed through realization of the coming judgment of the world. This is the time when William Miller began preaching about the soon coming of Christ and the prophecies in Daniel and Revelation being fulfilled. This lasted until 1844, when Adventists believe the heavenly sanctuary ministry of Jesus began. That leads us into Laodicea, the Christian church of the end times who is lukewarm up until the second coming of Christ.

Sardis is portrayed as dead in their faith. They are warned to wake up, or God will come and they will not even realize it or be ready. This is a reminder to stay faithful to God even when you cannot see Him working. Do not let your faith die and get caught up in worldly things. Instead, stay faithful and awake, ready for Jesus' coming.

The Philadelphia church chose not to deny Christ even when they could have. "I am coming soon. Hold fast what you have, so that no one may seize your crown" (Revelation 3:11). The message to Philadelphia reminds you to hold on to your hope in Jesus because He is coming soon! The pain and trials you are going through on this earth will not last forever. He is coming soon, and He will rescue you!

Lastly, Laodicea is known as being neither hot nor cold, but lukewarm. What is your relationship with God and your faith like? Are you only lukewarm? Or are you on fire for Him?

For further study

Nichol, Francis D. *The Seventh-day Adventist Bible Commentary.* Vol. 7, *Philippians to Revelation.* Washington, DC: Review and Herald®, 1980.

Pierce, Seth J. *What We Believe: Prophecies of Revelation for Teens.* Nampa, ID: Pacific Press®, 2013.

Stefanovic, Ranko. *Revelation of Jesus Christ.* Berrien Springs, MI: Andrews University Press, 2009.

Revenge

"This is evidence of the righteous judgment of God,
that you may be considered worthy of the kingdom of God,
for which you are also suffering."
—2 Thessalonians 1:5

The Christian believers in Thessalonica were heavily persecuted for their beliefs. Paul writes a second letter to them because the persecution has gotten worse. So, Paul gives them a message of hope at the beginning of the letter: "Therefore we ourselves boast about you in the churches of God for your steadfastness and faith in all your persecutions and in the afflictions that you are enduring. This is evidence of the righteous judgment of God, that you may be considered worthy of the kingdom of God, for which you are also suffering" (2 Thessalonians 1:4, 5).

Paul wants to remind them that this persecution will not last forever. They are being persecuted for their faith and commitment to Jesus, and they should let God be the one to bring justice to their persecutors. God's righteous justice will eventually take care of evil forces forever, and in 2 Thessalonians, Paul reminds the believers of this. When Jesus returns, He will bring judgment on those who have persecuted His followers.

When someone hurts you, do you tend to want to bring your own justice on them and get revenge for what they are doing to you? In some cases, it is appropriate to stand up for yourself and stop what is happening. But many times God does not want you to treat other people in the same evil way that they are treating you. He will bring justice on them, so let Him do it. Do not go seeking revenge on the friend that says mean things behind your back. Their own words will come back to bite them. Do not try to hurt the person who keeps shoving you around the court and fouling you on purpose in basketball. Let their own actions lead to their downfall. Retaliation is not what God calls you to. He is the only one who can bring perfect, righteous justice on other people for their actions. So let Him fight your battles for you!

Be Original

"You shall not steal."
—Exodus 20:15

My family once had our house broken into, and some very valuable things were taken, including the engagement watch my father had given to my mother when he proposed to her. It was a special watch she wore every Sabbath as a symbol of their commitment to each other and to God in a lifetime of love. Having someone take that away, even though it was just an object, was very painful. The commandment not to steal is important because taking things from others can cause them a lot of harm.

This commandment seems very simple at first reading—just do not steal! But while you might think of this as taking an object that does not belong to you, this commandment can extend into a lot of other areas as well. Has your teacher told you not to plagiarize on an essay you are writing for class? This commandment could easily apply to plagiarism today—do not take other people's words and claim they are your own. It could also apply to cheating—do not copy other people's assignments. And even to ideas—do not steal other people's thoughts and claim they are yours! Or song composition—do not take your talented friend's musical ideas and say you came up with them yourself!

What lies behind this commandment is the beautiful message that originality is important to God. He has given you your own talents and abilities, and He has blessed you with objects as well. And He wants you to use the things He has already given you. Do not try to take things from others for yourself. Be original! Use what He has already given you to bless others!

Jesus Gives Me Forgiveness

Then Peter came up and said to him,
"Lord, how often will my brother sin against me,
and I forgive him? As many as seven times?" Jesus said to him,
"I do not say to you seven times, but seventy-seven times."
—Matthew 18:21, 22

I am not generally a person who thinks unkindly toward others; I like to give people the benefit of the doubt and try not to judge them. However, there have been a few times in my life when my patience ran low and I did not get along with someone, causing some negative feelings toward them in my heart. I can think of one person that was so hurtful to me that I ended up hating them. And I mean that in the most serious sense of the word. I did not want anything bad to happen to them, but I did not want to see them, talk to them, interact with them, or be nice to them. I really hated them for how they had treated me, and I held a grudge for a long time.

Eventually I had to accept that this person might always be in the periphery parts of my life and that I would have to see the person again, so I had to learn to forgive. I wrestled with God over the grudge I held. In the end, He was the one who had to soften my heart by showing me some of the difficult things this person was going through, humbling me and making me realize that my hatred toward the person was unfair, even if the person had done something very unkind to me in the past. I prayed, gave it to God, and learned to let go. Over time I was able to switch my ill feelings to a sense of genuine care for that person's circumstance. Even though I may never be close friends with the person, I now wish the best for the person and hope God leads that person's life down a successful path.

One of the hardest lessons to learn and accept in your relationship with God is forgiveness. You must learn how to forgive people for the ways they have wronged you and move on without holding a grudge. As Jesus gives you that ability, you will begin to see your life change. You will be happier, people will like you more and want to be your friend, and your whole outlook on the world will be more positive!

We Believe: The Lord's Supper

*Now as they were eating, Jesus took bread, and after blessing it broke it
and gave it to the disciples, and said, "Take, eat; this is my body." And he took a cup,
and when he had given thanks he gave it to them, saying, "Drink of it, all of you,
for this is my blood of the covenant, which is poured out for many for the forgiveness of sins."*
—Matthew 26:26–28

Have you ever been to an agape feast? Sometimes we have them while we take part in a Communion service. The Greek word *agape* means "unconditional love." It is the kind of love that prompts you to care for the poor, help your neighbor, and be kind to the people in your youth group.

When Jesus had the Lord's Supper with His disciples, He was trying to teach them agape love, hoping they would be leaders who embraced this love. Thankfully, they did, and the early Christian church was known for agape love—caring for one another and supporting one another.

The Lord's Supper was a solemn event, though, because Christ was looking toward His soon death on the cross. He humbly washed His disciples' feet, then ate with them. As He passed the bread and wine around the table, He told the disciples that it represented His body and blood shed for humanity. He asked them to repeat this ceremony later in remembrance of His sacrifice. As you participate in your next Communion service or agape feast, take that time to remember Jesus' sacrifice and the love that He wants you to show.

Here is how the Fundamental Beliefs of Seventh-day Adventists describes this important event:

The Lord's Supper is a participation in the emblems of the body and blood of Jesus as an expression of faith in Him, our Lord and Savior. In this experience of communion Christ is present to meet and strengthen His people. As we partake, we joyfully proclaim the Lord's death until He comes again. Preparation for the Supper includes self-examination, repentance, and confession. The Master ordained the service of foot-washing to signify renewed cleansing, to express a willingness to serve one another in Christlike humility, and to unite our hearts in love. The communion service is open to all believing Christians. (Matt. 26:17-30; John 6:48-63; 13:1-17; 1 Cor. 10:16, 17; 11:23-30; Rev. 3:20.)*

---

* Seventh-day Adventist Church, "The Lord's Supper," in *28 Fundamental Beliefs* (General Conference of Seventh-day Adventists, 2015), 7, https://szu.adventist.org/wp-content/uploads/2016/04/28_Beliefs.pdf.

Revelation Studies 4:
The Throne Room

*And the four living creatures, each of them with six wings, are full of eyes all around and
within, and day and night they never cease to say, "Holy, holy, holy, is the Lord God Almighty,
who was and is and is to come!" And whenever the living creatures give glory and honor and
thanks to him who is seated on the throne, who lives forever and ever, the twenty-four elders fall
down before him who is seated on the throne and worship him who lives forever and ever.*
—Revelation 4:8–10

Revelation 4 gives a magnificent description of God's throne! The One sitting on the throne looks like jasper and carnelian, while the throne itself is like an emerald with a rainbow around it. Flashes of lightning and thunder come from the throne, and in front of the throne is a sea of glass. It is an epic scene. I dare you to try and draw it!

Each of the elements mentioned represents something. The rainbow represents God's perfection, holiness, and mercy. The twenty-four elders wearing white robes and gold crowns are a reminder of the priestly rotation of duties in the tabernacle. These may be literal people or representations of those on earth who have sinned but are saved by Jesus' grace because they chose to follow God.

The strangest part of this chapter is the mention of four different creatures also standing before the throne. They represent heavenly beings that work with God to help humans in the quest for salvation. They are guided by the Holy Spirit, and their mission is to call people to work for God and spread His kingdom on earth so that more people can learn about salvation and Jesus' sacrifice for them. In a strikingly similar vision in Ezekiel, Jesus' character is represented in these animals through being both powerful and gentle, human and divine, strong and serving.

Ultimately this chapter is an encouragement because it is a reminder that God is in control and is at work to give the assurance of salvation. Heaven is working to help you and guide you.

For further study
Nichol, Francis D. *The Seventh-day Adventist Bible Commentary*. Vol. 7, *Philippians to Revelation*. Washington, DC: Review and Herald®, 1980.
Pierce, Seth J. *What We Believe: Prophecies of Revelation for Teens*. Nampa, ID: Pacific Press®, 2013.
Stefanovic, Ranko. *Revelation of Jesus Christ*. Berrien Springs, MI: Andrews University Press, 2009.

Stand in Awe of God

Therefore fear God.
—Ecclesiastes 5:7, NIV

Where do you want to be in ten years? Twenty years? Fifty years? Think about what kind of life you want to lead. Do you want to be a world changer? Do you want to be someone who shapes society, who spreads love, and who helps the less fortunate? Dreaming of the future and who we want to become is wonderful. It helps us set goals, and it gives us something to hope and strive for. But sometimes what we need to do is take a step back and look at what God has already done, having faith that He will continue to do good things in our lives.

The book of Ecclesiastes is a very interesting one to read, and if you have the time, pull out your Bible and start reading through it now. Ecclesiastes 5 has some great advice. I was once struck by the section that says, "Why should God be angry at what you say and destroy the work of your hands? Much dreaming and many words are meaningless. Therefore fear God" (verses 6, 7, NIV). Does it strike you powerfully? "Stand in awe of God!" He is so magnificent and powerful! We really should spend more time simply standing in awe of His greatness.

Instead of spending our time dreaming uselessly or trying to accomplish things by our own abilities, we should instead stop and stand in awe of God and all He is. Have you ever done that? Have you ever had a moment where you could not help but stand in awe of how He was working in your life or the lives of people around you? I am sure you have witnessed it at least. Do you remember the joy that accompanied that moment? When God does something for you, it is amazing because it is often something you could not have done by your own strength. Maybe it was even something you did not dare believe was possible! Yet God made it happen! I think He loves to surprise us and do incredible things for us. We should really listen to these verses and let Him do it more often!

Today I invite you to take a step back and look at your life. Look at where you have been in the past and where you want to be in the future. How much more do you think you could accomplish with God's help? When you look to the past, can you see the powerful effects that God has had in your life? Now look to the future. Instead of trying to dream up your own useless plans, why not stand in awe of God and see where He takes you? I promise it will be better than anything you could ever imagine.

Air-Raid Sirens

And those who know your name put their trust in you,
for you, O LORD, have not forsaken those who seek you.
—Psalm 9:10

I wonder what that siren noise is? I thought. *I bet it's an ambulance coming since all the cars are stopping.* My two friends and I were hot, dusty, and sweaty, ready for a cool shower and a yummy dinner. When we got to the top of the Jerusalem hill, we realized what was going on, and it chilled us to the bone. It was an air-raid siren, and we were outside the compound! I shot up a quick prayer for safety, hoping the missile would be shot down before it reached us.

In the summer of 2014, I traveled with seventeen other students to study Hebrew in Jerusalem, Israel. One day two of the other students and I decided to spend the afternoon exploring the hills surrounding Jerusalem. We crossed the Kidron Valley, climbed the Mount of Olives, and crossed over to Mount Scopus, where we could see across the Jordan Valley and the Jordan River!

This would be a normal activity for a tourist in most cases. However, there was a war being waged between militant Hamas in Palestinian Gaza and the Israeli Army in the rest of the country. Missiles and rockets were launched from both sides, and some were aimed at Jerusalem. Air-raid sirens gave a ninety-second warning before the bombs were expected to hit. Thankfully, Jerusalem was protected by the Iron Dome system, which shot two small rockets into the air to intercept the incoming missile and make it explode in the air before it could hit the city. Still, when you heard an air-raid siren, you were supposed to go to a shelter or get in a safe place as quickly as possible.

But on that day we were outside the compound, with no way of contacting our fellow students and professor to let them know whether we were safe or not! As we got to the top of the hill and realized it was an air-raid siren, we frantically looked for a place to hide. Seeing nothing, we decided the best thing to do was just head toward the compound. The ninety seconds ticked by, and then we heard an explosion. I swung around just in time to see the missiles explode in the air, three spirals of smoke dancing in the sky. I realized that day how fragile life is. We made it back safely, and I thank God for that. Always be grateful for the life God has given you. Ask God for the strength to avoid evil. I hope you choose His way today.

Revelation Studies 5: The Scroll

And they sang a new song, saying,
"Worthy are you to take the scroll and to open its seals,
for you were slain, and by your blood you ransomed people for God
from every tribe and language and people and nation."
—Revelation 5:9

Scrolls are epic. They make my imagination run wild thinking about ancient mysteries, hidden treasure, secret messages, and complicated prophecies. In Revelation 5, a scroll with seven seals is held by the One sitting on the throne in heaven. An angel asks who is able to open the scroll, but no one is worthy . . . except "the Lion of the tribe of Judah, the Root of David," who has conquered (Revelation 5:5). Who is that talking about?

The imagery is clear: Jesus is the only one worthy to open this scroll. The reason He is the only one able to open it is that He is the one who conquered Satan in the war that had been playing out for thousands of years. Jesus is a warrior, and while on earth, He fought against Satan by healing the sick and preaching the gospel, and He ultimately won through His death on the cross under the weight of our sins. His resurrection from that death made it eternally impossible for Satan to win.

This scroll represents the history of the world and the way God has worked in it, including the life story of every person who has ever lived on earth. The fact that Jesus is the one holding this scroll should give you a sense of great peace. He loves you so much, and He holds your life in His hands. There is no safer place for you to be. He knows all the choices you have made, both good and bad, and He loves you anyway. He wants you in that beautiful heavenly throne room of Revelation 4 with Him. He is the Lion of Revelation 5. And He will protect and keep you as you continue living on this earth until He returns to take you home!

For further study

Nichol, Francis D. *The Seventh-day Adventist Bible Commentary.* Vol. 7, *Philippians to Revelation.* Washington, DC: Review and Herald®, 1980.

Pierce, Seth J. *What We Believe: Prophecies of Revelation for Teens.* Nampa, ID: Pacific Press®, 2013.

Stefanovic, Ranko. *Revelation of Jesus Christ.* Berrien Springs, MI: Andrews University Press, 2009.

Road Signs

First of all, then, I urge that supplications, prayers, intercessions, and thanksgivings be made for all people, for kings and all who are in high positions, that we may lead a peaceful and quiet life, godly and dignified in every way. This is good, and it is pleasing in the sight of God our Savior, who desires all people to be saved and to come to the knowledge of the truth.
—1 Timothy 2:1–4

I remember that we had a quiz on road signs and their meanings while taking my summer driver's ed class. I never realized how many different signs there are until I had to learn what they all meant and take that quiz! These signs along roadways help drivers find their way around, know what is about to happen on the roadway ahead of them, and give instructions on actions to take for safe traffic maneuvering. As a responsible driver, you must pay attention to these signs if you intend to drive safely and get where you are going efficiently.

Some signs on roadways are warnings. Signs that read "Dead End," "No Outlet," or "Private Driveway" warn you that going down that road may not be the best idea. The Bible is full of signs that help you navigate the roadways of your life experience. Memorizing Bible promises gives you hope and keeps fear away during the hard times. Prophecies warn about the future and give you direction on the choices you should make to be safe and follow Jesus. The Scriptures help prevent you from getting lost in life and taking wrong turns away from God.

Just like I needed a teacher in driver's ed to help me learn these signs and what they meant, you also need teachers that help you understand the signs of the Bible. Sometimes the message is easy to understand, like the Ten Commandments. Other times, you need help figuring it out, like the prophecies of Daniel and Revelation. So take advantage of the leaders around you that are willing to help you understand the Bible more deeply. Teachers, church leaders, and parents can help you navigate life and live happily by following what the Bible teaches.

Standing in the Ocean

If I take the wings of the morning and dwell in the uttermost parts of the sea,
even there your hand shall lead me, and your right hand shall hold me.
—Psalm 139:9, 10

On a beach in San Diego, I watched the sandpipers walk along the beach. They are smart little birds, flirting with the ocean but not letting it get the better of them. They knew when to stand firm when the waves came crashing in. And they knew when to jump back and to not go in too deep. As the water washed up on the sand, they would plant themselves firmly, waiting patiently for the water to recede.

The Christian worship band Hillsong United sings the famous song "Oceans." The lyrics talk about the sovereign hand of God guiding your feet across the deep waters, not letting you fail and fall into the sea. Go listen to the song, and reflect on what the words mean in your life.

God calls you to stand firm while the waves are crashing around you. He knows that they will eventually recede, and His hand will hold you firm during the trial. You might not be able to see how long that will take, but have faith that He can. And He will not let go of you in the meantime. Whether you are standing on the beach or you have ventured out too deep to hold yourself up any longer, His love can reach you, and His arms can steady you. Plant yourself firmly in Him and be patient. Wait for the water to recede.

Building Muscles

For while bodily training is of some value, godliness is of value in every way,
as it holds promise for the present life and also for the life to come.
—1 Timothy 4:8

Working out is great for you. Not only will you feel great from the endorphin rush you get after working out, but you will also look great too—healthy and strong! But building muscle takes time, and it can be painful in the process. Knowing the proper steps to take in a workout progression so that you do not injure yourself working toward a goal is important.

Similar to working out, making changes in your lifestyle can take time and require a progression of steps and goals along the way to be successful. Whether it's trying to maintain a vegan diet, making a goal of staying off social media for two weeks, or working to build healthier relationships with family or friends, God has some tips on how to make these things a bit easier and aid your mental health in the process:

- Fresh air
- Exercise
- Water
- Rest
- Abstinence
- Diet
- Sunshine
- Trust God's Word

These eight natural remedies will help you stay healthy and battle all kinds of problems in life. As school starts, you need to be prepared to overcome some big obstacles. That is just like weight lifting. You work out to build muscle so that you can do more things and become a stronger person. Facing the big obstacles at the beginning of a school year is tough, but if you prepare yourself by spending time with God and following the principles listed above, you will feel a whole lot less stressed and anxious. Take the time to strengthen your spiritual muscles as well as your physical ones. Both physical and spiritual exercise are important for a healthy mental outlook on life and response to the world around you.

Revelation Studies 6:
Thundering Hooves

Now I watched when the Lamb opened one of the seven seals,
and I heard one of the four living creatures say with a voice like thunder, "Come!"
—Revelation 6:1

Horses are magnificent and fearless creatures. They fight in wars, rushing into battle unafraid, following the command of their rider to the death. They are intelligent and caring animals, and their mention in Revelation 6 is significant. As the first four seals on the scroll from Revelation 5 are opened, four horses deliver the first four judgments on the world. Essentially, these represent historical events in the world.

The first is a white horse; the rider, a conqueror. This represents the early Christian church that won many people to Jesus. The second horse, bright red, has a rider that takes peace from the earth. This represents the next phase in earthly Christian history, when Christians were persecuted for their beliefs. The third horse, which is black, brings a set of balances to measure things on earth. At this time, paganism mixed with Christianity, and biblical literacy was at an all-time low. The fourth horse is pale like death, and it brings death. This represents the church of the Middle Ages, when the church became an evil political power. Meanwhile, many people died either from disease or war during this period in history.

The fifth seal is different, opening to reveal martyrs who were killed for their faith. Protestant Reformers tried to get the church back on track, but many were killed for their beliefs. The sixth seal reveals an earthquake, and the sun is darkened, while the moon turns red and a meteor shower happens. These events happened during the 1700s and 1800s. Jesus told His followers that these were signs of the end of the world, signs that history is drawing to a close and His return is close. Revelation 6 is a reminder that God knew the history of earth before it happened, and He predicted it in these prophecies. It gives us a marker of hope that this pain and suffering will not last forever but that Jesus is coming back soon to take us home!

For further study

Nichol, Francis D. *The Seventh-day Adventist Bible Commentary.* Vol. 7, *Philippians to Revelation.* Washington, DC: Review and Herald®, 1980.

Pierce, Seth J. *What We Believe: Prophecies of Revelation for Teens.* Nampa, ID: Pacific Press®, 2013.

Stefanovic, Ranko. *Revelation of Jesus Christ.* Berrien Spring,s MI: Andrews University Press, 2009.

Baking Bread

Oh, taste and see that the LORD is good!
Blessed is the man who takes refuge in him!
—Psalm 34:8

The smell of bread baking in the oven is a very comforting smell. All the ingredients combined together make a tasty loaf of bread that smells heavenly. However, there is one key ingredient that is the secret to a fluffy loaf: yeast! Yeast is what makes the bread rise. It is a leavening agent, which means it causes a chemical reaction while baking so that bubbles form in the dough. This is what gives your bread a light fluffiness and makes all those little air pockets you see when you cut a slice from the loaf.

The Holy Spirit is kind of like yeast in our lives. Without Him, our hearts are hard and tough. But with Him, we can be sensitive and kind to one another. Inviting Him into your heart will make your heart warm and fluffy! Sometimes understanding the Holy Spirit is confusing, but His voice can be a bit like those yeast bubbles in your mind. He can expand in your life when you let Him and pop an idea into your mind that you would not think of otherwise. Accepting the Holy Spirit is simple since He was already sent to earth two thousand years ago and is the primary form of God's presence here on earth. All you have to do is say yes to Him! Ask Him to be a constant presence in your life, and like yeast, which makes bread rise, He will raise your life from something hard and tough to something kind and wonderful!

Influence Your World

Do your best to present yourself to God as one approved,
a worker who has no need to be ashamed, rightly handling the word of truth.
—2 Timothy 2:15

Today's devotional is another time of experience for you and God. Find a comfortable, quiet spot where you can write and search through your Bible for a few moments alone with God. Answer these questions thoughtfully as you probe deeper into your relationship with your Savior:

What are three major problems you think teens face in today's world?

_____

_____

Do you feel like you have the ability to influence any of those areas, with God's help? How?

_____

_____

How do you think the Adventist Church can better minister to society?

_____

_____

What does your generation define as the most important things in life?

_____

_____

How can you lead the Adventist Church forward, *in your position as a young person*, in these issues?

_____

_____

Never Alone

On the day I called, you answered me;
my strength of soul you increased.
—Psalm 138:3

When I was young, I was afraid of the dark. I knew there were no monsters under my bed, no bogeymen in the closet, and that I was perfectly safe in my home. But sometimes, in the evening, my dad would go to the garage or basement to work on a project fixing something. If I could not find him, I would run around the house, yelling, "Daaaddy! Daddyyy!" until I found him. Even if I did not need anything, I just wanted to know where he was. I needed to know he was present to feel safe.

As you grow up, you begin to have a sense of independence, and you do not need your parents as much as you did when you were young. But in moments of panic, they are still often the first ones you call! God is the best parent ever, because He is always accessible, always near, and always ready to help and protect us. When you are going through a tough situation, it might feel like you are running around yelling for Him to help you, but do not worry, He is always listening. He may not answer when or how you want Him to, but that does not mean He has abandoned you. It simply means He can see the bigger picture, and He knows what path would be best for you to go down. Sometimes that means dealing with some heartache in the process toward a better future.

God's Firm Foundation

But God's firm foundation stands, bearing this seal: "The Lord knows those who are his,"
and, "Let everyone who names the name of the Lord depart from iniquity."
—2 Timothy 2:19

*H*ave you ever chopped and stacked firewood? I remember doing it a lot in Pathfinders as a kid. When kids who are not experienced chop it, you end up with lots of different shapes and sizes of wood. The big ones stack easily on the bottom. The small ones fit best in the cracks or on top. But if they are not all the same size, you have to be very careful how you stack them so that they will not all topple over when you are done. What is the most important layer of the stack? The base! You need a solid foundation if you want anything else to work on top.

The same is true of your life. You need a solid foundation to be successful and happy. The activities you choose to participate in and the people you surround yourself with form the foundation that ultimately shapes your life. If God is first in your life and at the base of your structure for life, then you have a firm foundation to build upon. You can be sure that no one will be able to topple you over. When the storms of life try to knock you down, you can be secure knowing you are built on a solid base.

Do you trust Jesus to be that firm foundation for you? Once you accept Him as your base, what will you choose to build on top? Pick friends who will lead you back to Him. Pick activities that focus on uplifting Him. Praise Him in everything you are involved with, and your life will be solid!

Revelation Studies 7: 144,000

After this I looked, and behold, a great multitude that no one could number, from every nation,
from all tribes and peoples and languages, standing before the throne and before the Lamb,
clothed in white robes, with palm branches in their hands, and crying out with a loud voice,
"Salvation belongs to our God who sits on the throne, and to the Lamb!"
—Revelation 7:9, 10

Revelation 7 presents some interesting numbers and a beautiful heavenly scene. The chapter starts by naming the number of those who are "sealed," then every tribe of Israel is listed. The last half of the chapter shows a "great multitude" of people from every race, language, and nation clothed in white and proclaiming words about salvation in the throne room of Jesus. The angels, elders, and living creatures worship God, while an angel asks John who the people are and where they have come from. John's reply is short, and the angel clarifies by saying they are those who have come out of the great tribulation by choosing Christ and washing their robes in His blood to make them clean.

The 144,000 in this chapter is not a literal number of the people who will be in heaven. It is a representation of how the twelve tribes of Israel were scattered throughout the world and how God's message was also scattered throughout the world by the early Christian church, bringing people from every language and nation into God's family. So this number represents all people on earth who are saved, and there will probably be way more than 144,000 people in heaven!

The beauty of Revelation chapter 7 can show you how loved you are by God. The nation of your family origin does not matter, the language you speak or race you identify with does not matter, none of your earthly identifying factors matter when it comes to heaven. God will have people from every nation, tribe, people, and language in heaven. He is the God who created diversity, and He loves you no matter what your family background is. You can be a part of that symbolic 144,000 in heaven simply by believing in Jesus!

For further study

Nichol, Francis D. *The Seventh-day Adventist Bible Commentary.* Vol. 7, *Philippians to Revelation.* Washington, DC: Review and Herald®, 1980.

Pierce, Seth J. *What We Believe: Prophecies of Revelation for Teens.* Nampa, ID: Pacific Press®, 2013.

Stefanovic, Ranko. *Revelation of Jesus Christ.* Berrien Springs, MI: Andrews University Press, 2009.

A Mother's Love

Give thanks to the God of heaven,
for his steadfast love endures forever.
—Psalm 136:26

A mother's strength goes far beyond any other human experience. Her love is more powerful than any other human emotion. Mothers are fearless and bold, giving life through an incredibly painful process and loving their tiny baby more than they love themselves. When a mother delivers her baby, the chemical oxytocin is emitted, creating a powerful bond between a mother and her child. This chemical is responsible for the way a mother looks after her children with intense care. This is what makes giving up a child for adoption, for any reason, heartbreaking. And it's why your mom bugs you constantly to be a better, more responsible person—her discipline is a result of her intense love for you and desire for you to live the best life possible.

In the Bible, God's love is sometimes compared to that of a mother. His love for us is intense, fierce, powerful, and never-ending. He will chase us down, discipline us when we mess up, kiss our boo-boos, and hug us tightly while we cry, just as a mother does. His love is displayed in the affection your mother has for you, and He lets His love shine through mothers so that we can experience how loving and serious He is about us.

Today, take the time to figure out your mother's, or mother figure's, love language and spend time demonstrating love to her—whether it's talking to her about how thankful you are for her care, spending time doing a fun activity with her, or serving her in a meaningful way. The most special thing for a mother is to receive love back from the person she loves most in the world: you.

We Believe: Spiritual Gifts

To each is given the manifestation of the Spirit for the common good.
—1 Corinthians 12:7

Have you ever thought about your spiritual gifts? Typically, the most glorified spiritual gifts are preaching, teaching, evangelism, or serving others in obvious ways. That makes it easy to forget the lesser thought of gifts, such as hospitality, encouragement, technology management, and so on. The Holy Spirit can use you in hundreds of ways to inspire others. Take some time today to pray and figure out what your top spiritual gifts are.

Spiritual gifts are described by the Fundamental Beliefs of Seventh-day Adventists in this way:

God bestows upon all members of His church in every age spiritual gifts that each member is to employ in loving ministry for the common good of the church and of humanity. Given by the agency of the Holy Spirit, who apportions to each member as He wills, the gifts provide all abilities and ministries needed by the church to fulfill its divinely ordained functions. According to the Scriptures, these gifts include such ministries as faith, healing, prophecy, proclamation, teaching, administration, reconciliation, compassion, and self-sacrificing service and charity for the help and encouragement of people. Some members are called of God and endowed by the Spirit for functions recognized by the church in pastoral, evangelistic, and teaching ministries particularly needed to equip the members for service, to build up the church to spiritual maturity, and to foster unity of the faith and knowledge of God. When members employ these spiritual gifts as faithful stewards of God's varied grace, the church is protected from the destructive influence of false doctrine, grows with a growth that is from God, and is built up in faith and love. (Acts 6:1-7; Rom. 12:4-8; 1 Cor. 12:7-11, 27, 28; Eph. 4:8, 11-16; 1 Tim. 3:1-13; 1 Peter 4:10, 11.)*

---

* Seventh-day Adventist Church, "Spiritual Gifts and Ministries," in *28 Fundamental Beliefs* (General Conference of Seventh-day Adventists, 2015), 8, https://szu.adventist.org/wp-content/uploads/2016/04/28_Beliefs.pdf.

Revelation Studies 8: Silence in Heaven

When the Lamb opened the seventh seal, there was silence in heaven for about half an hour. Then I saw the seven angels who stand before God, and seven trumpets were given to them. And another angel came and stood at the altar with a golden censer, and he was given much incense to offer with the prayers of all the saints on the golden altar before the throne, and the smoke of the incense, with the prayers of the saints, rose before God from the hand of the angel. Then the angel took the censer and filled it with fire from the altar and threw it on the earth, and there were peals of thunder, rumblings, flashes of lightning, and an earthquake.
—Revelation 8:1–5

The scene of silence in heaven described in Revelation 8 is very strange because Revelation shows us that heaven is not a quiet place! There are thundering voices, trumpets, angels, voices singing, and things happening all the time! But this seventh seal brings silence. What does this all mean?

Think of it like the calm before the storm—something big is about to happen. Seven angels blow their trumpets, and one by one, plagues come on the earth. Hail, fire, blood, burning, creatures dying, ships destroyed, stars falling, and one-third of everything is destroyed. This one-third reminds us of the one-third of heaven's angels that followed Lucifer when he rebelled against God and was thrown out of heaven. And yet it also shows God's mercy on earth by not destroying all of it immediately. The trumpets are a sign that the end is near. They also represent God's judgment on earth's sins.

The purpose of this whole chapter is to show what choosing sin has caused on earth and what the fate of a fallen race of humans is. God has allowed sin to exist for a time so that the universe can see what the result of choosing evil is. When God destroys Satan and evil completely, He will be justified as a good, loving, and righteous God for not forcing His creation to follow Him in fear but letting us choose to follow Him out of love. Have you made that choice?

For further study

Nichol, Francis D. *The Seventh-day Adventist Bible Commentary.* Vol. 7, *Philippians to Revelation.* Washington, DC: Review and Herald®, 1980.

Pierce, Seth J. *What We Believe: Prophecies of Revelation for Teens.* Nampa, ID: Pacific Press®, 2013.

Stefanovic, Ranko. *Revelation of Jesus Christ.* Berrien Springs, MI: Andrews University Press, 2009.

Finding Acceptance

"All that the Father gives me will come to me,
and whoever comes to me I will never cast out."
—John 6:37

Do you look for validation based on your acceptance in social circles? Popularity is a big deal in high school. Making a good name for yourself and not being the uncool kid is a top priority for many people. But there is a good reason to not base your value on what others think of you. That is because people are imperfect, so people will fail you. You cannot look for true acceptance in the opinions of the people around you.

The truest form of acceptance comes from God. The most beautiful thing about God's acceptance is that it has nothing to do with how you perform in His presence. His acceptance of you is not based on your merits, your goodness, your popularity, your style, or what movies you saw most recently. His approval comes from looking into your heart and seeing what direction you are walking in. Are you choosing to walk toward Him? He would love that! Are you choosing to walk away? He still loves you and will continue calling you back to His heart. Your value in His eyes is not based on earthly things. Every good thing we have here is nothing compared to the glories of heaven, so that is not what God looks at in us! He simply wants you to choose to follow Him and the principles He has laid out for you in the Bible. That is how to get true acceptance.

Surround yourself with people who have learned not to care what others think but instead to find their acceptance in God's love for them. If there are not any people like that around you, be the first one to have that attitude. Create an atmosphere of seeking God's approval instead of the approval of your peers. Trust God's love for you, and lean on Him today.

Musically Frustrated—Part 1

A fool vents all his feelings, but a wise man holds them back.
—Proverbs 29:11, NKJV

Music is a passion of mine. I took classical piano lessons from grade school through high school, sang in multiple choirs, was involved in band, loved singing on the praise team or playing music for church, and even got to play for some weddings! Though I know I am not the best praise band leader in the world by far, I still feel like I know enough to get by with any other musicians I need to work with.

At one church where I helped with music, my patience was really tested, though. The person leading the praise team was disorganized, never did things in a timely manner, would sometimes play in the wrong key during church, and seemed somewhat clueless as to how to successfully lead a group of people in praise. And since music is such an important part of my relationship with God, naturally, this really bothered me! I let it fester by getting upset and annoyed after our one-hour practices became two-hour practices and I got to bed later than planned. I would be annoyed after church when the music did not go well, and I felt embarrassed about how we did. I let it stir around in my heart and almost got to the point where I wanted to quit and not even help with praise music anymore because the process was so frustrating.

While this story does have some redemption in tomorrow's devotion, today, spend some time thinking about what frustrates you or which person always seems to get under your skin. Why does that situation or person bother you so much? What are those hard feelings doing to your heart and to your view of that person? How do these thoughts affect you and influence your relationships with the people around you when you are annoyed?

Proverbs 29:11 tells us, "A fool vents all his feelings, but a wise man holds them back" (NKJV).

Musically Frustrated—Part 2

I will ponder the way that is blameless. . . .
I will walk with integrity of heart within my house.
—Psalm 101:2

Yesterday I described my frustration with someone I felt was not musically gifted enough to be the praise team leader at church. Well, after a few of those incidents, something happened. The praise leader told everyone they were planning to move to a different church. I started realizing all the areas of ministry this individual was involved in and how much passion they put into everything they did. The church would really miss them when they left! I realized that my sour attitude had caused something gross to grow in my heart, and I did not want it to be there anymore.

The next Sabbath that we played music together, the practice went surprisingly well, and the delivery of the songs at church was one of the best we had ever done! Obviously, I felt embarrassed about my negative thoughts. Though outwardly I had never let feelings of annoyance show, inwardly, I continued to let them fester.

Thankfully, the praise leader decided to stay at that church and continue leading. I decided from that moment forward I would have a good attitude about working together and I would go into each practice with a gracious mind-set. And the results were incredible! The music was great, and the friendship grew too.

God has given us the ability to choose our attitude, but letting a bad attitude about someone fester can negatively affect our hearts. If you have an annoying person like this in your life who really frustrates you, pray and ask God to give you a better perspective and a gracious attitude when you interact with them.

Insecurities

I praise you because I am fearfully and wonderfully made;
your works are wonderful, I know that full well.
—Psalm 139:14, NIV

Recently I went to my high school reunion. While there, I talked with one of my best friends about something strange that happens when we walk into that building. Even though we are now both grown women who are much more confident than we were in high school, when we walk into that building, we both feel like all our old high school insecurities come creeping back. Feeling so insecure seems silly, but it's something everyone deals with, whether they admit it or not!

What are your biggest insecurities right now? Be honest with yourself and write them below:

_____

_____

Though you may feel like you are the only one who feels left out, unpopular, not pretty or handsome enough, not good enough at sports, not smart enough, not talented enough, or not cool enough—you are not the only one! Most likely everyone in your class or friend group feels the same way. Each person has their own insecurities, and sometimes the people who seem like they have it all together have the most insecurities of all.

This is why you cannot look to other people to find your worth and value. You must get that from God and let Him be the source of your confidence and inner strength. When you are feeling insecure about yourself or your abilities. remember who made you. God has put in you a special strength of your own. You are valuable and full of worth because He made you! Let His love be what nurtures your heart, not whether the person's eye you catch in class thinks you are cool or not. God's love is faithful and with you, no matter how you look or feel. Find your confidence in Him!

Speaking With Dignity

Likewise, urge the younger men to be self-controlled. Show yourself in all respects to be a model of good works, and in your teaching show integrity, dignity, and sound speech that cannot be condemned, so that an opponent may be put to shame, having nothing evil to say about us.
—Titus 2:6–8

Sometimes it seems that young people get railed on for being young. You have probably have had a time or two when you were frustrated by older people telling you that you could not do something because you were young or getting annoyed about something youth like doing. Choosing to respond with grace, kindness, and patience in those moments can be extremely difficult.

Titus was a young minister of the gospel. Paul wrote to encourage him in his ministry to other young people so that they would not be "put to shame" and so that people would have nothing evil to say about them or about Paul and his mentorship of Titus. So take the words of this verse to heart when someone says something negative about youth. Turn their negativity into goodness in how you choose to respond.

Holding high the value of self-control will keep you from doing something that could cause more harm. Being a role model for doing good will cause parents to trust you and want their kids to be like you. Being honest and walking with dignity shows that you have a good character and are strong enough to recognize your weaknesses and learn from them. Think before you speak, and research topics you are passionate about—this will help you have intelligent conversations with professionals in every field. They will respect you for learning well and thinking critically about issues you choose to discuss or debate. Above all, put God first in your heart and mind so that what comes out of your mouth is from Him.

We Believe: The Prophetic Gift

And he said, "Hear my words: If there is a prophet among you,
I the LORD make myself known to him in a vision; I speak with him in a dream."
—Numbers 12:6

Do you believe prophets still exist? We see them all over the Bible. Many prophets even wrote significant portions of the Old Testament. Prophets are people chosen by God to share messages from Him with humans on earth. God speaks to prophets in a much more direct way than how He usually speaks to other people. This puts a lot of stress and pressure on them, and though it is a special gift to be spoken to by God or His angels, do not be jealous—most prophets had tough lives! They had to choose to make sacrifices in their life in order to be His prophet.

The prophet Joel made a prophecy about prophets at the end of time: "And it shall come to pass afterward, that I will pour out my Spirit on all flesh; your sons and your daughters shall prophesy, your old men shall dream dreams, and your young men shall see visions. Even on the male and female servants in those days I will pour out my Spirit" (Joel 2:28, 29).

Adventists see this passage as a promise that the gift of prophecy is not over. We believe the Holy Spirit gave this prophetic gift to a teenage girl named Ellen, who joined with other teenagers and young adults to study the Scriptures and learn more about God. When they would discover something in the Bible, God often gave her a vision of confirmation, letting them know that what they understood Scripture to mean was correct! Always be open to His guidance and quick to study the Scriptures!

The Fundamental Beliefs of Seventh-day Adventists describes Ellen White and her gift of prophecy in this way: "The Scriptures testify that one of the gifts of the Holy Spirit is prophecy. This gift is an identifying mark of the remnant church and we believe it was manifested in the ministry of Ellen G. White. Her writings speak with prophetic authority and provide comfort, guidance, instruction, and correction to the church. They also make clear that the Bible is the standard by which all teaching and experience must be tested. (Num. 12:6; 2 Chron. 20:20; Amos 3:7; Joel 2:28, 29; Acts 2:14-21; 2 Tim. 3:16, 17; Heb. 1:1-3; Rev. 12:17; 19:10; 22:8, 9)."*

---

* Seventh-day Adventist Church, "The Gift of Prophecy," in *28 Fundamental Beliefs* (General Conference of Seventh-day Adventists, 2015), 8, https://szu.adventist.org/wp-content/uploads/2016/04/28_Beliefs.pdf.

Revelation Studies 9: Atheism

The first woe has passed; behold,
two woes are still to come.
—Revelation 9:12

Revelation 9 continues the journey through the seven angels blowing trumpets, describing the fifth and sixth trumpets. They seem intense and scary, with locusts preparing for battle and plagues and demons. But remember, this is all in symbols. These are not literal things happening; they symbolize events throughout history!

In the fifth trumpet section, a star falls from heaven, and locusts come on the earth and are given power. They try to harm God's people, but they are not allowed to bother them for more than five months. This is not a physical battle that took place in history but rather an intellectual one—a moment in the great controversy when Satan was battling for people's minds, trying to convince them that there was no reason to believe in a God. This is when atheism increased in societal beliefs.

In the sixth trumpet section, a heavenly voice commands four angels to kill one-third of humankind. Horses ride forward, plagues descend, and people worship demons and idols. It's a very dark scene. What does it mean? This trumpet describes the end of time when Satan is trying to deceive the whole world. If you have chosen to follow God, you are safe from the devil's schemes. But for those who have chosen not to follow God, they will be subject to Satan's powers. However, hope is not lost here just because things look dark and scary. This is a time when God will work hard to help His people spread the gospel of His kingdom of love and safety on earth. Once again, this section is not so much about a physical battle taking place but a spiritual one—the war over your mind and choices. You get to choose whom you follow: a God of love and peace or the devil and evil. God wants to protect and love you; choose to let Him do that today.

For further study

Nichol, Francis D. *The Seventh-day Adventist Bible Commentary.* Vol. 7, *Philippians to Revelation.* Washington, DC: Review and Herald®, 1980.

Pierce, Seth J. *What We Believe: Prophecies of Revelation for Teens.* Nampa, ID: Pacific Press®, 2013.

Stefanovic, Ranko. *Revelation of Jesus Christ.* Berrien Springs, MI: Andrews University Press, 2009.

The False Witness

"You shall not bear false witness against your neighbor."
—Exodus 20:16

When my sister and I were young and would get into a typical sibling fight, our parents would send us to our rooms and talk to us separately about what happened. What do you think each of us said in those moments? It was always, "Well, she started it! She said this, and she did this, so it's not my fault!" And regardless of what *really* happened, we would make up whatever we had to in order to blame the other person. At least, I would do that sometimes. (Sorry, Sis!)

Our parents were smarter than we were and could usually discern what actually happened, despite our false tales. They would give us the punishments we deserved, and they would help us learn how to forgive and make up, becoming best buddies again.

When the Ten Commandments are listed, the ninth one says, "Do not lie." But this commandment goes deeper than just telling a little lie here and there to get your way out of something. Bearing false witness against your neighbor means throwing them under the bus for something they did not do or placing blame on them that is not deserved. How often do you find yourself working on a group project and it does not get done right or is not turned in on time, so you tell the teacher it was because another person in your group did not do their part? Sadly, I still sometimes find myself blaming my colleagues when things do not go well or our programming does not turn out right. Everyone struggles with "bearing false witness."

God wants you to be humble and willing to tell the truth. Take responsibility for your own actions. And when you have the chance, lift people up instead of saying something false about them or their actions. Treat your neighbor or friend with love and respect, and likely, they will respond in kind!

Grandparents Day

Grandchildren are the crown of the aged,
and the glory of children is their fathers.
—Proverbs 17:6

Dear Grandparents,

You taught me to believe. You taught me to serve. You taught me what mission looks like. You taught me what loving the poor and needy looks like. You taught me to be unafraid to travel the world for God's cause. Your faithfulness to Jesus inspired me to follow Him with my life. Your wisdom bought by many years of experience has shown me what a successful life of winning souls on this earth looks like. Thank you for your grace and love for me. May God continue to bless you as you serve Him!

With love,
Your Grandchild

Today is Grandparents Day! Send a letter to your grandparents expressing thanks to them for all they have taught you. God gives wisdom to the elderly, and He wants us to respect them and the path they have paved for us young people. Show care for them, love them with all your heart, and while you have time left with them, ask them to tell you all their stories about the "good old days"! You might be surprised at some of the stories they have to tell, and how much they actually can relate to what you go through as a teenager. Everyone was a teenager once, and everyone dealt with the same things teenagers deal with. They may not have had smartphones at your age, but they certainly dealt with very similar social circumstances and probably have a lot of wisdom to give about dating, friendships, and developing a walk with God.

God gives us wiser elders to show us the way to Him and to be an example of what a God-filled life looks like. Follow their example, and trust the experiences they share with you. God got them through the trials of life, and He will get you through as well.

You Are Worthy

For we are his workmanship, created in Christ Jesus for good works,
which God prepared beforehand, that we should walk in them.
—Ephesians 2:10

Striving for self-worth is a huge struggle for most teens. When I was a teenager, I had a hard time looking in the mirror and believing I was a beautiful person with some awesome, God-given talents. I looked at myself and saw all my failures. I thought my nose was too big. I saw the pimples that stuck out everywhere, the eyelashes that were too light, the stomach that had no abs, the moles I thought were ugly, and the hair that would not cooperate. And when I

looked at my character, I felt insignificant, unpopular, too shy, unconfident, and never good enough. My self-worth was at an all-time low when I was in high school. Maybe you have felt the same way.

God wants us to look in the mirror and see a different story. He wants you to see yourself the way He sees you and to hear His voice affirming you. He wants you to know you are valuable. You are strong. You are precious. You are handsome. You are worthy of love on your worst days and worthy of His blessings even though you are not perfect. Your insecurities and confusion are worth loving. You are worthy not because of all the good things you do or because of how talented you are but simply because you are His. You belong to Him, and His love is what makes you worthy.

Your heart is worth fighting for, and your salvation was worth His death on the cross. So when you feel down and want to beat yourself up inside for an area you think you failed in, remember who you belong to and why you are worth it to Him.

Revelation Studies 10:
An Angel and a Scroll

So I went to the angel and told him to give me the little scroll. And he said to me,
"Take and eat it; it will make your stomach bitter, but in your mouth it will be sweet as honey."
And I took the little scroll from the hand of the angel and ate it. It was sweet as honey in my
mouth, but when I had eaten it my stomach was made bitter. And I was told, "You must again
prophesy about many peoples and nations and languages and kings."
—Revelation 10:9–11

To summarize Revelation 10, an angel comes down from heaven holding a little scroll and calling out while seven thunders sound. But John is not allowed to write down what the thunders said. Instead, he is told to seal it up. Then the angel swears that there will no longer be a delay in the mystery of God being fulfilled. Then John is instructed to eat the scroll, and it tastes good but gives him a stomachache. What on earth is happening here?

This is a strange vision, to be sure! It's talking about the church at the end of earth's history. John stands in the place of the church, and we Christians are supposed to preach the gospel to the world. During this time, God warns His people about the judgment, which most Adventists identify as starting in 1844. Believers thought Jesus was coming back in 1844—a sweet taste! But they were disappointed when Jesus did not return—a bitter stomachache.

As you grow in your own personal relationship with God, remember that our purpose as Christians is to spread the message of the gospel to the entire world. Since we know that the end of earth's history is near, we must urgently spread the message! This is not out of a sense of fear but rather because we want to see as many people as possible in heaven with Jesus! So we share with others the love of God for the world.

For further study

Nichol, Francis D. *The Seventh-day Adventist Bible Commentary.* Vol. 7, *Philippians to Revelation.* Washington, DC: Review and Herald®, 1980.

Pierce, Seth J. *What We Believe: Prophecies of Revelation for Teens.* Nampa, ID: Pacific Press®, 2013.

Stefanovic, Ranko. *Revelation of Jesus Christ.* Berrien Springs, MI: Andrews University Press, 2009.

Service in Chaos

Now there are varieties of gifts, but the same Spirit; and there are varieties of service, but the same Lord; and there are varieties of activities, but it is the same God who empowers them all in everyone.
—1 Corinthians 12:4–6

I remember watching the TV screen in our classroom as the news flashed video clips of the Twin Towers of the World Trade Center in New York crumbling to the ground and people plummeting to their death. I continue to see news stories scare people, relating terror incidents around the world. In these moments of horrific pain and unexplainable grief and shock, there are silent heroes who ignore the panic and chaos and rush in to save people. In the moments of terror, these people of solid resolve fight terror with service, choosing to risk their lives in order to save the lives of others.

Service is an underrated gift, but it takes a lot of strength and willpower to do anything uncomfortable in order to help others. Yet a heart of service makes people feel fulfilled when they do good deeds and change the world around them one person at a time. No question about it, service is a necessary part of the Christian life. Your walk with God will flourish the more you find ways to serve others.

Ask yourself these questions, and prayerfully answer them:

What is something you have done to serve others that you are really proud of, something that made you feel fulfilled and happy for making a difference?

_____

What type of service is hardest for you? Why?

_____

Who is a good example of someone with a servant's heart that you could ask to mentor you?

_____

What are some upcoming service projects you could get involved with?

_____

F-

So that, as sin reigned in death, grace also might reign
through righteousness leading to eternal life through Jesus Christ our Lord.
—Romans 5:21

When I was in elementary school, my best friend and I had our hearts set on being scientists. We told everyone how when we grew up we would invent things, do experiments, explore, dig up dinosaurs, and go on all kinds of other exciting adventures! One day for class, our teacher had us do dot-to-dot pictures of dinosaurs, which we then colored. Since we admired our teacher so much and loved the stickers she would put on our papers when we did a good job, we asked if we could grade the papers for her during recess time. She kindly agreed, and she wrote examples on sticky notes of nice things we could write on our classmate's papers. She also gave us the prized sticker box to reward everyone for their beautiful artwork. Then she put us in "big people" chairs at her desk and gave us free reign to grade!

We quickly shuffled through and found our own artwork first, giving large red A++'s and 100%'s as well as shiny stickers and notes of "Good job!" or "Amazing!" written at the top. As we went on to the rest of the kids' pictures, we decided it would be really funny if we wrote mean things instead of nice things. I remember sifting through paper after paper of carefully drawn dinosaur dot-to-dots and circling all the mistakes where they missed a dot or colored outside the lines. We drew large frowny faces, did not give them any stickers, and wrote "F-" and "Bad job" at the tops of the papers. We were terrible!

Once we were finished, we stacked the papers in a nice, neat pile and told our teacher we were done, then fled outside to play. I can only imagine her horror when she saw what we did!

What struck me about remembering this story from my childhood was the grace our teacher treated us with. She still gave them stars and smiley faces, unlike we had. God's grace is not complicated. Whether we have lived the perfect life and always colored inside the lines and followed the rules or have made tons of obvious mistakes, God still gives everyone grace equally. Jesus died for everyone, and He gives us that grace for our mistakes. He writes "100%" at the top of our papers and helps us do better when we mess up. Grace is a simple thing. God gives it to us freely. Accept that grace today, and live your life sharing it with others.

Team Spirit

Let everything that has breath praise the LORD! Praise the LORD!
—Psalm 150:6

It's football time! Get out your team spirit gear, wear the number of your favorite player, sit on the couch yelling at the TV screen, or, if you are lucky, join the crowds in the stadium! Watching football is an exciting event that involves lots of energy and often an intense spirit of support for the team you love most. You would defend them at any cost, would you not? If you are an avid football fan, you probably spend lots of your energy arguing with your friends about why your team is the best or why your favorite player is the best on the team. Even if you do not like sports, you can still relate to seeing those die-hard fans who come to school wearing only the select colors of their favorite team, right?

I am a pretty big football fan, and I definitely show my support when my team is playing. But while I was watching one of their games, I had an interesting thought. Why is it so important to us to put all this time and energy into a group of people I do not know personally? Why do we like to rally behind something or someone and cheer them on? Why do we enjoy and almost need something to get so excited about that we cannot contain it? I think a lot of it has to do with the feeling of connectedness and fellowship we have with those who like the team as much as we do. We like to feel connected to something greater than ourselves, especially when we have fun watching them play and win! So why do we not get that excited about God? Why are we not absolutely stoked that He already won the spiritual battle against the devil?

No, Christianity is not mainstream, hipster, or all that popular right now in our society. I am not saying we need to go out on street corners and cheer Jesus' name or else we are bad Christians. But I do think we should not be so afraid of doing the unpopular thing and actually sharing about God once in a while or getting excited over what He has done in our lives. In high school, I became close to one of my best friends simply by sharing Bible verses I thought were really cool with her. Sometimes I would be struggling with something, come across a Bible verse that spoke directly to the situation, and then run to her and show her—genuinely excited that God had spoken to me in that way. Be open to getting excited about God. He has done some epic things—just read the Bible and you will see it all over the place! And look at your own life—no doubt He has worked some miracles for you too! He is a God worthy of our praise, so let's get out there and do a little more praising!

Read Psalm 150

Philemon and Onesimus

For this perhaps is why he was parted from you for a while, that you might have him back forever, no longer as a bondservant but more than a bondservant, as a beloved brother— especially to me, but how much more to you, both in the flesh and in the Lord.
—Philemon 1:15, 16

Philemon is another short, one-chapter book in the New Testament. It's an easy read, so I suggest reading it now!

Paul and Timothy wrote this letter to a man named Philemon, a woman named Apphia, a man named Archippus, and the church that met in their house. Paul is very happy with the work they have done for the gospel. Yet he has a bold request for them: that Philemon accept back a servant named Onesimus who had run away from his master. As you study the text, you can learn a few behind-the-scenes things about this story:

- Paul is in prison because of his preaching about Jesus.
- Onesimus is a young man Paul has taken under his wing.
- Paul is sending Onesimus back to Philemon.
- Paul is calling on Philemon's Christian heart to do what is right toward Onesimus.
- Paul is asking Philemon, the master, to take back Onesimus, the slave, as a brother!

The radical message of Christianity is clearly demonstrated in this short letter. Normally, if a slave or servant ran from their master, when they returned, they would be severely punished—if not killed! But Paul sends Onesimus back, asking Philemon not to punish him and not even to take him back as a servant. Instead, Paul expects Philemon to accept Onesimus as an equal—a Christian brother—not as someone from a lower class. When Philemon read this letter, he had a choice to make: accept the radically transforming message of Christianity and make his slave his equal, his brother, or reject Christian love and punish Onesimus terribly.

What does this story suggest about Jesus' power to transform society? At a time when racism is high, we are called to show Christian love by accepting all people as equals. No matter what circumstances people are in, they are still your siblings in Christ, and He expects you to extend the same love to them that you would to your best friend.

Revelation Studies 11: Biblical Gospel

*"The kingdom of the world has become the kingdom of our Lord
and of his Christ, and he shall reign forever and ever."*
—Revelation 11:15

Revelation 11 shares a vision of two witnesses and the angel sounding the seventh trumpet. John is told to measure the temple, except for the courtyard, because nations will trample the holy city for forty-two months. Meanwhile, the two witnesses will prophesy for 1,260 days, which represents years in prophetic language.* Near the middle of the chapter, a wonderful verse states, "The kingdom of the world has become the kingdom of our Lord and of his Christ, and he shall reign forever and ever" (verse 15).

The world is finally Christ's! And the devil cannot reign over it again. The background of this chapter makes the most sense in light of the Day of Atonement, which was the day when a spiritual measuring occurred. The 1,260-year prophecy, in conjunction with studies from other prophetic books such as Daniel, ends in 1798, when Napoleon's general Berthier took the pope captive and ended the 1,260-year domination of the papacy. The two witnesses mentioned in Revelation 11 represent the Word of God found in the Old and New Testaments. Study the history of the Middle Ages, and you will see that the message of the gospel and truth of the Bible was distorted by Christian faith at the time and underwent a lot of persecution! Though the Bible was rejected for a period of time, it was eventually accepted again and once again was viewed as the sole authority. The fact that the Bible survived the period of rejection is incredible! It demonstrates the importance God places on His Word.

This chapter reminds us that the only way to salvation is through Jesus and His sacrifice. There is nothing you can do to make your way into heaven. The only way is through belief in Jesus Christ as your Lord and Savior. And your job once you accept His gift of salvation is to then go and spread that gospel to everyone you meet—in how you live your life, in the choices you make, and in your own devotional time with Him.

For further study

Nichol, Francis D. *The Seventh-day Adventist Bible Commentary.* Vol. 7, *Philippians to Revelation.* Washington, DC: Review and Herald*, 1980.

Pierce, Seth J. *What We Believe: Prophecies of Revelation for Teens.* Nampa, ID: Pacific Press*, 2013.

Stefanovic, Ranko. *Revelation of Jesus Christ.* Berrien Springs, MI: Andrews University Press, 2009.

---

* See Numbers 14:34 and Ezekiel 4:6.

We Believe: Guidebook to Life

And God spoke all these words, saying, "I am the Lord your God, who brought you out of the land of Egypt, out of the house of slavery. You shall have no other gods before me."
—Exodus 20:1–3

Read how the Fundamental Beliefs of Seventh-day Adventists describes the importance of the Ten Commandments:

The great principles of God's law are embodied in the Ten Command-ments and exemplified in the life of Christ. They express God's love, will, and purposes concerning human conduct and relationships and are bind-ing upon all people in every age. These precepts are the basis of God's covenant with His people and the standard in God's judgment. Through the agency of the Holy Spirit they point out sin and awaken a sense of need for a Savior. Salvation is all of grace and not of works, and its fruit is obedience to the Commandments. This obedience develops Christian character and results in a sense of well-being. It is evidence of our love for the Lord and our concern for our fellow human beings. The obedience of faith demonstrates the power of Christ to transform lives, and therefore strengthens Christian witness. (Exod. 20:1-17; Deut. 28:1-14; Ps. 19:7-14; 40:7, 8; Matt. 5:17-20; 22:36-40; John 14:15; 15:7-10; Rom. 8:3, 4; Eph. 2:8-10; Heb. 8:8-10; 1 John 2:3; 5:3; Rev. 12:17; 14:12.)*

Do you get excited by the Ten Commandments? Do you prefer having par-ents who love each other and are committed in their marriage? What about living where people do not murder others on the street? Do you like it when your friends get jealous, upset, and mean when you achieve something or get something they cannot? Life is a lot happier when loved ones care about one another—people live, and jealousy is not a problem. That is why God gave us the Ten Commandments, not as a set of rules to prod us with but as a guide-book for how to live a happy life. And God wants to have a relationship with us first anyway, which is the whole point of the first four commandments!

---

* Seventh-day Adventist Church, "The Law of God," in *28 Fundamental Beliefs* (General Conference of Seventh-day Adventists, 2015), 8, https://szu.adventist.org/wp-content/uploads/2016/04/28_Beliefs.pdf.

Groomsmen and Candles

But the path of the righteous is like the light of dawn,
which shines brighter and brighter until full day.
—Proverbs 4:18

My cousin's wedding was at an idyllic venue—a beautiful beach on the Pacific Ocean. Everything looked perfect, from the couple getting married to every tiny, thoughtful decoration. The more weddings you attend, the more quickly you discover that nothing ever goes smoothly. At this wedding, the battle was the wind! Beaches are beautiful but always windy. As the couple stepped over to the unity candle to light it, the wind began to pick up speed, blowing the flame out every time they tried to light it. How could you solve that on a beach? Then something special happened. All the groomsmen walked over and huddled around the couple, creating a barrier between them and the wind. Because of the wall the groomsmen created, they were able to light the unity candle and have a special moment that brought tears to everyone's eyes!

When you see someone whose light is going out, step up and block the wind, bringing other friends with you to help support them. When the winds of depression, failed relationships, lost friendships, family strife, or unkind classmates beat against you, ask God for a wall. When you see someone else going through those things, be that wall for them. Prevent the wind from breaking through and destroying their flame. Be a part of what makes that flame grow and burn brighter. Be the support they need by praying with them, sitting with them, encouraging them, writing kind notes to them, and letting them know how special and important they are. Everyone needs friends who will be a wall against the wind for them. Be the start of that wall, and when you are in need, you will find that others will step up and be that wall for you, protecting you from the winds trying to blow out your flame.

Preparing for College

"How can a young man keep his way pure?
By guarding it according to your word.
With my whole heart I seek you;
let me not wander from your commandments!
I have stored up your word in my heart,
that I might not sin against you."
—Psalm 119:9–11

College is starting soon for some of you! This is the time of year when future college students start panicking about their freshman classes and the new stresses that are ahead. College brings with it freedom—you are away from your parents, often far away from home, where you are making the most of your own decisions for the first time. Go into college with a clear head and a solid conscience. You will be surrounded by people from all walks of life. There will be people who believe similarly to you and practice religion similarly to you. Others will be quite different, inviting you to parties and offering you alcohol and drugs. Making a firm resolve to stay away from compromising situations is important, and it will keep you safe and healthy during your college years. College is expensive! These are the years when your decisions are thousand-dollar decisions, and every moment of your education counts toward your future in a huge way.

If you are unsure about your major choice for college, get some experience shadowing people in fields you are interested in. Choose general classes that will apply to lots of majors, and trust God to lead you down a clear path. Start a prayer journal for your career, writing down your life goals, things that inspire you, and what you want to get involved in. Ask God to give you wisdom as you revise and update your list, trusting Him to show you which path you should take. College is exciting, so enjoy it! But make sure you do not leave God behind in the process. He will make it the best experience of your life if you choose to walk with Him by your side.

Revelation Studies 12:
Satan Defeated

"Now the salvation and the power and the kingdom of our God
and the authority of his Christ have come, for the accuser of our brothers
has been thrown down, who accuses them day and night before our God."
—Revelation 12:10

The first thing to note when reading Revelation 12 is what certain symbols stand for in the Bible. The woman represents the church. The dragon represents Satan. And the heads and horns represent kingdoms and political powers in history. The beginning of Revelation 12 describes much of sin and salvation's history, from Satan being cast out of heaven for rebelling against God to the Messiah's birth on earth to the struggle the Christian church went through during the Middle Ages. After the birth of her child, the woman goes through some trouble because the dragon wants to devour her and her child. But in verse 5, the "child was caught up to God," and the woman is protected during the 1,260 days, also known as years in prophetic language.

God did not forsake His people. Instead, Christianity spread throughout the world. Unfortunately, over time political powers entered the church and began to rule it like a kingdom, persecuting those who followed the Bible and trying to reform the church for 1,260 years. When Satan tries to make war with the remnant toward the end of Revelation 12, two special characteristics are mentioned: they keep the commandments of God and hold to the testimony of Jesus. Adventists believe that these characteristics identify the Seventh-day Adventist movement as playing a role in end times because we believe in keeping God's law and following God's teachings in the Bible, especially those concerning Jesus. In Revelation 12, there is a definite sense of hope and God's power as well as the promise of the devil being defeated forever!

This chapter gives a sense of urgency for the message about Jesus' soon return to be spread! What do you think your role in that job may be? Pray about it today, and ask Him to reveal a portion of His plan to you.

For further study

Nichol, Francis D. *The Seventh-day Adventist Bible Commentary*. Vol. 7, *Philippians to Revelation*. Washington, DC: Review and Herald®, 1980.

Pierce, Seth J. *What We Believe: Prophecies of Revelation for Teens*. Nampa, ID: Pacific Press®, 2013.

Stefanovic, Ranko. *Revelation of Jesus Christ*. Berrien Springs, MI: Andrews University Press, 2009.

Birds

"Look at the birds of the air: they neither sow nor reap nor gather into barns,
and yet your heavenly Father feeds them. Are you not of more value than they?"
—Matthew 6:26

Birds sing to one another in order to communicate a message. Their songs are beautiful to our ears and delightful to listen to. The songs we hear communicate messages of warning, courtship, and calling out to one another. Some birds can sing while flying through the air, while others prefer sitting on a high branch to be heard by the whole forest. If you take the time to sit and listen to the songs of the birds, you will begin to be able to identify birds by their song. Next time you are in nature, take some time to listen to the different birdsongs you hear.

God gives you the ability to enjoy music and songs through playing or singing them. Through praising Him with your voice, you bring joy to God and grow in your relationship with Him. It is just one of the many ways we can experience God's presence and praise Him! Sharing your gifts, like music, with someone who is feeling low can give you joy and happiness and a way out when you are confused and lost.

Today, for the remainder of your devotional time, find a Christian song to listen to or play some music yourself. Your praise and musical talent bring glory to God! He loves to hear you praise Him, and He knows your unique voice, just as all the birds have unique voices that communicate different messages.

Call out to Him, and He will hear you. You are never alone, and spending time in song can draw you closer to God and gain you other musical friends as well! May God be praised through your life!

Fulfilled

Know the love of Christ that surpasses knowledge,
that you may be filled with all the fullness of God.
—Ephesians 3:19

School has been going long enough by now that you have probably developed a crush if you did not already have one. Maybe some of your friends are getting into relationships, or maybe you have started dating someone! When you begin a relationship with someone, you may think this will be the person that will finally fulfill all your emotional needs. You may have certain expectations of them—how they will be the perfect person for you, how they will make you happy forever, and how nothing could ever go wrong.

Hopefully, in the back of your mind, you know this is not true. People cannot be completely emotionally fulfilling for one another. While God has placed in humans the ability to love one another and form deep relationships, because every person is sinful, fulfilling one another is totally impossible.

God must be the only source for meeting your emotional needs. You can place expectations on Him because He is strong enough to handle them! Do you have a need to feel safe and secure? Place that on God and know that it is His responsibility. Do you want your crush to be the one who gives you endless joy and happiness? Place that on God instead because He is the only one who can give you true happiness and joy that will last.

While relationships will teach you how to love another person selflessly, having a boyfriend or girlfriend will not solve all your problems or make you feel completely fulfilled. God is the only One who can do that. And He is excited and ready to have that kind of relationship with you! Commit to letting Him be the One who fulfills all your needs.

The Gospel for the Hebrews

Now faith is the assurance of things hoped for,
the conviction of things not seen.
—Hebrews 11:1

The book of Hebrews was written to Hebrew Christian believers who cultur-ally and racially were Jewish. Since they had been raised in the Jewish reli-gion, they naturally wanted to continue their Jewish customs as they practiced the Christian faith. And oftentimes, since Christianity had its roots in Judaism, they also wanted Gentiles to adopt those Jewish ways. The book of Hebrews is meant to help expand their knowledge and let those believers see how Jesus was the Messiah, the fulfillment of all their prophecies in Scripture, our Old Testament.

The author of Hebrews indicates throughout the book that these Judeo-Christian believers had gone through persecution, perhaps from their own Jew-ish community. As a result, it would be very easy to abandon faith in Jesus and revert back to their old Jewish ways. That is why the author of Hebrews works so hard to prove Jesus as the fulfillment of every prophecy of the Messiah and as superior to every Old Testament hero. For example, in Hebrews 10 we see this solemn set of verses: "Anyone who has set aside the law of Moses dies without mercy on the evidence of two or three witnesses. How much worse punishment, do you think, will be deserved by the one who has trampled underfoot the Son of God, and has profaned the blood of the covenant by which he was sanctified, and has outraged the Spirit of grace?" (verses 28 and 29).

The readers would be reminded of the penalties of not following the Mosaic Law and realize the seriousness of giving up Christ, because He is God! While you might not relate to the wording of some parts of Hebrews, understanding its cultural setting and who it was written to will help you see why it was written that way. The famous chapter on faith (Hebrews 11) is a central message of hope in the book, reminding us that we must have a solid faith and trust Jesus even though we cannot see Him. Do you?

Revelation Studies 13: Beasts

And the beast that I saw was like a leopard; its feet were like a bear's,
and its mouth was like a lion's mouth. And to it the dragon gave his power
and his throne and great authority. One of its heads seemed to have a mortal wound,
but its mortal wound was healed, and the whole earth marveled as they followed the beast.
And they worshiped the dragon, for he had given his authority to the beast,
and they worshiped the beast, saying, "Who is like the beast, and who can fight against it?"
—Revelation 13:2–4

If you have read through Revelation 13, you will be familiar with the first beast that rises out of the sea, the dragon who gives it power, and the second beast that rises from the earth. These are all symbols of things on earth and historical events, some of which have already taken place!

As we saw earlier, the dragon always represents Satan and his powers on earth. The first beast is often seen as a symbol of the system of popes during the Middle Ages, in power for 1,260 years, which equates to the forty-two months mentioned in Revelation 13:5. During the Middle Ages, the Catholic Church persecuted Protestant Christians. The sea and ten horns represent the many nations Europe and the rest of the world split into. The second beast is traditionally viewed as the United States (US), founded on the separation of church and state, a country without a king or pope, ruled by the people. Adventists, through the study of history, Scripture, and the visions of Ellen White, believe at the very end of the world the US and the papacy will unite in some way, causing persecution for those keeping the Sabbath. Again, Revelation 13 provides hope that God will not leave His people to suffer for their faithfulness. He will save them by coming back to earth at the Second Coming! So even though this chapter sounds a bit scary, do not be afraid. No matter what the future brings, Jesus is coming back soon to save you and end sin.

For further study

Nichol, Francis D. *The Seventh-day Adventist Bible Commentary.* Vol. 7, *Philippians to Revelation.* Washington, DC: Review and Herald®, 1980.

Pierce, Seth J. *What We Believe: Prophecies of Revelation for Teens.* Nampa, ID: Pacific Press®, 2013.

Stefanovic, Ranko. *Revelation of Jesus Christ.* Berrien Springs, MI: Andrews University Press, 2009.

Jesus Gives Me Trust

Trust in the LORD with all your heart, and do not lean on your own understanding.
In all your ways acknowledge him, and he will make straight your paths.
—Proverbs 3:5, 6

Do you know what it means to trust Jesus completely? I learned my lesson in complete trust while overseas studying Hebrew in Jerusalem. Because of the Fifty-Day War between the Israeli Defense Forces and militants in Gaza in the summer of 2014, getting out of the country safely when it was time to go home proved very difficult. All international airlines had canceled their flights in and out of the country. Only the local airline El Al was flying out, so when I got word that my flight was canceled, I frantically started searching for a way out, along with the other students on the trip. Due to the hundreds of cancellations, ticket prices skyrocketed, and our internet service would go in and out, so finding a spot on a flight and buying it seemed impossible. We prayed, I Skyped with my parents, and finally, a flight with the exact number of seats we needed popped up. I bought the tickets, and the second after the confirmation for the transaction was made, the internet cut out! I think God performed a miracle to let us get those tickets in time before all the seats were taken.

Trusting Jesus is easy when times are good and everything makes sense. But when life gets tough and you are brought low by the situations going on around you, truly trusting Him to work it out is difficult. And that is normal, so as you go through those feelings, do not beat yourself up about it. But a thriving relationship with Jesus will help you make it through those times. The verses He brings to your mind, the songs He allows you to hear, the sermons preached on Sabbaths, and many other things will draw your mind to Him and soothe your worried heart.

Dealing With Prejudice and Stereotypes

There is neither Jew nor Greek, there is neither slave nor free,
there is no male and female, for you are all one in Christ Jesus.
—Galatians 3:28

Y ou cannot sit here because you are _____." (Fill in the blank with what you have heard.) From racism to sexism to stereotypes about disabled or mentally impaired people, many kids experience being left out at the lunch table. In my high school, there were well-defined areas that certain groups of people sat—the jocks ate on the gym stage, wanting to spend the rest of the lunch period playing basketball. The popular girls huddled in their corner, whispering and laughing as they looked around the room. The ones who were left out sat on the couches on the other side of the room, laughing about silly jokes.

Sometimes the lunch tables are split by race. Other times by gender. The harm that comes from negative comments and treatment based on prejudice or a stereotype can be very damaging. Think before you speak, and observe before you act.

Jesus' ministry was characterized by His inclusion of those who had prejudices held against them. He talked to prostitutes. He debated with religious leaders. He intentionally ministered to Samaritans. He picked disciples from the lower levels of society—tax collectors, fishermen, and Zealots. When you find yourself judging someone based on a stereotype, pause for a moment and ask yourself whether that is a worthy reason to make a quick decision about who someone is and what defines them. You do not want to be defined by a stereotype. Treat others with the same respect. And if others are treating you poorly based on some prejudice they have, kill it with kindness! Show love, care, and concern for them as an individual, and you will be amazed at what God can do!

The Subtle Savior

This, the first of his signs, Jesus did at Cana in Galilee,
and manifested his glory. And his disciples believed in him.
—John 2:11

John 2 reveals one of Jesus' first miracles to us. The story of the famous wedding in Cana unfolds with Jesus' mother bustling around the feast trying to make sure everything is just perfect! Can you imagine Mary rushing Jesus and His friends to their seats and then scurrying about in the background, perfecting every piece of the meal? I get the sense from this story that Mary was a bit of a perfectionist. To refresh your memory, read through the chapter now!

Mary was concerned when they ran out of wine to serve at the wedding, but inwardly she seems to have had something else on her mind as well. She raised Jesus, she had taught Him the Scriptures, and she and His earthly father, Joseph, had carefully instructed Him on how to live His life in Jewish society. He was the perfect Son, and she knew it! But the rest of the world didn't yet. They didn't know who He was. No doubt He had been bullied growing up, perhaps even called an illegitimate child. But Mary knew the truth in her heart, and she wanted to finally show off her Son to her community!

So Mary instructs the servants to go do whatever He says. And He performs a miracle! Not something flashy to show off His abilities but rather something subtle that would make the wedding better for everyone. Although Jesus didn't take credit for the miracle, people noticed. John tells us that the servants and His disciples saw what He did, and they believed.

Jesus never tried to show off to the rich and mighty people in His society, or even the most important individuals at that wedding. Instead He let the lowliest people of all–the servants—see His miracle. His disciples, many of them lower class citizens, witnessed this miracle as well, and they believed in His divinity. Don't expect Jesus to only do flashy things to get your attention—that's not how He works. Pay attention to the subtle ways He works in your life. Watch how He draws you closer to Him in the little moments—and believe.

We Believe: The Sabbath

And on the seventh day God finished his work that he had done,
and he rested on the seventh day from all his work that he had done.
—Genesis 2:2

*L*et's look at how the Fundamental Beliefs of Seventh-day Adventists describes the importance of the Sabbath:

The gracious Creator, after the six days of Creation, rested on the seventh day and instituted the Sabbath for all people as a memorial of Creation. The fourth commandment of God's unchangeable law requires the observance of this seventh-day Sabbath as the day of rest, worship, and ministry in harmony with the teaching and practice of Jesus, the Lord of the Sabbath. The Sabbath is a day of delightful communion with God and one another. It is a symbol of our redemption in Christ, a sign of our sanctification, a token of our allegiance, and a foretaste of our eternal future in God's kingdom. The Sabbath is God's perpetual sign of His eternal covenant between Him and His people. Joyful observance of this holy time from evening to evening, sunset to sunset, is a celebration of God's creative and redemptive acts. (Gen. 2:1-3; Ex. 20:8-11; 31:13-17; Lev. 23:32; Deut. 5:12-15; Isa. 56:5, 6; 58:13, 14; Ezek. 20:12, 20; Matt. 12:1-12; Mark 1:32; Luke 4:16; Heb. 4:1-11.)*

Jesus declared Himself as Lord of the Sabbath in the New Testament, joyously proclaiming His gospel of love, peace, kindness, and doing good on the Sabbath to everyone around Him. His treatment of the Sabbath angered the Pharisees but enlightens us as to how we should keep it: not worried about rules and laws and breaking things but as a day to glorify God, enjoy His creation, fellowship with others, worship Him, and grow in our relationship with Him. Spend this Sabbath doing those things and find delight in it!

---

* Seventh-day Adventist Church, "The Sabbath," in *28 Fundamental Beliefs* (General Conference of Seventh-day Adventists, 2015), 9, https://szu.adventist.org/wp-content/uploads/2016/04/28_Beliefs.pdf.

Revelation Studies 14:
Three Angels

Then I saw another angel flying directly overhead, with an eternal gospel to proclaim to those who dwell on earth, to every nation and tribe and language and people. And he said with a loud voice, "Fear God and give him glory, because the hour of his judgment has come, and worship him who made heaven and earth, the sea and the springs of water."
—Revelation 14:6, 7

Revelation 14 describes the three messages central to Adventism's roots. In this chapter, we watch as John sees three angels flying above him. The first says to worship God only. The second proclaims that Babylon is fallen. And the third says beware of the beast, do not worship him, but instead keep the commandments of God and have faith in Jesus.

The first angel reminds us that God's judgment has already begun, and Jesus is going over the lives of those who have died. Some people fear that they must live an almost perfect life to get into heaven, but that is not what salvation is all about! Salvation is a gift given by Christ, so His blood covers your sin at judgment time. When you accept this gift, your life will naturally change as a result, and you will keep the commandments and follow Him out of love, not as check marks to get into heaven.

The second angel's message points to Babylon as the Roman Catholic papacy and Sunday replacing the Sabbath. Paired with the third angel's message, sometimes the message of avoiding persecution from non-Sabbath keepers and the coming of a Sunday law has scared people. As a kid, I was terrified of the "end times" and the thought of being hunted through the woods. While the end of the world will be a troubling time, I now realize we do not need to fear it. We do not know what events will actually take place or how quickly they might pass, but we do know one thing: God never abandons His children. He loves you, and He will not forsake you. You do not have to live in fear because He is with you and will give you strength.

For further study
Nichol, Francis D. *The Seventh-day Adventist Bible Commentary.* Vol. 7, *Philippians to Revelation.* Washington, DC: Review and Herald®, 1980.

Pierce, Seth J. *What We Believe: Prophecies of Revelation for Teens.* Nampa, ID: Pacific Press®, 2013.

Stefanovic, Ranko. *Revelation of Jesus Christ.* Berrien Springs, MI: Andrews University Press, 2009.

Pizza DNA?

And God said, "Behold, I have given you every plant yielding seed that is on the face
of all the earth, and every tree with seed in its fruit. You shall have them for food."
—Genesis 1:29

Eating healthy matters. What you eat literally affects what your body is made of. Think about it . . . if you put chips, pizza, and soda pop into your body, then your body is regenerating your cells and making new ones out of whatever nutrients it can find in chips, pizza, and soda pop. Gross much? Sure,

those things might taste great in the moment, but do you really want to be made out of greasy, oily, fatty, cheesy, sugary, salty things? Eating a plant-based diet, similar to what God provided for Adam and Eve in the Garden of Eden, is ideal because then your body is making new cells out of the best ingredients on earth. Imagine the difference between building your house out of wood versus feathers. I am sure you could get creative and figure out a way to use the feathers to make a house, but really, the wood is going to do a whole lot better job, just as fruits, vegetables, nuts, grains, legumes, and plant-based foods will be much better building blocks for your body.

This week I dare you to look up a vegan restaurant in your area and go try it with your friends and/or family. If there is not one nearby, go online and find some creative vegan recipes to try—make it a fun event creating something new! There are some incredible recipes out there, and you can eat a well-balanced, filling, and tasty meal out of completely plant-based foods! If you are worried about bodybuilding or staying strong on a vegan diet, you have nothing to fear. Go look up some vegan bodybuilders and research how they are often healthier in the long run because of their good diet! Now read these verses about Daniel and his diet choices, and be encouraged in your attempts at healthy eating: "Test your servants for ten days; let us be given vegetables to eat and water to drink. . . . At the end of ten days it was seen that they were better in appearance and fatter in flesh than all the youths who ate the king's food" (Daniel 1:12–15).

Do Not Jump Without Training!

I will meditate on your precepts
and fix my eyes on your ways.
I will delight in your statutes;
I will not forget your word.
—Psalm 119:15, 16

Whether it is white-water rafting, climbing a mountain, or skydiving, if you want to participate in the sport, you must go through training and acquire the appropriate gear. You would not jump out of an airplane without a parachute on your back! Likewise, you would not start climbing a mountain in your swimsuit, or jump into a river raft without any paddles! In order to participate in thrilling and life-threatening sports, you have to be well trained and have a guide with you that can teach you how to stay safe and have tons of fun while you are at it.

The journey of life has rough moments, times when you will feel like you are stranded on the glacier of a mountain, unsure of the safest way down. The Bible is like our tour guide, providing us with ways to be safe—like putting on the whole armor of God, following the Ten Commandments, and living like Jesus. Going through rigorous biblical training for spiritual warfare will strengthen us to face difficult times and be prepared.

When I was in Pathfinders, I got to participate in a Bible Bowl/Bible Achievement/Bible Experience event. One year we memorized the entire book of Jeremiah, each of us taking about ten chapters. To this day, I still have verses from my chapters that will pop up into my mind at exactly the right moment, giving me an answer that I did not realize I needed. Training yourself in biblical knowledge is not just about memorizing the facts so that you can get them right in class. You train so that when the battle is real and you are on your knees begging God for an answer or standing by the bedside of a dying grandparent or holding the hand of your abused friend, you will have an answer and know what to do because God's Word has been etched into your heart. I have been in those moments, and it is only through God giving me strength and recalling certain Bible verses to mind that I was able to get through them and lead other people through those uncertain moments as well.

Should I Date in High School?

So flee youthful passions and pursue righteousness, faith, love, and peace,
along with those who call on the Lord from a pure heart.
—2 Timothy 2:22

When I was a teen, I used to read Christian articles for high school students that said you should never date in high school. *Whatever*, I would think. *They are just old-fashioned. I am smart enough to make good dating choices now. If I wait until college, I might never find someone!*

My parents met in high school, so I assumed it was normal for people to meet their future spouse in those four hormone-filled years. And let me tell you, even though you might not want to hear it, boy, was I wrong! I dated a few guys, got to college, had my heart broken, and graduated without a husband. *What?* I thought I knew everything there was to know about dating and how to do it right!

Nope. While dating in high school did let me know what it was like to kiss someone on the lips for the first time, it also opened my heart to being influenced by another person in a completely different way. While there is nothing wrong with dating in high school, when you get to college, you will look back and see how much you changed during those four years.

Throughout high school, your likes and dislikes, talents, and career choices will change. You will challenge the hierarchy of everything. You will question who you are and everything your parents have taught you. While it is fun to date someone during this time, it also causes lots of complications—especially when you both change in different ways.

It is rare to find a couple that dated in high school, made it through college, and then got married. So I encourage you to choose wisely. There is no shame in waiting until college to date. It is probably smart, actually. You will learn a lot, change a lot, and grow up a lot. Wait to find someone who has the same values and life goals as you, not just the cutest guy or girl in your class.

Revelation Studies 15:
Glass and Fire

Then I saw another sign in heaven, great and amazing, seven angels with seven plagues, which are the last, for with them the wrath of God is finished. And I saw what appeared to be a sea of glass mingled with fire—and also those who had conquered the beast and its image and the number of its name, standing beside the sea of glass with harps of God in their hands. . . . After this I looked, and the sanctuary of the tent of witness in heaven was opened, and out of the sanctuary came the seven angels with the seven plagues, clothed in pure, bright linen, with golden sashes around their chests. And one of the four living creatures gave to the seven angels seven golden bowls full of the wrath of God who lives forever and ever, and the sanctuary was filled with smoke from the glory of God and from his power, and no one could enter the sanctuary until the seven plagues of the seven angels were finished.
—Revelation 15:1–8

Since this chapter is so short, I decided to include most of it for you above. In this chapter, we are once again in heaven, witnessing those who overcame the beast and its image standing around the sea of glass, praising God. The last seven plagues presented here are going to happen on earth at the end of time while God's people are still on earth, but they will be brought through them and have victory over them, so you do not need to be afraid of them. At this point in history, Jesus is about to come back to earth, so everyone on earth has already made the decision in their heart as to who they will follow: Christ or Satan. You will hear the phrase "probation is closed" used, but do not be scared of that—it just means that at that point, everyone will have clearly decided whom they will follow.

This chapter closes Jesus' mediation in the heavenly sanctuary. However, He is not going to cut you off mid-decision. All who will accept salvation have chosen it, and the others have chosen against it. You have no reason to fear these "end-time events." If you have already chosen God in your heart, then you are secure in salvation!

For further study

Nichol, Francis D. *The Seventh-day Adventist Bible Commentary.* Vol. 7, *Philippians to Revelation.* Washington, DC: Review and Herald®, 1980.

Pierce, Seth J. *What We Believe: Prophecies of Revelation for Teens.* Nampa, ID: Pacific Press®, 2013.

Stefanovic, Ranko. *Revelation of Jesus Christ.* Berrien Springs, MI: Andrews University Press, 2009.

We Believe: Stewardship

"Be fruitful and multiply and fill the earth and subdue it."
— Genesis 1:28

*L*et's read how the Fundamental Beliefs of Seventh-day Adventists views the topic of stewardship:

We are God's stewards, entrusted by Him with time and opportunities, abilities and possessions, and the blessings of the earth and its resources. We are responsible to Him for their proper use. We acknowledge God's ownership by faithful service to Him and our fellow human beings, and by returning tithe and giving offerings for the proclamation of His gospel and the support and growth of His church. Stewardship is a privilege given to us by God for nurture in love and the victory over selfishness and covetousness. Stewards rejoice in the blessings that come to others as a result of their faithfulness. (Gen. 1:26-28; 2:15; 1 Chron. 29:14; Hag. 1:3-11; Mal. 3:8-12; Matt. 23:23; Rom. 15:26, 27; 1 Cor. 9:9-14; 2 Cor. 8:1-15; 9:7.)*

What is a "steward"? The word *stewardship* in Christianity refers to taking care of the things God has given you. It is in our DNA to care for God's creation because that is one of the primary responsibilities He gave Adam and Eve in the Garden of Eden: "And God blessed them. And God said to them, 'Be fruitful and multiply and fill the earth and subdue it, and have dominion over the fish of the sea and over the birds of the heavens and over every living thing that moves on the earth' " (Genesis 1:28).

Being good stewards also means participating in returning tithe, which is giving 10 percent of anything we earn to God. This tradition was started early in the Old Testament. Tithe in Israelite times was used to support God's ministry and the priests' livelihood. In the Adventist Church today, we use tithe to spread the gospel message. Offerings are separate from tithe. Any percentage beyond that 10 percent that you choose to give to the church or a ministry helping other people is an offering.

While money is not essential to God getting work done on earth, for those of us who are blessed with it, we are called to be unselfish and use what we have to help serve others. Start practicing giving tithe and offerings now. You will see God's blessings come as a result!

---

* Seventh-day Adventist Church, "Stewardship," in *28 Fundamental Beliefs* (General Conference of Seventh-day Adventists, 2015), 9, https://szu.adventist.org/wp-content/uploads/2016/04/28_Beliefs.pdf.

Plane Malfunction

May the God of hope fill you with all joy and peace in believing,
so that by the power of the Holy Spirit you may abound in hope.
—Romans 15:13

I once heard a man share his testimony, and it was not the usual story about drug addicts and secular hippies coming to the Lord. This man was an Adventist, a wealthy and successful CEO in his company. He told about a frightening plane ride where they had to turn the plane around halfway through the flight due to malfunctioning equipment. They were told that the plane's brakes were engaged, meaning the wheels might be locked on impact and could explode when they hit the runway. It would be a rough landing, they had to brace for impact, and it could be a life-threatening experience. This man and those around him had to sit on that plane for hours before landing, thinking about their families on the ground, about the lives they had lived, and whether they had made the right choices. The first thing on people's minds was death and what comes after it. For some, they were confident in their salvation. But most were questioning, some extremely emotional about the possibility of dying and not knowing what was next. Our CEO friend had a conversion experience, fully giving himself to God. In that moment on the plane, with the end literally in sight, people had to make a choice about who they wanted their heart to belong to and whether they wanted that owner to be God.

Who does your heart belong to today? Is Jesus the owner of your heart? Does the Holy Spirit reside within you? Or do you feel lost, unsure of what lies ahead, and unsure of life after death? Heaven is real, and God has invited you to join in it with Him. All you need to do is believe, and leave the rest up to Him.

As the passengers braced for impact and the plane landed, to their surprise, the wheels did not explode. The plane landed smoothly, and they taxied to a halt safely on the ground. Trust in Jesus, and He will help you land your life safely in Him.

Celebrate Diversity

"My brothers, show no partiality as you hold faith in our Lord Jesus Christ."
— James 2:1

The produce department of the grocery store is made up of various types of fruits and vegetables. What makes the displays so beautiful and attractive is the wide variety of colors, shapes, and sizes of the produce. Each item is different, and they each serve a different purpose in how they nourish the body when you eat them. If everything looked the same and did the same thing, the grocery store would be very boring, and you would probably go somewhere else to look for more variety.

God has made all of us unique. And God wants a church full of diversity. He wants us all to be brothers and sisters, celebrating the various cultures we come from, yet all serving to nourish the body of the church. We each have different unique qualities that are like no other person. And when we come together as one church family, we make a beautiful display of God's love, grace, and handiwork in the ways He has made us.

The early Christian church struggled with diversity, and it has been a battle ever since to celebrate the various ways we can worship God and use our different gifts for Him. All should be welcome in your church. Let's be a church of diversity, celebrating the different gifts God has given us!

Look at how James describes the importance of diversity in the church:

My brothers, show no partiality as you hold the faith in our Lord Jesus Christ, the Lord of glory. For if a man wearing a gold ring and fine clothing comes into your assembly, and a poor man in shabby clothing also comes in, and if you pay attention to the one who wears the fine clothing and say, "You sit here in a good place," while you say to the poor man, "You stand over there," or, "Sit down at my feet," have you not then made distinctions among yourselves and become judges with evil thoughts? Listen, my beloved brothers, has not God chosen those who are poor in the world to be rich in faith and heirs of the kingdom, which he has promised to those who love him? But you have dishonored the poor man. Are not the rich the ones who oppress you, and the ones who drag you into court? Are they not the ones who blaspheme the honorable name by which you were called?

If you really fulfill the royal law according to the Scripture, "You shall love your neighbor as yourself," you are doing well. But if you show partiality, you are committing sin and are convicted by the law as transgressors (James 2:1–9).

Armor of God: Belt of Truth

Finally, be strong in the Lord and in the strength of his might.
Put on the whole armor of God, that you may be able to stand against the schemes of the devil.
—Ephesians 6:10, 11

One of the first sermons I ever preached in grade school was about the armor of God. Many kids memorize the six different parts of the armor, songs are written about them, and they are pictured on classroom walls in Christian schools. But how deeply have you honed in on their message and purpose? They are essential if you plan to have a relationship with God that is protected from the devil's attacks.

Ephesians 6 holds the description of the armor of God:

Finally, be strong in the Lord and in the strength of his might. Put on the whole armor of God, that you may be able to stand against the schemes of the devil. For we do not wrestle against flesh and blood, but against the rulers, against the authorities, against the cosmic powers over this present darkness, against the spiritual forces of evil in the heavenly places. Therefore take up the whole armor of God, that you may be able to withstand in the evil day, and having done all, to stand firm. Stand therefore, having fastened on the belt of truth. (verses 10–14)

The purpose of the armor of God is clearly stated: so you will have the strength to stand up to the devil. Our greatest battles on earth are not the ones that can be seen or are fought in hills and valleys. The greatest battles are fought in the realm of spiritual forces that cannot be seen with the eyes.

The first piece of the armor of God is the "belt of truth." A belt is something that holds your whole outfit together and keeps it from falling off. So having truth as a primary weapon must be incredibly important! Being able to speak words of truth as well as hear words of truth and take them to heart makes your faith strong and confident. It is easy to lie but difficult to tell the truth. Speaking words of truth will grow your spiritual maturity and help you lead your peers in the same direction. Today, commit to putting on the belt of truth.

Revelation Studies 16: Keep Your Garments On

"Behold, I am coming like a thief! Blessed is the one who stays awake,
keeping his garments on, that he may not go about naked and be seen exposed!"
—Revelation 16:15

Revelation 16 is painful to read because it is full of violence and death. The seven plagues take place, represented in this chapter by seven bowls poured out on the earth. Remember that you do not need to be afraid of this time in earth's history. If you are alive when it begins, because you have already made your choice to follow God, your salvation is secure eternally. God has promised to be with the people who choose Him! Do not become obsessed with the scary, terrible things that seem to be happening. They are consequences for sin and choosing to follow Satan. So if you choose to follow God, you do not need to worry!

Amid all this chaos is Revelation 16:15, which is actually serving as a reminder that Jesus' second coming is moments away! He gives us this verse to help us remember that all these plagues happen right before He returns. The plagues will not last forever, and we do not need to be afraid because He is about to come back and save us from sin forever!

The verse in this chapter that describes Satan's powers preparing for the battle on the great day of God the Almighty is a symbol for the spiritual battle between God and Satan (Revelation 16:14). It is not talking about a literal battle in a literal place like we normally imagine. The location of the battle is in our hearts and minds, the spiritual warfare between the forces of evil and God. This is why having a relationship with Jesus is important. He is what will keep you rooted in your faith. Essentially, in this chapter, we see the intensity of this spiritual warfare as Satan realizes that Jesus' coming is near and his time is running out. You do not need to fear this time, though, because it will not be as scary as the symbols make it sound. If you are rooted in God, you will see Him do miracles on your behalf, and He will carry you through any trial!

For further study

Nichol, Francis D. *The Seventh-day Adventist Bible Commentary.* Vol. 7, *Philippians to Revelation.* Washington, DC: Review and Herald®, 1980.

Pierce, Seth J. *What We Believe: Prophecies of Revelation for Teens.* Nampa, ID: Pacific Press®, 2013.

Stefanovic, Ranko. *Revelation of Jesus Christ.* Berrien Springs, MI: Andrews University Press, 2009.

The Day of Atonement

"He shall make atonement for the holy sanctuary, and he shall make atonement
for the tent of meeting and for the altar, and he shall make atonement for the priests
and for all the people of the assembly. And this shall be a statute forever for you,
that atonement may be made for the people of Israel once in the year
because of all their sins." And Aaron did as the LORD commanded Moses.
—Leviticus 16:33, 34

While the children of Israel were wandering in the desert, God used this time to instruct them and give them certain religious rituals to perform. This is when He gave the Ten Commandments and the instructions for sacrificing animals as burnt offerings for their sins. One of the most important days of the year for the Hebrew people was the Day of Atonement, which God gives instructions for in Leviticus 16. This day came once a year, and for Jews that still celebrate it, Yom Kippur, or the Day of Atonement, begins today.

On this day God instructed that the priest offer certain sacrifices for the sins of the people and the priests in order to forgive all sins entirely and then cleanse the sanctuary. Aaron, Moses' brother, was the first priest, and he gave a sin offering for himself and his household. Then he cast lots over two goats—one would become the goat for sacrifice, the other the scapegoat. He sacrificed the first goat, a symbol of Christ, for the sins of all the people of Israel. Then the interesting part: Aaron would lay his hands on the live goat and confess the sins of the people, representing all the sins that had been laid in the sanctuary throughout the year, and transferring their blame to the live goat. Then that goat was taken out into the wilderness and set free, where it would likely die.

These two goats represent our Savior, Jesus, who died on behalf of all our sins, taking their consequence on Himself. But the origin of sin is not God, is it? No, it came from Satan. The second live goat represented the blame for all those sins being given back to the originator, just like how at the end of time Satan will have to bear the final consequence for causing sin to infect the universe, and God will destroy him forever. The meaning behind this yearly ritual is incredible, and it shows us another way to understand salvation, the great war between God and Satan, and the ultimate victory by Jesus because He rose again. Trust Him and accept the sacrifice He already made for you!

Jesus Gives Me Confidence

"Is not your fear of God your confidence,
and the integrity of your ways your hope?"
—Job 4:6

A relationship with Jesus is truly life-transforming. One of the most powerful things He can give you is confidence. So often we struggle with our self-worth and feeling like we are not enough. This can affect how we live our lives and how confident we are in the things we do.

Do you struggle with feeling that you are not good enough? In Christ, you can find the confidence to get up every day and be the best version of yourself because He made you an incredible human being. He wants the best for you.

So how can you grow in your confidence when you are feeling down? First, start by realizing how much you need Jesus. We are not good enough by ourselves, but with Him, we have everything we could ever need. Then, think about all the gifts He has given you. Appreciate how He has made you, and recognize your best qualities. He loves you, He is proud of you, and He wants you to feel special and accomplished!

When you walk into a room, instead of hanging your head or being worried about what others might think of you, have confidence in the love God has for you and the abilities He has given you. In my relationship with Him, I have gained confidence in the fact that He alone determines my true value. I can go into any situation with confidence because I know He is right there with me, guiding my every step and giving me words when I cannot think of what to say.

Armor of God:
Breastplate of Righteousness

Stand therefore, having fastened on the belt of truth,
and having put on the breastplate of righteousness.
—Ephesians 6:14

In a romantic relationship, part of your job is to hold up the other person's heart, put them before yourself, and love them as Jesus does. You choose to stay committed and not cheat because you love them, and you are the protector of their heart. They have given you access to their emotions, and you have the power to crush them or lift them up.

The second piece of the armor of God is the breastplate of righteousness. In battle, a breastplate was worn to protect the chest of the warrior. What important organ lies within the chest, behind the ribs? Your heart, of course! Taking a stab to the heart from your foe could kill you, so soldiers wore a breastplate of strong armor to try and deflect blows to the chest.

Righteousness is the ability to be morally correct or being able to justify your actions before God. Being righteous means you have a clear conscience and are able to stand before God without blame. Obviously, every one of us has sinned, but God still wants us to strive for a righteous life, one in which we follow Him and do our best to live righteously.

So the breastplate of righteousness protects your heart by having a moral compass by which you make your decisions. When the devil throws temptations at you, you can deflect them because you have chosen to make moral decisions based on God's ideals. You can resist the devil by living a righteous life. And in doing so, you will protect your heart from unnecessary hurt. Choose to protect your heart with righteousness today.

Who Cares?

"You shall not covet your neighbor's house; you shall not covet your neighbor's wife, or his male servant, or his female servant, or his ox, or his donkey, or anything that is your neighbor's."
—Exodus 20:17

Who cares what other people have, right? Don't you wish that was your perspective all the time? If it already is, that is great! But for most people, the struggle not to be jealous of others is very real. Covetousness, or wanting something someone else has that you do not, is a sin. Why? Because jealousy will eat you from the inside out and turn you into a nasty person! Growing up, you may have heard kid stories that talk about the "green-eyed monster." Those stories are often referring to when a child is overtaken by jealousy and does something unkind or rude, like taking their sibling's toy.

While jealousy for you could look like wanting the Nikes your friend got or those Gucci sunglasses, covetousness can look like the desire to buy more things, or it can make it sound like money is all there is to success in life. Or jealousy could look like you disliking someone for whom they are dating because you have a crush on the person they are dating. It could look like hating your friend for their good grades or being jealous of someone for their looks or talents. Sometimes it seems unfair when some people get things you think they do not deserve, but jealousy will just eat you up inside and make life miserable.

To combat it, write down three things you are thankful that you have and three things you are thankful your parent, sibling, or friend has that you do not. Be happy for other people, and you will remove jealousy from your life!

Fall to Spring

Now may our Lord Jesus Christ himself, and God our Father,
who loved us and gave us eternal comfort and good hope through grace,
comfort your hearts and establish them in every good work and word.
—2 Thessalonians 2:16, 17

Fall can be a depressing time of year if you do not like seeing death in the trees and plants as winter begins. However, Ellen White reminds us that this is a time of hope for the new growth and beauty that spring will bring. In her book *Education*, she shares about how fall and winter eventually turn into spring:

Though marred by sin, [nature] speaks not only of creation but of redemption. Though the earth bears testimony to the curse in the evident signs of decay, it is still rich and beautiful in the tokens of life-giving power. The trees cast off their leaves, only to be robed with fresher verdure: the flowers die, to spring forth in new beauty; and in every manifestation of creative power is held out the assurance that we may be created anew in "righteousness and holiness of truth" (Ephesians 4:24). Thus the very objects and operations of nature that bring so vividly to mind our great loss become to us the messengers of hope.*

Our relationship with Jesus goes through times that may feel a bit like fall. Yet there is always a springtime coming! I often get asked by students how to keep a relationship with Jesus fresh and relevant. Here is what I tell them:

- Continue reading Scripture, or try listening to an audio Bible.
- Listen to Christian music.
- Journal.
- Go on walks and pray.
- Read Christian books about growing a relationship with Jesus. I really enjoyed the book *A God Named Desire* by Ty Gibson when I was in high school.

The promise of spring is just around the corner. He will see you through the winter months.

---

* Ellen G. White, *Education* (Nampa, ID: Pacific Press®, 2002), 27.

Revelation Studies 17:
The Lamb Will Conquer

"The Lamb will conquer them."
—Revelation 17:14

Welcome to the strange part of Revelation. Time for the judgment of the "prostitute"! The scene starts with an angel taking John to the wilderness in vision, showing him a woman on a beast that has seven heads and ten horns. She is called a prostitute. But the angel gives us hope for the end of this evil woman and beast, saying in Revelation 17:8, "The beast that you saw was, and is not, and is about to rise from the bottomless pit and go to destruction." Let's unpack the symbols used in this chapter.

A "woman" always represents a church in biblical prophecy. So this woman represents an unfaithful church. Describing her as a mother means she has existed for a long time. Waters represent people of the world. So this is a worldwide, old church. It is also a church that has made people "drunk," meaning its doctrines follow man's traditions and false teachings rather than God's Word. The last descriptor in verse 6, drinking the blood of saints, means the church has persecuted God's people.

Next, the beast. It is a kingdom of some kind, a political power. Since it is united with the woman, it is a religious and political power. Together, this power blasphemes against God (verse 3) and represents a church that has tried to take the place of God on earth. Since verse 9 describes this church as sitting on "seven mountains," many believe this represents papal Rome: the Vatican, known as the city sitting on seven mountains.

What happens at the end of the chapter when all these evil powers come together to make war against the Lamb? Verse 14 says, "The Lamb will conquer them, for he is Lord of lords and King of kings, and those with him are called and chosen and faithful." For today, remember this: Even amid all the chaos of religious-political powers rebelling against God, Jesus still has a spot of peace and calm in the world in His relationship with you. He will protect and keep you, and since He will conquer these powers, you do not need to fear them. Just stay faithful to Jesus, and you will experience heaven with Him someday very soon!

For further study
Nichol, Francis D. *The Seventh-day Adventist Bible Commentary.* Vol. 7, *Philippians to Revelation.* Washington, DC: Review and Herald®, 1980.
Pierce, Seth J. *What We Believe: Prophecies of Revelation for Teens.* Nampa, ID: Pacific Press®, 2013.
Stefanovic, Ranko. *Revelation of Jesus Christ.* Berrien Springs, MI: Andrews University Press, 2009.

We Believe:
Smart Body

And try to discern what is pleasing to the Lord. Take no part in the unfruitful works of darkness, but instead expose them.
—Ephesians 5:10, 11

Before we discuss this belief in detail, look at how the Fundamental Beliefs of Seventh-day Adventists describes having a modest, healthy lifestyle:

We are called to be a godly people who think, feel, and act in harmony with biblical principles in all aspects of personal and social life. For the Spirit to recreate in us the character of our Lord we involve ourselves only in those things that will produce Christlike purity, health, and joy in our lives. This means that our amusement and entertainment should meet the highest standards of Christian taste and beauty. While recognizing cultural differences, our dress is to be simple, modest, and neat, befitting those whose true beauty does not consist of outward adornment but in the imperishable ornament of a gentle and quiet spirit. It also means that because our bodies are the temples of the Holy Spirit, we are to care for them intelligently. Along with adequate exercise and rest, we are to adopt the most healthful diet possible and abstain from the unclean foods identified in the Scriptures. Since alcoholic beverages, tobacco, and the irresponsible use of drugs and narcotics are harmful to our bodies, we are to abstain from them as well. Instead, we are to engage in whatever brings our thoughts and bodies into the discipline of Christ, who desires our wholesomeness, joy, and goodness. (Gen. 7:2; Exod. 20:15; Lev. 11:1-47; Ps. 106:3; Rom. 12:1, 2; 1 Cor. 6:19, 20; 10:31; 2 Cor. 6:14-7:1; 10:5; Eph. 5:1-21; Phil. 2:4; 4:8; 1 Tim. 2:9, 10; Titus 2:11, 12; 1 Peter 3:1-4; 1 John 2:6; 3 John 2.)*

God has given you an amazing body that He created with intricate detail. And God wants you to be as healthy as possible. To do that, He knows what will keep you safe from harm and help you be effective in your ministry for Him as well.

---

* Seventh-day Adventist Church, "Christian Behavior," in *28 Fundamental Beliefs* (General Conference of Seventh-day Adventists, 2015), 9, https://szu.adventist.org/wp-content/uploads/2016/04/28_Beliefs.pdf.

Armor of God: Gospel of Peace

And, as shoes for your feet, having put on the readiness given by the gospel of peace.
—Ephesians 6:15

Developing your relationship with God includes many pieces. This month we have started looking at the armor of God as outlined in Ephesians 6. Speaking words of truth and protecting your heart with righteousness are two important factors, and the third gives us an even bigger picture of God's plan for a protected relationship with Him. The gospel of peace is the third piece of your armor. Strap up! It's time to march!

Once you have put on your clothes in the morning (belt of truth), read a devotional and prayed (breastplate of righteousness), it is time to do one more thing before going out the door—besides eating breakfast! You need a good pair of shoes to slip your feet into. When you face the world, does an attitude of hostility or divisiveness get you very far? Of course not! A peaceful attitude, on the other hand, can do wonders in smoothing over rough friendship moments or even in getting a teacher to like you more. If you enter every situation at school with a peaceful mind-set, people are more likely to trust you and listen to you. They will feel accepted and heard in your presence.

Especially in a public setting where not all your friends are Christians, this could give you the opportunity to share the gospel with a friend. The gospel of peace means not only entering situations peacefully or not only sharing about Jesus but also sharing that in Jesus you can have peace in your life. When you give your heart to Him, He can give you a peaceful spirit and calm any nerves you may have. When your heart is in turmoil, His gospel of peace can calm you down and help you get through the day. So put on your peaceful shoes today, and go change the world one step at a time!

Do Not Be a Prisoner

*To put off your old self, which belongs to your former manner of life
and is corrupt through deceitful desires, and to be renewed in the spirit of your minds,
and to put on the new self, created after the likeness of God in true righteousness and holiness.*
—Ephesians 4:22–24

I remember walking into a prison, its walls closing in around me. I was scared, yes, but not because I was a prisoner there. I was observing chaplaincy work that day, but seeing all those prisoners locked inside, some for the rest of their lives, made me realize how intense the choices that you make are. For those prisoners, their past defined them. They let their decisions take them to the point of no return, a point where they could no longer turn back, and their only option was to accept the consequences of their past choices.

I read a quote somewhere that said: "Do not become a prisoner to your past. It was just a lesson, not a life sentence." Let that sink in. Every one of us has a past. The decisions you made that you later regret. The things you have done you would rather no one find out. And it can be very easy to get swallowed up by those things, letting them consume you and steal your joy in life. But God does not want you to be a prisoner to your past. He does not want your past to define you. *He* wants to be what defines you! The things that happened in your past are not a life sentence; you are not stuck in a high-security prison somewhere. You are free, so you can look back at those things in your past as life lessons to learn from and not repeat, not things that define your existence or imprison your future. Give your past to God, and let Him free you.

Let It Go

For I do not understand my own actions. For I do not do what I want,
but I do the very thing I hate. . . . Now if I do what I do not want,
it is no longer I who do it, but sin that dwells within me. . . .
For I delight in the law of God, in my inner being,
but I see in my members another law waging war against the law of my mind
and making me captive to the law of sin that dwells in my members.
—Romans 7:15–23

Shame and guilt are feelings everyone can understand. They creep up first when you are a child and deliberately choose to do something your parent told you not to do. When you hurt someone intentionally, the guilt enters your heart. When you secretly do something that you know is bad for you, the shame starts to eat you from the inside out. You may have something eating away at you right now. As you read this, you know exactly what you have done, and you feel the conviction of the wrongness of that action in your heart. Dealing with feelings of shame and guilt can be difficult. Often we try to numb the feeling instead of taking responsibility for it and refusing the temptation to do it again. How can you change the pattern and avoid those feelings of shame and guilt? Give it to God.

Start by recognizing the sinfulness of your actions and choose to give it to God. Ask Him to help you forgive yourself, avoid that temptation or particular sin, and move forward in grace to a happier future free of shame. Jesus' death on the cross covers every sin, and His love and forgiveness heal the deepest wounds of your heart. If you are struggling with something and have been holding on to those feelings of shame for too long, you need to give them up and let God heal you.

This also means being intentional about avoiding sin. You know what triggered it in the first place, so avoid those triggers or think of ways to overcome them. Whatever is causing you shame and guilt, trust that Jesus can heal you and help you overcome.

Goodbye to the Wise

For the Lord himself will come down from heaven . . . and the dead in Christ will rise first.
—1 Thessalonians 4:16, NIV

Death is confusing and foreign. Deep down, humans know it was not supposed to be something we had to deal with. We grieve for long periods of time after the death of a loved one because we feel a loss that our deepest senses want to reject as impossible. I lost my grandma when I was in second grade, and I felt numb. I did not know how to say goodbye. I kept the bouquet of tissue paper flowers that my second-grade class made for me for years afterward.

Grandparents are the wise ones in our lives who traditionally love and spoil us regardless of our relationship with our parents. Maybe you grew up with your grandparents as the ones who raised you, or perhaps they were your biggest cheerleaders as you grew up and accomplished your dreams! If yours are still alive, take time to ask them about what the world was like when they were growing up and the things they have learned from their years on this planet.

Recently a great-grandmother passed away in my church. One of her little great-grandbabies, only a few years old, kept asking when grandpa was going to let grandma out of the box. She was too young to understand that when death occurs, there is no longer any consciousness, reaction, or conversation. Death is the end of life, and her little mind could not wrap around why grandma was stuck sleeping in the box. When would she wake up and get out and have a tea party again?

Do you find yourself asking God the same questions about your grandparents or other loved ones who have died? Though the pain takes time to heal from, God's Word gives us some hope about our loved ones who have died in Him: "For the Lord himself will come down from heaven, with a loud command, with the voice of the archangel and with the trumpet call of God, and the dead in Christ will rise first. After that, we who are still alive and are left will be caught up together with them in the clouds to meet the Lord in the air. And so we will be with the Lord forever" (1 Thessalonians 4:16, 17, NIV).

Revelation Studies 18: Fallen Babylon

"Fallen, fallen is Babylon the great!"
—Revelation 18:2

Revelation 18 brings us closer to the second coming of Christ. It describes the time just before the close of probation and before the end-time plagues are poured out. An angel flies from heaven, proclaiming, "Fallen, fallen is Babylon the great!" (Revelation 18:2). Babylon is described as detestable, immoral, demonic, and luxurious. Another voice from heaven in verse 4 echoes Revelation 14, saying, "Come out of her, my people, lest you take part in her sins, lest you share in her plagues." It is clear that God does not want His people to be in Babylon!

This prophetic voice reveals that in the end times, some churches will have aligned themselves with the Babylonian power mentioned in Revelation 18. This "Babylon" is a spiritual power, not the literal Babylon of ancient times. So any Christian church that combines biblical teachings with pagan ideas and anything spiritual that is not of God has aligned itself with Babylon. Babylon is the system of religion throughout time that has departed from God's direction. The idea of Babylon and what it represents is apostasy and rebellion against God.

The message of Revelation 18 is clear: Babylon will be destroyed. Satan's use of this power over God's children on earth to confuse them and lead them away from God will not last forever. While it sounds like a sad message, it's actually something to rejoice about if you are a Christian trying to follow God's truth in your life! The devil will not rule over the earth forever. His power will not last forever. God has promised Satan's destruction and the destruction of everything evil along with him. So have hope! The hard things you are going through right now, the hypocrisy you see in people you once looked up to, the evil in this world—it will not last forever. God will cast out the devil and his schemes very soon!

For further study

Nichol, Francis D. *The Seventh-day Adventist Bible Commentary.* Vol. 7, *Philippians to Revelation.* Washington, DC: Review and Herald®, 1980.

Pierce, Seth J. *What We Believe: Prophecies of Revelation for Teens.* Nampa: ID: Pacific Press®, 2013.

Stefanovic, Ranko. *Revelation of Jesus Christ.* Berrien Springs, MI: Andrews University Press, 2009.

Spiritual Maturity

For this very reason, make every effort to supplement your faith with virtue, and virtue with knowledge, and knowledge with self-control, and self-control with steadfastness, and steadfastness with godliness, and godliness with brotherly affection, and brotherly affection with love. For if these qualities are yours and are increasing, they keep you from being ineffective or unfruitful in the knowledge of our Lord Jesus Christ.
—2 Peter 1:5–8

I love 2 Peter 1:5–7! It includes a step-by-step guide for how to be effective in ministry and fruitful in your knowledge of and relationship with Jesus:

1. *Supplement your faith with virtue:* This means if you have faith in God, you will follow it up by living with high moral standards.
2. *Supplement virtue with knowledge:* Once you have those standards, you will gain a higher understanding of theology and practical ways to use your faith.
3. *Supplement knowledge with self-control:* Just knowing about faith and high moral standards is not enough. You also need to be self-disciplined, paying attention to how you approach others, being self-controlled in how you live and what you choose to do.
4. *Supplement self-control with steadfastness:* Once you have good emotional control in your life, you will be able to stand strong, be unwavering in your faith, and be a dependable person for others to turn to as they go through their spiritual journey.
5. *Supplement steadfastness with godliness:* Once you have developed a mature, unwavering faith, you will be a godly person, someone God is proud of and others look up to for a spiritual example.
6. *Supplement godliness with affection:* This means using your spiritual position to help others—showing them brotherly love and caring for people in your church and community.
7. *Supplement affection with love:* And when you have gone through all this in your relationship with God, then you will finally understand what God's love for you is like, and you will naturally reflect that to the world!

Armor of God: Shield of Faith

In all circumstances take up the shield of faith,
with which you can extinguish all the flaming darts of the evil one.
—Ephesians 6:16

The shield of faith may be one of the most epic pieces of the armor of God. It is described in such a fierce way, with fiery darts being shot at it. Archery is a sport that has been popularized by recent movies. Most kids make their own string and long stick bow, with little sticks for arrows, at some point in their childhood playtime. I remember making one and hiding it stealthily in my room because I knew my mom would not want sticks in the house. I would take it out when I wanted to play a make-believe game, and I would pretend to shoot my little arrows all over the backyard.

Making a shield was never quite as epic, however. And if you were to pick a weapon, would you likely go on defense with the shield or on offense with

the bow and arrows? Many would pick a bow and arrow because the offense seems like it gives you more control over the situation. Yet that is not something God includes in His list of armor. Instead, He instructs to take up the *shield* of faith *in all circumstances*. A barrier of strong faith is the only way to defeat the devil's attacks. You cannot attack back with your own arrows and expect to win—you cannot beat him at his own game. However, if you have faith in God, you have a stronger defense than he does. And no matter what he shoots at you, you can withstand it through faith that God will protect you and get you through! So take up your shield today, and do not be afraid of anything Satan might try to do to you. Your faith in God will see you through.

The Great Disappointment

"But concerning that day and hour no one knows,
not even the angels of heaven, nor the Son, but the Father only."
—Matthew 24:36

Just wait! A little while longer, and we will see Jesus' face!"

"Look! Do you see anything in the clouds?"

"It's getting dark. Do you think it will be much longer?"

"He is coming, I know He is; just be patient, and the trials of this earth will all be over soon . . ."

Voices must have echoed long into the night as the believers waited. On this day in 1844, throngs of Christians who believed that Jesus was coming back on October 22 waited patiently to see their Lord coming in the clouds to take them home. They had clung to the preaching and teachings of William Miller, a man convicted from his studies of Scripture that 1844 was the year when Christ would return to take His children home to heaven. But He did not come on October 22, 1844. Miller was incorrect—we cannot know the day or hour when Jesus will come back.

This day in Adventist history is often called the Great Disappointment because so many early Advent believers were disappointed by the fact that Jesus did not come back. However, as hard as that day was, it was only the beginning of what would become a worldwide movement to tell people about Jesus' love and His soon return. Just a few months later, in December, a seventeen-year-old girl named Ellen would have a vision that would be the catalyst for the beginning of the Seventh-day Adventist Church. Her vision gave hope because it depicted Jesus leading believers forward and showed a beautiful picture of the Second Coming.*

---

*Andrew McChesney, "Great Disappointment Remembered 170 Years On," *Adventist Review*, updated Oct. 22, 2014, https://www.adventistreview.org/church-news/great-disappointment-remembered-170-years-on; "Life and Times—The Great Disappointment," The Truth About Ellen G. White, accessed June 19, 2018, https://www.ellengwhitetruth.com/life-times/two-great-disappointments/the-great-disappointment.

Reviewing the Relationship

"I have loved you with an everlasting love;
therefore I have continued my faithfulness to you."
—Jeremiah 31:3

Part of developing your relationship with God is looking at your strengths and spiritual gifts and determining how you will use them. Reviewing where you have been with God so far this year can also be valuable in helping you understand where you are in your relationship with Him and where you are going. Below are some questions for you to ponder as you spend time praying today, and space is given for you to write your own answers. Feel free to grab your prayer journal and use space there as well!

What is the most significant thing that God has done in your life this past year?

_____

_____

How do you see God working in your school and church?

_____

_____

What spiritual gift has God grown in you this past year, and how have you used it?

_____

_____

What spiritual gift would you like to have that you do not see in your life currently?

_____

_____

Where do you feel God calling you to go with Him this winter?

_____

_____

Revelation Studies 19:
Faithful and True

Then I saw heaven opened, and behold, a white horse!
The one sitting on it is called Faithful and True,
and in righteousness he judges and makes war.
—Revelation 19:11

The beginning of Revelation 19 is filled with glorious praise to God. Imagine the best orchestral or choir concert you have ever heard, times a million! The multitude is singing, "Hallelujah! Salvation and glory and power belong to our God" (Revelation 19:1). They sing about the defeat of evil and the marriage of the Bride and the Lamb. Then there is a familiar reference to the parable Jesus told about the ten virgins and the marriage feast. Those who were prepared were invited in to the wedding feast, while those who were unprepared were not (see Revelation 19:9).

Then the scene transitions in verse 11, which tells of heaven opening and a rider on a white horse bursting forth—this is a vision of Jesus coming as a mighty conqueror. Verse 13 says His robe is dipped in blood, a reference to His death on the cross. And He is the Word of God (read the first chapter of the Gospel of John)! The beast and the false prophet are destroyed, and the wicked are killed. Though it's a gory scene, it does let us know that hell is not so much a state of everlasting torment but rather a point at which Jesus destroys sin and wickedness.

So to recap: Jesus returns to earth triumphantly. He raises the righteous from the grave, and they rise to meet Him in the air with their loved ones who are righteous and alive. Then Jesus destroys all the living wicked, which leaves Satan angry and alone on earth, stuck as we enter the millennium. Again, the message remains: Choose Jesus and eternal life. He is your Victor and Savior who offers you a way out of this sinful world. Choose Him, and choose life!

For further study
Nichol, Francis D. *The Seventh-day Adventist Bible Commentary*. Vol. 7, *Philippians to Revelation*. Washington, DC: Review and Herald®, 1980.
Pierce, Seth J. *What We Believe: Prophecies of Revelation for Teens*. Nampa, ID: Pacific Press®, 2013.
Stefanovic, Ranko. *Revelation of Jesus Christ*. Berrien Springs, MI: Andrews University Press, 2009.

Praying Boldly

If any of you lacks wisdom, let him ask God, who gives generously to all without reproach, and it will be given him. But let him ask in faith, with no doubting, for the one who doubts is like a wave of the sea that is driven and tossed by the wind. For that person must not suppose that he will receive anything from the Lord; he is a double-minded man, unstable in all his ways.

—James 1:5–8

Prayer is a multifaceted way to communicate with God. There are many different ways to pray, and many things we have yet to learn about it! This verse in James gives us a clear picture of what it looks like to have confidence in our prayers, however. His instruction to be bold in asking God for things we lack goes against how we commonly pray. How often do you hear bold prayers?

Fear cannot be what prevents us from praying bold prayers to God. According to James, let us ask in faith, with no doubting! We cannot be unstable, double-minded people—we must believe that what we ask for is going to happen! Think about the last time you prayed publicly, like for a meal or in front of your class. Think about how you used your words, and what you asked God for. Did you pray boldly?

Whether or not you did, today you can start trying this new method of prayer. Ask God for wisdom. If there is another quality you need Him to grow in you, ask boldly for Him to clear the path for growth in that area of your life. Write down a few bold prayer requests you have for God here:

_____

_____

_____

_____

_____

_____

_____

Armor of God:
Helmet of Salvation

Stand therefore, having fastened on the belt of truth, and having put on the breastplate of righteousness, and, as shoes for your feet, having put on the readiness given by the gospel of peace. In all circumstances take up the shield of faith, with which you can extinguish all the flaming darts of the evil one; and take the helmet of salvation.
—Ephesians 6:14–17

Your senses tell you about the world around you, but all of those things are experienced through neurons and chemicals in your brain. God created you with an incredible ability to gather information and think critically about what you can sense not only through sight, sound, smell, touch, and taste but also through logic and philosophy—entirely within your own headspace. Your mind is a battlefield in the war between good and evil. The devil wants to do anything he can to stomp out any hope you have of a better future than what this world has to offer.

That is why God's next piece of armor is the helmet of salvation. A helmet protects your brain. If you were to get hit hard enough in the head, you could have permanent brain damage, which would complicate everything from your ability to speak to your ability to walk. Since the brain controls your entire body system, it is essential to survival, both physically and spiritually. The helmet of salvation is protecting your mind through the assurance you have in Christ's salvation for you. Since He has already saved you, you have nothing to worry about. You are protected from eternal death by putting on that helmet of salvation and accepting that gift from Christ. When the devil tries to make you doubt God's true love and care for you, rely on that helmet, that assurance in salvation, to get you through the mental battle. God gave you a mind powerful enough to understand the depth of these things, and He gives you the choice to use it wisely.

Confession Time

*If we confess our sins, he is faithful and just to forgive us our sins
and to cleanse us from all unrighteousness.*
—1 John 1:9

irst John 1:9 is as popular as it is unfollowed advice. It is recited by second-grade and high-school students and memorized for Bible credit but too often ignored when it comes to the workings of daily life. How many times have you actually confessed your sins, not just to God, but to other people?

Confession is powerful. When you confess something to someone, you are sharing a secret with them, an intimate detail of your life, something you may be ashamed of. Sharing your burdens with others helps lighten the load on your back and gives you the support you need to right the wrongs you have done. Confession is good for you because it relieves the pressure in your mind of whatever is weighing you down. When you are able to share openly with someone about what you have done, you will naturally start to feel better about it and begin the road to forgiving yourself and recovering from your poor choices.

God is a God of forgiveness. As the verse says, He will not only be faithful in always forgiving your sins but also cleanse you from *all* unrighteousness. He can help you to be even better after you have confessed a sin you committed. If you have been gossiping about someone in your school and they found out, going to the person and apologizing personally for what you did could lead to the two of you becoming friends instead of enemies. If you took money from your parent's wallet without asking or cheated on a test, confessing what you did and making it right will relieve the guilt on your heart and actually gain you more trust in the eyes of your parent or teacher because you were honest enough to tell them about it. So do not be afraid to confess your sins to others and to God, and gain righteousness as a result!

Jesus' Reputation in Nazareth

He went away from there and came to his hometown, and his disciples followed him.
And on the Sabbath he began to teach in the synagogue, and many who heard him
were astonished, saying, "Where did this man get these things? What is the wisdom given to
him? How are such mighty works done by his hands? Is not this the carpenter, the son of Mary
and brother of James and Joses and Judas and Simon? And are not his sisters here with us?"
And they took offense at him. And Jesus said to them, "A prophet is not without honor,
except in his hometown and among his relatives and in his own household." And he could do no
mighty work there, except that he laid his hands on a few sick people and healed them.
—Mark 6:1–5

Going home or visiting family is supposed to be a happy occasion! For Jesus, however, going back to His hometown of Nazareth, where He grew up, was not always an exciting occasion. Think about what His childhood was like: Most people thought He was an illegitimate child of a woman who should have been stoned to death for her sin. After all, His mother, Mary, had become pregnant as a teenager while she was engaged to Joseph, so people questioned Jesus' parentage. Only a few people, such as Mary's cousin Elizabeth, believed Jesus was actually the Son of God placed in her womb. Growing up, Jesus was probably called names and left out of certain social circles because of His perceived illegitimate origins.

But He decided to take His disciples to Nazareth anyway. On the Sabbath when He preached in their synagogue, can you imagine the shock people must have had? Seeing Him come into town like a rabbi with His followers must have been surprising! Sadly, their unbelief prevented Him from doing much there. We can learn a few things from this story: First, we must not let our doubt prevent God from doing miraculous things. Second, Jesus experienced ridicule and bullying, so if you have been there, so has He, and He can understand what you have been through. Give Him the benefit of the doubt, and let Him show His power to you.

We Believe:
Family Time

*Then the L*ORD *God said, "It is not good that the man should be alone;*
I will make him a helper fit for him."
—Genesis 2:18

Here's how the Fundamental Beliefs of Seventh-day Adventists describes marriage and family:

Marriage was divinely established in Eden and affirmed by Jesus to be a lifelong union between a man and a woman in loving companionship. For the Christian a marriage commitment is to God as well as to the spouse, and should be entered into only between a man and a woman who share a common faith. Mutual love, honor, respect, and responsibility are the fabric of this relationship, which is to reflect the love, sanctity, closeness, and permanence of the relationship between Christ and His church. Regarding divorce, Jesus taught that the person who divorces a spouse, except for fornication, and marries another, commits adultery. Although some family relationships may fall short of the ideal, a man and a woman who fully commit themselves to each other in Christ through marriage may achieve loving unity through the guidance of the Spirit and the nurture of the church. God blesses the family and intends that its members shall assist each other toward complete maturity. Increasing family closeness is one of the earmarks of the final gospel message. Parents are to bring up their children to love and obey the Lord. By their example and their words they are to teach them that Christ is a loving, tender, and caring guide who wants them to become members of His body, the family of God which embraces both single and married persons. (Gen. 2:18-25; Exod. 20:12; Deut. 6:5-9; Prov. 22:6; Mal. 4:5, 6; Matthew 5:31, 32; 19:3-9, 12; Mark 10:11, 12; John 2:1-11; 1 Cor. 7:7, 10, 11; 2 Cor. 6:14; Eph. 5:21-33; 6:1-4.)*

The Adventist belief on marriage and family is the *ideal* situation that we believe people should strive for. What God wants most is two people who love each other to stay committed to each other in a marriage.

---

* Seventh-day Adventist Church, "Marriage and the Family," in *28 Fundamental Beliefs* (General Conference of Seventh-day Adventists, 2015), 10, https://szu.adventist.org/wp-content/uploads/2016/04/28_Beliefs .pdf.

Dear Wormwood

Beloved, do not be surprised at the fiery trial when it comes upon you to test you,
as though something strange were happening to you.
—1 Peter 4:12

C. S. Lewis was a Christian author who tackled issues of faith and belief in ways that have been life-changing for many people. In his book *The Screwtape Letters*, he comes at Christianity from a different perspective. The "letters" are correspondence between two of Satan's demons, Wormwood and his uncle, Screwtape. Lewis reminds readers that since the letters are written by devils, they may not always be telling the truth. But the book gives a unique view into the other side of the great controversy in the war between God and Satan, and it sheds light on areas of weakness in the human experience. Screwtape, the older demon, is counseling Wormwood in these letters as to how to tempt his newly assigned "patient," a human being, into sinning.

If you ever read the book, you will be struck by the truth that Lewis sews into it about the human experience with sin and some of the things we are most easily tempted by. From being a hypocrite in church to ruining family relationships to questioning God's existence to making prayer boring to encouraging self-reliance—there are hundreds of ways to tempt a human, as Screwtape instructs.

Although the plotline may seem a bit humorous, it's a reminder of what is really going on around us all the time. Right now there are angels and demons battling over your mind and the choices you will make today. The evil angels want you to listen to their deception and fall into temptation. God's angels are warring for your soul, reminding you that every choice is eternal and that choosing God will give you a much happier outcome!

Luther's Ninety-Five Theses

For I delight in the law of God, in my inner being,
but I see in my members another law waging war against the law of my mind
and making me captive to the law of sin that dwells in my members.
—Romans 7:22, 23

*H*appy All Saints' Eve! Nope, not Halloween. Originally October 31 was the eve of All Saints' Day, a celebration put in place by the Catholic popes to commemorate martyrs and, eventually, all saints. It was a day to celebrate the unity of the church and the saints the people believed in. Martin Luther, a monk who protested certain things he saw wrong with the church, decided that All Saints' Eve was the perfect time to nail his Ninety-Five Theses to the church door in Wittenberg, Germany, in 1517. This was a bold act because his Ninety-Five Theses were basically ninety-five things he found wrong with the indulgences sold by the church. His original goal was to reform the church, not to create the Protestant Reformation and the new denominations that came from it. He just wanted the church to recognize what it was doing wrong and correct its evils, going back to the Bible as the root of faith and belief.

However, the leaders of the Catholic Church did not respond well to Luther's boldness. His actions triggered the Protestant Reformation, which swept across Europe and was used by God to bring to light things Christianity was ignoring. Through his study of the Scriptures as a monk, Luther became convinced of the idea of *sola gratia*, or justification by grace alone. This means salvation not by works but by faith in Jesus and His grace toward us. At the time of Luther's ministry, many Christians thought they needed to work hard and pay money to get a spot in heaven—grace was not in their vocabulary! Luther became convinced that Jesus' death on the cross meant there is nothing we can do to get ourselves into heaven—it is only through accepting Jesus' grace and gift of salvation to us that we receive heaven!

Martin Luther was a bold pioneer for God, fighting for truth. He was un-afraid of the persecution he received as a result, and he stood up for his beliefs anyway. He paved the way for you to have your own Bible, not have to believe in works to get into heaven, and to have a personal relationship with Jesus. Thanks, Martin Luther! God definitely used him. And He can use you too! Always stand up for your faith and be firmly rooted in Scripture so that you have a reason for what you believe.

Cinnamon Roll Hearts

Create in me a clean heart, O God,
and renew a right spirit within me.
—Psalm 51:10

Fall is the best time to dig in to some tasty comfort foods. One of my favorites is a huge cinnamon roll! They have that slightly crisp exterior and are covered in gooey goodness, and everyone knows the best part is the center—filled with cinnamon sweetness!

People are sometimes like cinnamon rolls. They might seem to have a hard exterior or walls built up around their heart. They may seem callous, harsh, or reserved. But when you take the time to get to know people, you will begin to understand their heart. And like a cinnamon roll's sweet interior, getting to know someone's heart is worth the time and effort it takes to make a new friend.

I became best friends with a girl in college because she decided to try this on me. She pursued a friendship with me, took time to get to know me, and really made an effort to understand my heart. Because of her kindness and willingness to put herself out there and make a new friend, she became one of my closest friends! I even got to officiate her wedding a few years later!

You are a few months into school now and have probably set up the group of people you usually hang out with by now, but do not be afraid of new opportunities and getting to know someone at your school or youth group that you do not know very well. Maybe pick someone whom you have seen around a lot but do not know very well and try to make friends with that person. Find out what is important to this person, what he or she is passionate about, and what desires God has placed on the person's heart to achieve in life.

False Teachings

I rejoiced greatly to find some of your children walking in the truth, just as we were commanded by the Father. And now I ask you, dear lady—not as though I were writing you a new commandment, but the one we have had from the beginning—that we love one another.
—2 John 4, 5

Second John is one of the shortest books in the Bible, with only one chapter and thirteen verses total! This little letter was written by the apostle John to an "elect lady and her children" (verse 1), and though scholars do not know exactly who this is referring to, it is evidently written to a Christian church family John was familiar with. Perhaps the woman receiving the letter was the "pastor" for that church, leading the congregation, and that is why John warned her specifically in the letter to watch out for false teachers and not let them sway her people.

After the start of the early Christian church, false teachings about Jesus began to spread. Some people would travel around spreading throughout local churches the rumor that Jesus did not actually come to earth in the flesh. This was mainly a group who had not actually seen Jesus in real life, and because of this, they were more easily swayed to believe these false teachings.

I remember that when I was in college, a group of former Adventists and Adventist-bashing Christians would come and stand just off the campus limits and lure students into theological debates, trying to convince them that the teachings of Adventism about the Bible were wrong. Some theology majors would debate with them for hours, upset by their false claims. Unfortunately, these people could not be reasoned with. They were not going to come back to the faith; they just wanted to lure unsure college students away from it. Opening up a debate with people like that is never profitable, and Ellen White even cautions against it multiple times in her writings. Instead, focus your attention on growing your faith, understanding the Scriptures well, and being certain of what you believe so that if your faith is ever threatened by false teachings, you will be able to recognize them for what they are: false.

We Believe: The Sanctuary

He is the radiance of the glory of God and the exact imprint of his nature,
and he upholds the universe by the word of his power.
After making purification for sins, he sat down at the right hand of the Majesty on high.
—Hebrews 1:3

et's dive into the doctrine of the heavenly sanctuary:

There is a sanctuary in heaven, the true tabernacle that the Lord set up and not humans. In it Christ ministers on our behalf, making available to believers the benefits of His atoning sacrifice offered once for all on the cross. At His ascension, He was inaugurated as our great High Priest and began His intercessory ministry, which was typified by the work of the high priest in the holy place of the earthly sanctuary. In 1844, at the end of the prophetic period of 2,300 days, He entered the second and last phase of His atoning ministry, which was typified by the work of the high priest in the most holy place of the earthly sanctuary. It is a work of investigative judgment which is part of the ultimate disposition of all sin, typified by the cleansing of the ancient Hebrew sanctuary on the Day of Atonement. In that typical service the sanctuary was cleansed with the blood of animal sacrifices, but the heavenly things are purified with the perfect sacrifice of the blood of Jesus. The investigative judgment reveals to heavenly intelligences who among the dead are asleep in Christ and therefore, in Him, are deemed worthy to have part in the first resurrection. It also makes manifest who among the living are abiding in Christ, keeping the commandments of God and the faith of Jesus, and in Him, therefore, are ready for translation into His everlasting kingdom. This judgment vindicates the justice of God in saving those who believe in Jesus. It declares that those who have remained loyal to God shall receive the kingdom. The completion of this ministry of Christ will mark the close of human probation before the Second Advent. (Lev. 16; Num.14:34; Ezek. 4:6; Dan. 7:9-27; 8:13, 14; 9:24-27; Heb. 1:3; 2:16, 17; 4:14-16; 8:1-5; 9:11-28; 10:19-22; Rev. 8:3-5; 11:19; 14:6, 7; 20:12; 14:12; 22:11, 12.)*

Because Jesus took our place, we do not need to worry about the judgment! Your salvation is secure in Him!

---

* Seventh-day Adventist Church, "Christ's Ministry in the Heavenly Sanvtuary," in *28 Fundamental Beliefs* (General Conference of Seventh-day Adventists, 2015), 5, https://szu.adventist.org/wp-content/uploads/2016/04/28_Beliefs.pdf.

Revelation Studies 20:
Satan Defeated

Blessed and holy is the one who shares in the first resurrection!
Over such the second death has no power, but they will be priests of God and of Christ,
and they will reign with him for a thousand years.
—Revelation 20:6

Finally, we reach the end of sin! Revelation 20 is one of the most hopeful chapters in the book.

Here is the setting: The earth is uninhabitable. All the righteous people have been taken to heaven, and all the unrighteous are dead on the earth. Satan and his evil angels are stuck on the earth, roaming around and not allowed to tempt any other beings for a thousand years.

Meanwhile, in heaven, all those righteous people who were alive or raised at Jesus' second coming sit on thrones with God and go through earth's history, asking questions and reviewing the events of their lives. The purpose of this time of judgment is not to judge people and their actions but to actually judge God's justice! We will get to decide whether God was just in allowing sin to exist as long as He did and for choosing to deal with it in the way He did. We will cry, we will question, we will search. But this chapter tells us that by the end of the thousand years, we will be satisfied with God's justice and ready for Him to destroy sin and Satan forever!

Now we come to the end of the millennium, and the rest of the dead people are resurrected, those who intentionally chose Satan. Satan gathers his forces together, planning his final attempt to overthrow God. He convinces them that he has given them life and that they have the power to overthrow God and conquer the New Jerusalem. But fire from God finally destroys them, and Satan is obliterated from existence.

All will see that God has been just, and even the wicked will agree. So all who choose sin will be completely destroyed. This chapter is violent and graphic, yes, but also hopeful. It reminds us that we have a choice to make: Will you choose God's side?

For further study

Nichol, Francis D. *The Seventh-day Adventist Bible Commentary*. Vol. 7, *Philippians to Revelation*. Washington, DC: Review and Herald®, 1980.

Pierce, Seth J. *What We Believe: Prophecies of Revelation for Teens*. Nampa, ID: Pacific Press®, 2013.

Stefanovic, Ranko. *Revelation of Jesus Christ*. Berrien Springs, MI: Andrews University Press, 2009.

Cornerstone

As you come to him, the living Stone—rejected by humans but chosen by God and precious to him—you also, like living stones, are being built into a spiritual house to be a holy priesthood, offering spiritual sacrifices acceptable to God through Jesus Christ. For in Scripture it says: "See, I lay a stone in Zion, a chosen and precious cornerstone, and the one who trusts in him will never be put to shame." Now to you who believe, this stone is precious. But to those who do not believe, "The stone the builders rejected has become the cornerstone."
—1 Peter 2:4–7, NIV

While driving one day, my mother told me about something she noticed. The neighborhood she was going through had a variety of rock walls, some stable and sturdy, while others were crooked and falling over. Some had obviously stood the test of time, and others would not handle the weight much longer. The ones that lasted had a solid foundation built up from the main cornerstone that supported the whole structure.

In order for us to have a thriving relationship with God, Jesus must be our strong Cornerstone. He is the one we must run to when life is overwhelming and the going gets rough. Peter promises us that if we trust in Jesus, we will never be put to shame. Jesus is our precious Cornerstone, and if we build our hopes and dreams on Him, we will be built up into a spiritual house, chosen by God and precious to Him. This promise is powerful! Not only do we have access to the Creator, but He has promised that if we trust Him, He will be our Builder and make us into something incredible!

Listen to the song "Cornerstone" by Hillsong Worship, and think about Jesus. Christ is our Cornerstone, and He is the one who makes us strong. Trust in Him, and your life will be made complete.

Climbing Out of the Pit—Part 1

When the righteous cry for help, the LORD hears
and delivers them out of all their troubles.
—Psalm 34:17

*A*ny time I go on a cave tour deep into the earth, I have fears of the earth closing in on top of us. Caves are dark, and my skin gets cold and clammy. Claustrophobia starts creeping over me, and all I want to do is get out. Instead, I try to ignore the feelings and focus on the amazing underground rivers and the stalactites and stalagmites jutting through the ceiling and floor of the cave. In one cave, the guide asked us to turn out our lights and experience the darkness for a minute. In that darkness, I was reminded of something else that too many young people experience.

Depression. The word itself looms over you and threatens to take you down with it. For some people, it can feel like being in a cave or pit that you just cannot seem to climb out of. A constant darkness surrounds you and will not let you escape. Mental illnesses are very real, just like the physical cuts and bruises you get from injuries. And they can also be healed, just like injuries. If you or someone you know suffers from depression, get professional help. Tell a trusted adult who can help you find a counselor to help you work through what you are experiencing.

Depression has many faces, and similar to the stalagmites in a cave, it can cut through your life in unexpected ways. For some, an outward sign of depression may be cutting or other types of self-harm. For others, it may be an entirely inward struggle that you would not see in a typical school day. God promises us that He can help through these times of darkness: "When the righteous cry for help, the LORD hears and delivers them out of all their troubles" (Psalm 34:17).

Climbing Out of the Pit—Part 2

"It is the LORD who goes before you.
He will be with you; he will not leave you or forsake you.
Do not fear or be dismayed."
—Deuteronomy 31:8

The most important thing to remember if you or a friend is going through depression is that you are not alone and there are a lot of safe places and people to turn to for help. When a friend of mine opened up to me about cutting herself in grade school, I did not know what to do. I freaked out and ran to the bathroom, hiding there until I could compose myself and figure out the next step to take. I ended up having the sense to tell a teacher. At the time, she was extremely mad at me for sharing something she wanted to be kept private. But she was able to get the help she needed. Much later in life, when we were in college, this same friend and I became close, and she was able to confide in me about hard things she was going through and how she was trusting God to help get her on the right track again.

Do not give up. You are not alone. You are valuable to your Creator. He made you for a purpose, and He loves you very much! First, get professional help to deal with your depression. You can get out of this—it will not last forever! Next, take some practical steps to get well. Spend time in prayer every day, and write down things you are thankful for—intentionally thank God for those things. Go outside and take a walk. Are you eating healthfully? Are you sleeping enough? Focus on getting those simple things put together and let your counselor help you with the rest.

God has amazing plans for your life, and He can use your story of going through this dark time to shed light on someone else's story. You can be the flashlight into the dark cave of someone else's life and help them climb out of the pit too.

Armor of God: Sword of the Spirit

And take the helmet of salvation, and the sword of the Spirit,
which is the word of God, praying at all times in the Spirit,
with all prayer and supplication. To that end, keep alert with all perseverance.
—Ephesians 6:17, 18

To conclude our miniseries about putting on the armor of God so that we can resist the devil, we are reading about the last piece of armor, the sword of the Spirit. God has given you tools to resist temptation and attacks that the devil uses to try to bring you down. From the belt of truth to the breastplate of righteousness protecting your heart to the helmet of salvation protecting your mind, each piece of the armor has a role to play in your spiritual development and ultimate victory in this life. If you use each piece, you will conquer the trials of your earthly existence!

The sword is different from the other pieces of armor because it is the first one that goes on the offensive. Everything else was geared for defense. But notice, even though it is a sword you would hold in your hand, you are not the one actually doing any fighting. It is actually the Holy Spirit! *God Himself* is the sword, and by putting Himself in the only offensive position in the set of armor, He is letting you know that only He can fight your battles and win. And He will win them for you! If you try and fight by your own strength, you will lose. The devil can beat you. But he cannot beat God! That is why God has to be the one fighting for you. He is your sword, and He is the only one who can conquer the devil and outsmart his schemes.

So when you see a battle coming or you feel beaten down by the devil, do what the end of the verse says: *pray.* And through prayer, you will call all the powers of heaven to your side, and God and His angels will fight for you! The greatest battles you will ever fight will be won on your knees while God conquers for you. Guard yourself by putting on the armor of God, and let Him fight for you!

Do Not Be Like Diotrephes

Beloved, do not imitate evil but imitate good.
—3 John 11

Third John is a short letter written to a man named Gaius. John's three epistles were written to warn about false teachers who were traveling around trying to convince people of false things about Jesus. Gaius was clearly known as a faithful Christian because in the first few verses John praises him as someone who is "walking in the truth" (3 John 3).

Sadly, a man named Diotrephes apparently liked to put himself first and would not acknowledge the authority of the apostles, as verse 9 mentions. Diotrephes was talking "wicked nonsense" against them and would not welcome "the brothers," likely other Christian apostles and teachers of Jesus, into that local church (verse 10). He was unfriendly, unkind, and definitely not a reflection of the message of Christianity. What can we learn from this message? John sums it up nicely in verse 11: "Beloved, do not imitate evil but imitate good. Whoever does good is from God; whoever does evil has not seen God."

In too many churches, people forget to reflect the character of Christ, instead using their power and position to put themselves first and be a bit like Diotrephes. Be respectful of your elders and those leading the church, but if you do see people in leadership acting directly against what God has called us to do, talk to the pastor about it if you do not feel comfortable approaching them yourself. It's OK to hold our leaders accountable for their position. And if you are in a position where you have some say in your local church and how it treats people, make sure you are welcoming to guests and following Jesus' example of how to treat people. Imitate good, for that is from God.

We Believe:
Jesus' Return

"Men of Galilee, why do you stand looking into heaven? This Jesus, who was taken up from you into heaven, will come in the same way as you saw him go into heaven."
—Acts 1:11

Here's how the Fundamental Beliefs of Seventh-day Adventists describes the importance of Jesus' second coming:

The second coming of Christ is the blessed hope of the church, the grand climax of the gospel. The Savior's coming will be literal, personal, visible, and worldwide. When He returns, the righteous dead will be resurrected, and together with the righteous living will be glorified and taken to heaven, but the unrighteous will die. The almost complete fulfillment of most lines of prophecy, together with the present condition of the world, indicates that Christ's coming is near. The time of that event has not been revealed, and we are therefore exhorted to be ready at all times. (Matt. 24; Mark 13; Luke 21; John 14:1-3; Acts 1:9-11; 1 Cor. 15:51-54; 1 Thess. 4:13-18; 5:1-6; 2 Thess. 1:7-10; 2:8; 2 Tim. 3:1-5; Titus 2:13; Heb. 9:28; Rev. 1:7; 14:14-20; 19:11-21.)*

This is the moment we all have been waiting for! The moment when the sky finally breaks open and Jesus comes back to take us home. It's such an encouraging hope that I wish it would happen right this second! The whole of history has pointed forward to the moment when perfection will happen for humanity, at Jesus' return. Loved ones will be reunited with those who died before them. Joy will reign as believers in Christ join together in the air and begin the journey to heaven. While we do not know exactly what it will look and feel like, we know it will be an incredible day—a day when all our hopes and dreams are fulfilled.

At that point, every worry will be gone. The issues we have on this earth will not matter anymore because Jesus is there to take us home with Him. Everyone will have made their choice whether to follow the Holy Spirit's nudging in their hearts or to live purposefully against Him. Yet even with that, it will be a joyful day when we are united with our Creator, never again to leave His side. Take comfort in His soon return!

---

* Seventh-day Adventist Church, "The Second Coming of Christ," in *28 Fundamental Beliefs* (General Conference of Seventh-day Adventists, 2015), 11, https://szu.adventist.org/wp-content/uploads/2016/04/28_Beliefs.pdf.

Revelation Studies 21:
Earth Made New

Then I saw a new heaven and a new earth, for the first heaven and the first earth
had passed away, and the sea was no more. And I saw the holy city, new Jerusalem,
coming down out of heaven from God, prepared as a bride adorned for her husband.
And I heard a loud voice from the throne saying, "Behold, the dwelling place of God is with
man. He will dwell with them, and they will be his people, and God himself will be with them
as their God. He will wipe away every tear from their eyes, and death shall be no more, neither
shall there be mourning, nor crying, nor pain anymore, for the former things have passed away."
—Revelation 21:1–4

*F*inally, we get to a part of Revelation that does not sound confusing! Revelation 21 is filled with hope and joy, looking into a blissful eternity filled
with happiness and perfection, sin forever wiped from the universe. The New
Jerusalem, God's Holy City, is described as a city of beautiful jewels. The most
beautiful thing about it is that it is lacking a temple. Wait . . . lacking a temple?
Was not that the *most* significant part of Jerusalem? This chapter is a reminder
to the early church reading it at the time it was written, as well as believers
today, that a temple is no longer needed because we will have direct access to
God Himself! Verses 22 and 23 say, "And I saw no temple in the city, for its
temple is the Lord God the Almighty and the Lamb. And the city has no need
of sun or moon to shine on it, for the glory of God gives it light, and its lamp
is the Lamb."

Again, the Revelation of Jesus Christ points us back to Him and the sacrifice He made to give us this beautiful, eternal experience with Him! The great
controversy between good and evil is over. Sin is gone. And the universe is
finally restored to perfection and peace! As the war is waged in your mind as to
whether you will choose to follow God's way or Satan's way, remember these
hopeful pictures the Bible gives us and the glorious eternity that awaits you if
you choose God!

For further study

Nichol, Francis D. *The Seventh-day Adventist Bible Commentary*. Vol. 7, *Philippians to Revelation*. Washing-
    ton, DC: Review and Herald®, 1980.
Pierce, Seth J. *What We Believe: Prophecies of Revelation for Teens*. Nampa, ID: Pacific Press®, 2013.
Stefanovic, Ranko. *Revelation of Jesus Christ*. Berrien Springs, MI: Andrews University Press, 2009.

Revelation Studies 22: Jesus Is Coming

"And behold, I am coming soon. Blessed is the one
who keeps the words of the prophecy of this book."
—Revelation 22:7

Revelation 22 begins with a beautiful picture of the river of life in heaven, flowing from God's throne through the middle of the city. The leaves of the tree of life are healing, and it has twelve kinds of fruit. God is the light of the city, and it is a paradise!

Then the promise we have been holding on to from Genesis rings through: "Behold, I am coming soon." Jesus promises that He is coming back for us; He will not leave us on this desolate planet forever. The curse of sin will be gone, and perfection has taken its place on the new earth. The connection between creation and Creator is restored, as we see symbolized by God's name being on our foreheads, meaning His character and image are finally made complete in us.

"The Spirit and the Bride say, 'Come.' And let the one who hears say, 'Come.' And let the one who is thirsty come; let the one who desires take the water of life without price" (verse 17). This is the invitation for everyone to drink of the water of life that Jesus talked about while He was on earth. The fact that at the very end of the Bible, in this prophetic book, God still signifies that the water of life is *without price* reminds us that there is nothing we can do to earn salvation. Eternal life comes only through Jesus Christ! And in this chapter, you are given a personal invitation to accept that gift: "Let the one who is thirsty come." Do you thirst for Jesus today? Answer His call to accept His gift, and live with Him forever.

For further study

Nichol, Francis D. *The Seventh-day Adventist Bible Commentary*. Vol. 7, *Philippians to Revelation*. Washington, DC: Review and Herald®, 1980.

Pierce, Seth J. *What We Believe: Prophecies of Revelation for Teens*. Nampa, ID: Pacific Press®, 2013.

Stefanovic, Ranko. *Revelation of Jesus Christ*. Berrien Springs, MI: Andrews University Press, 2009.

Believing What You See

Jesus said to him, "Have you believed because you have seen me?
Blessed are those who have not seen and yet have believed."
—John 20:29

Do you ever doubt God? Since you cannot see Him right in front of you, or touch His hand, or hear His voice speaking out loud, it is easy to doubt how involved He is with your life on this earth. One of Jesus' disciples struggled with doubt even though he had been with Jesus for three years!

Now Thomas, one of the twelve, called the Twin, was not with them when Jesus came. So the other disciples told him, "We have seen the Lord." But he said to them, "Unless I see in his hands the mark of the nails, and place my finger into the mark of the nails, and place my hand into his side, I will never believe."

Eight days later, his disciples were inside again, and Thomas was with them. Although the doors were locked, Jesus came and stood among them and said, "Peace be with you." Then he said to Thomas, "Put your finger here, and see my hands; and put out your hand, and place it in my side. Do not disbelieve, but believe." Thomas answered him, "My Lord and my God!" Jesus said to him, "Have you believed because you have seen me? Blessed are those who have not seen and yet have believed." (John 20:24–29)

God works with each of us according to our faith. Jesus said that those who believe in Him even though they cannot see Him will be blessed. Yet because Jesus cared so much for His disciple's faith, He showed Himself in a very miraculous way to Thomas and told him to believe because of what he was seeing. Jesus will work with you based on your faith, too. He may not show up in a vision to you or ask you to put your hands where the nail marks are like He did for Thomas, but if He knows your faith is in need of reassurance, He will provide ways for you to see His presence in your life. Keep your eyes open, and watch for how God is working. The Holy Spirit will enter your heart and inspire you to believe if you ask Him to. Do not worry when you doubt. Simply take those moments to ask God to help your unbelief.

Rewards

But when you pray, go into your room and shut the door and pray to your Father
who is in secret. And your Father who sees in secret will reward you.
—Matthew 6:6

What is the greatest reward you have ever received? When I was a kid, my teachers would give their students fun stickers to signify a job well done. In Sabbath School class, I remember receiving gold stars when we recited a memory verse correctly. In high school, you get rewards like an A+ on an assignment you do correctly or a trophy in sports when you win a championship or recognition at various types of reward ceremonies. We all like rewards. Rewards motivate us. But why?

I think God instilled in all people the desire to do well and achieve greatness. We know that there is something amazing out there to achieve, and the

idea of gaining a reward for doing good work motivates us to try our hardest to accomplish big things. The best reward that has been promised to us is heaven. But how do we get that reward? Is it through doing good works and making sure we follow every rule in the Bible? Is it by climbing some ladder of spiritual holiness through feeding the poor, being involved in local church leadership, and being seen as a good person by others? Often that is what we strive for, and that is not bad, but it is also not how we get to heaven.

Your reward is always waiting for you, like a gift Jesus put under the Christmas tree. He already died for your sins, and He has already made eternal life a possibility for you. The only thing you have to do to get that reward is to believe in Him! It's super easy—accepting Jesus gets you the reward of heaven!

Youth in the Bible:
Sons of Thunder

He appointed the twelve: Simon (to whom he gave the name Peter); James the son of Zebedee and John the brother of James (to whom he gave the name Boanerges, that is, Sons of Thunder); Andrew, and Philip, and Bartholomew, and Matthew, and Thomas, and James the son of Alphaeus, and Thaddaeus, and Simon the Zealot, and Judas Iscariot, who betrayed him.
—Mark 3:16–19

One verse in Mark 3 has defined James and John, the sons of Zebedee, and given them their reputation. Perhaps it is slightly unfair that we judge these two young men based on one verse, but the lesson behind that verse is powerful. While we do not entirely know why Jesus nicknamed these two brothers the "sons of thunder," you can imagine what that nickname indicates! They likely had a temper, were impulsive, and liked to have their own way. They were fishermen, so, like Peter, they probably had a rough way of living and speaking to people.

In Luke 9, after Jesus had already sent the disciples out on their own to preach and perform miracles, they were traveling, and the disciples began arguing about which one of them was the greatest. John said, "Master, we saw someone casting out demons in your name, and we tried to stop him, because he does not follow with us" (verse 49). John wanted to be exclusive in his relationship to Jesus and special because of his proximity to Jesus. Another time, John and James get frustrated when a village of Samaritans rejected them because they were going to Jerusalem, and they said, "Lord, do you want us to tell fire to come down from heaven and consume them?" (verse 54). But both times, Jesus rebuked them. During their time with Jesus, something incredible happened—they began to turn from their thunderous ways into showing loving kindness and compassion for others. John even calls himself "the disciple Jesus loved" multiple times in his gospel, reminding us how he was transformed through Jesus' love as a man of thunder to a man of love.

Proximity to Jesus will change you. You may not notice it at first, or you may be resistant to it, but spending time with Him daily will change your heart and actions. If you relate to the sons of thunder and their struggles with anger and impulsiveness, Jesus can change your heart to one of love and patience. Stay close to Him and be changed!

Jude

Beloved, although I was very eager to write to you about our common salvation,
I found it necessary to write appealing to you to contend for the faith
that was once for all delivered to the saints. For certain people have crept in unnoticed
who long ago were designated for this condemnation, ungodly people, who pervert the grace
of our God into sensuality and deny our only Master and Lord, Jesus Christ.
—Jude 3, 4

Jude, also known as "Judah" or "Judas" in Jesus' time, was actually one of Jesus' own brothers. We often learn about the disciples and apostles of Jesus, forgetting that while He was on earth He had siblings! Though they likely did not believe in Him as the Messiah during His ministry, after His death and resurrection, they saw Him and realized who He was. Then Jesus' siblings became some of the most powerful advocates for His divinity. Jude was one of these.

Since the book of Jude is so short, I encourage you to read it now. This letter was written by Jude to a church struggling with corrupt teachers preaching false theology. The readers were most likely Jewish Christians because the stories he includes come from ancient Jewish texts that are not included in the canon of Scripture. The readers would have to be Jewish to understand the metaphors he used. They were being taught that since Jesus forgives our sins, we can now do anything we want because we are already forgiven. Jude is counseling them to "contend for the faith," meaning he wants the believers to stand up for correct theology and not be confused. Throughout this short book, you get a sense of what Jude believes a true Christian community should be built on: faith in Jesus and His soon return, dedication to prayer, and love for God through obedience. By doing these things, we can stay faithful to Jesus, just as the book of Jude counsels early Christian believers.

Get Away and Pray

And after he had dismissed the crowds,
he went up on the mountain by himself to pray.
—Matthew 14:23

After his second cousin John was killed, Jesus needed some time away. In Matthew 14:13, after hearing about John the Baptist's death, He left in a boat and went to a desolate place all alone to grieve and pray. But Jesus, like many of us, was not given the luxury of taking some time off to be alone with God.

When people heard where He had gone, they followed Him. When they found Him, they wanted something from Him—His power to heal. Though He was grieving, Jesus had compassion on them, verse 14 says, so He healed the sick all day long. The rest of the day was filled with miracle after miracle.

Even though His sorrow was deep, Jesus did not let it consume Him; instead He did good and helped people. He was not selfish with His power, reserving it for when He felt comfortable and happy. He gave even when He did not have the energy. After healing people, He performed the miracle of feeding the five thousand—probably more like ten thousand or more people because there were also women and children. Then, when the day was done, He finally had time to be alone. In verse 22, He made the disciples get into a boat and leave Him as He dismissed the crowds. Then He finally took time to be alone: "And after he had dismissed the crowds, he went up on the mountain by himself to pray. When evening came, he was there alone" (verse 23).

Jesus gives us a solid example of what we need to do when we face great sorrow in the midst of our busiest times in life. We cannot always get away from everyone and everything, but taking time away to pray and be alone with God is important for healing and processing the pain of loss or sorrow. Find your "mountain" to go to and pray. In high school, there was a spot on a high hill in a neighborhood near my house where I could see out across the land for miles and miles, and I would often go there to reflect and pray. I also found two huge trees a few blocks down from my house where it was quiet and I could be alone and pray to God. Find your "God place" where you can get away from everyone for a few moments and process with God what you are going through.

Remembering Mimi

"The LORD is near to those who have a broken heart,
and saves such as have a contrite spirit."
—Psalm 34:18, NKJV

The wood floor was cool under her feet as she sped through the kitchen and rounded the corner into the hallway. In a few leaps, she landed on the carpet, raced through the living room, then the dining room, and rounded the last bend back into the kitchen again. Seated happily in a kitchen chair near the entrance to the kitchen was her doting grandmother, a Dixie cup of dried cranberries in her hand.

The child slid to a halt, taking one shriveled craisin from her grandmother's weathered hand and popping it in her mouth, barely taking time to chew before rushing off to race around the corners again.

This is the scene that has played in my mind over and over since my grandmother's death. I called her "Mimi," her chosen name for herself as a grandmother, taken from the French Canadian name for a grandmother: Mémé. When I returned to school after her death, my second-grade class made a tissue paper flower bouquet for me. I kept that bouquet for many years, both in memory of my grandmother and in memory of the kindness they had shown to me in my young sorrow.

Since my grandmother's death, I have had many hard moments. My memory is that she was one of my biggest supporters, and what I have learned from her death is that although the pain never goes away, it does get easier. If you have lost someone you love, you know the sharpness you feel in your heart when you miss them. But we have Someone to lean on, as Psalm 34:18 reminds us. And those around us can sometimes be a way He holds our broken heart. Write down your memories, treasure those good times, and comfort one another in grief.

Internet Identity

Turn my eyes from looking at worthless things;
and give me life in your ways.
—Psalm 119:37

nternet safety" is probably one of the most annoying phrases to come out of your parent's mouth. Likely, you have had a few lectures about being safe online or on your phone and good and bad ways to use it. As annoying as it might seem, their advice is important.

Sadly, there are creepy predators out there, people who will take advantage of you if they can. Being safe about how you set up social media profiles and what information you share online is important. Getting likes is not worth getting a stalker, so keep your privacy settings on and be careful about whom you add as a "friend."

When I got my first email in grade school, I was thrilled. All my friends were getting email addresses too. Unfortunately, my class had a lot of girl drama, and my little circle of friends often fought with one another. That quickly transferred over into our online lives. When my parents discovered the cyberbullying that was going on, my dad printed out a list of instructions for what I was allowed to do and not do online. He printed off the emails of the things we had said to one another and made me go over them, making me see what was wrong with my words and actions. It was humiliating to disappoint my dad in that way, but I never did it again. Do not be a part of cyberbullying or making fun of someone online. If you witness it, talk to the people involved *in person* about their behavior, and stand up for those being bullied. Bring it to the attention of school administrators. Be a good online citizen, just like in the real world.

Snapchat, Instagram, Facebook, Twitter, and other social media platforms are fun ways to connect with people online—there is nothing wrong with being a part of the digital world. Just pay attention to how you use it. What are you looking at on those platforms? What discussions are you involved in? What does your profile say about you, who can access it, and could they find you in person, if they wanted to, based on what you post? Do you post things that are provocative to get attention? How much time do you spend online or on your phone in comparison to doing other things in life? Once it is out there, you cannot take it back. So ask God to give you wisdom about how you use social media and the internet.

Jesus Gives Me Joy

David also commanded the chiefs of the Levites to appoint their brothers
as the singers who should play loudly on musical instruments,
on harps and lyres and cymbals, to raise sounds of joy.
—1 Chronicles 15:16

Worship is meant to be a joyful experience! A relationship with Jesus is meant to ultimately bring you joy and happiness. And church should be a joyful place! Sometimes we get bogged down in the ritual of how we do church and forget that we gather to praise our God and Savior and be in awe of His majesty.

God wants you to express joy when you worship. In 1 Chronicles we see a special moment during King David's reign when the ark of God is finally brought to Jerusalem and placed in a special tent that David had prepared for it. The Levites carried the ark, while hundreds of Israelites came to rejoice at its return. As the ark is approaching, David commands that singers and musicians "raise sounds of joy" to celebrate God's presence in the ark being brought into the city. "So the priests and the Levites consecrated themselves to bring up the ark of the LORD, the God of Israel. And the Levites carried the ark of God on their shoulders with the poles, as Moses had commanded according to the word of the LORD. David also commanded the chiefs of the Levites to appoint their brothers as the singers who should play loudly on musical instruments, on harps and lyres and cymbals, to raise sounds of joy" (1 Chronicles 15:14–16).

Jesus wants us to have a relationship of joyfulness with Him. Our God is not a solemn, angry God who only values reverence in the sense of a quiet style of worship. He also values joyful noise, rejoicing, and praising Him! When you involve joyful praise in your worship of Him, privately or publicly, you will feel His blessings showering down on your life. So take a moment to praise Him now, maybe by listening to your favorite Christian song, or in your prayer time.

I Forgive You Anyway

"Pay attention to yourselves! If your brother sins, rebuke him,
and if he repents, forgive him, and if he sins against you seven times in the day,
and turns to you seven times, saying, 'I repent,' you must forgive him."
—Luke 17:3, 4

What is the name of the person who has hurt you the worst in this world? What did they do to cause so much damage to your life? As the holidays approach, it is normal to have feelings of dread if you have an estranged relationship with a family member. Maybe your dad left when you were young, and you no longer consider him your father. Maybe your mom took off and left you with your grandparents, who have struggled to raise you. Maybe your brother or sister whom you thought the world of has abandoned you and you feel alone and lost without your sibling's guidance. Dealing with deep hurts from a blood relative takes courage and strength. But healing is possible.

Healing does not always mean reconciliation and the rebuilding of that relationship, however. For most people, at some point, it would be wonderful to have that moment take place. But for some, the hurt runs too deep. In situations of abuse in particular, it's OK to get away and never go back to the person who hurt you or your parent or sibling.

If it is possible to reconcile, do not give up on God. The Holy Spirit moves in mighty ways, and He has the power to change hearts and restore lives. Though you may have grown up acquainted with the feelings of loneliness, God can step into that space as your Father and fill the gaps in your heart. He can spur on those words to the family member you thought would never return to your life or care about you: "I forgive you anyway." Despite what has happened and how you have been hurt, forgiveness and healing are possible if you let Christ take the lead.

Obey and Live Long

Children, obey your parents in the Lord, for this is right.
"Honor your father and mother" (this is the first commandment with a promise),
"that it may go well with you and that you may live long in the land."
—Ephesians 6:1–3

The teenage years are one of the most difficult times in life to honor your parents. You are growing into a young adult, beginning to make choices for yourself apart from your parents, and choosing your own path of morality. Whether you are living at home or in a dorm, whether have a great or terrible relationship with your parents, it's still important to honor them as your mother and father.

If you have ever been a babysitter or spent time leading a group of Vacation Bible School kids around, you know that disciplining and having patience with kids is not always the easiest thing to do. Parents have a difficult job. They are tasked with raising a human being to know God, to have a moral compass, and to go out into the world as a successful, kind, and loving person who will serve in their community. Can you imagine the responsibility they must feel?

Taking care not only to respect them but to also make them feel appreciated and loved is so important, and it can dramatically change the relationship you have with your mom or dad. If you have a father who always seems to be upset at you, figure out a way to show him you love him anyway. If you have a mom who works really hard to provide a home for you, show her love by doing some extra chores to help her out or giving her a nice back rub. Honoring your parents means listening to them when they give you wise counsel, recognizing that they are human too, and realizing they are learning to be more like Jesus every day, just like you. If you take the time to build a good relationship with them, you will be thankful for it later on.

We Believe:
Death Is Not the End

For the living know that they will die, but the dead know nothing, and they have no more reward, for the memory of them is forgotten. Their love and their hate and their envy have already perished, and forever they have no more share in all that is done under the sun.
—Ecclesiastes 9:5, 6

During my first year of pastoral ministry, a tragedy struck our local Adventist grade school and church. One of our kindergartners passed away due to a pediatric stroke. Previously, I did not know kids could have strokes because it is so rare. But after that event, everyone in our church and school became aware of the signs and symptoms, as well as the aching hole in all of our hearts from the loss of that sweet child.

After his death, there were a few things that gave me peace and helped fill the hole. I found peace in our belief as Adventists that in death, people cease to exist until Jesus returns, their mind is no longer active, they are not up in heaven or down in hell. Death is like a sleep—they have no experience of it or realization of the passage of time or events on earth. When someone dies, the next thing they will know is Jesus raising them to life at the Second Coming! And that promise in Jesus' soon return to raise our loved ones from death gives me hope.

The Fundamental Beliefs of Seventh-day Adventists describes the death and resurrection of our loved ones like this:

The wages of sin is death. But God, who alone is immortal, will grant eternal life to His redeemed. Until that day death is an unconscious state for all people. When Christ, who is our life, appears, the resurrected righteous and the living righteous will be glorified and caught up to meet their Lord. The second resurrection, the resurrection of the unrighteous, will take place a thousand years later. (Job 19:25-27; Ps. 146:3, 4; Eccl. 9:5, 6, 10; Dan. 12:2, 13; Isa. 25:8; John 5:28, 29; 11:11-14; Rom. 6:23; 16; 1 Cor. 15:51-54; Col. 3:4; 1 Thess. 4:13–17; 1 Tim. 6:15; Rev. 20:1-10.)*

---

* Seventh-day Adventist Church, "Death and Resurrection," in *28 Fundamental Beliefs* (General Conference of Seventh-day Adventists, 2015), 11, https://szu.adventist.org/wp-content/uploads/2016/04/28_Beliefs.pdf.

Where's Dad?

*"Have I not commanded you? Be strong and courageous. Do not be frightened,
and do not be dismayed, for the* LORD *your God is with you wherever you go."*
—Joshua 1:9

After the September 11 terror attacks in 2001, I was a very scared little girl. I was frightened by planes in the sky, and I did not like being up high in tall buildings with no quick way of escape. I found security in my parents, especially my dad. He was the safest person in the world to me, and I knew that if he was around, everything would be OK.

So when my mom was at work and he was home in the evening with my sister and me, we would often play upstairs while he worked on a project in the garage, did some yard work, or fixed something in his basement workshop. As it would get dark, I would get nervous, and my first thought would be: *Find Daddy.*

So I would go look in my parent's bedroom, saying, "Dad? Daaaaddy?" I would run to the top of the stairs and call down to the main level as loud as I could, "Daaaaddyyyyyy!" I would listen carefully for an answer, and if there was none, I would start to panic. I would frantically search the whole house, trying to find him.

My child thoughts would think he had disappeared, or something had happened to him, or maybe he had been kidnapped. Usually, he was just outside cleaning things up before coming inside. I had a serious fear of being abandoned as a child!

For some people, that feeling does not leave, even as you get older. Maybe your father or mother has walked out on you and left you, and you feel completely alone, panicking at the loss of their presence and the security it brought. God is a good Father in these moments because He *never* leaves you. He will always keep you safe and hold you close. You might not be able to see Him, but His Spirit is always with you, in your heart, protecting you from evil.

The Perfect Sinner

When the LORD saw that [Moses] turned aside to see, God called to him out of the bush,
"Moses, Moses!" And he said, "Here I am." Then He said, "Do not come near;
take your sandals off your feet, for the place on which you are standing is holy ground."
—Exodus 3:4, 5

Moses is revered as one of the great patriarchs of the Old Testament, a man who walked closely with God. Ask any kid to name some Bible heroes, and Moses will be one of the first ones they name, along with people such as David, Esther, and Noah. We usually think of these people like the celebrities of today—virtually untouchable and seemingly perfect. They are not seen as normal people like you and me.

The truth of their stories is far darker than we care to admit—many of our greatest Bible heroes did some seriously twisted things! Moses was a murderer before God called Him to take off his sandals and be a leader at the burning bush. David slept with one of his loyal soldier's wives and got her pregnant, not to mention all the blood he shed, which was why God would not let him build the temple. Esther was essentially prepped for a year to have sex with a king who was picking a queen based on his night with the candidates. Noah got drunk and passed out naked, all this witnessed by his sons. Name any Bible hero, look at their story, and you will find a story of terrible sin and glorious redemption.

The point of all these stories is that God does not pick perfect people to do His work. In fact, the less qualified, the more likely God is to use them! We are all huge sinners, but our God uses us even in our weakness to reach other weak ones for His glory. God can use you no matter what you have done, and He can forgive the biggest of sins. Take off your shoes and stand on His holy ground today, and see what He can use you for!

Church History— Who Was Ellen White?

Let no one despise you for your youth,
but set the believers an example in speech,
in conduct, in love, in faith, in purity.
—1 Timothy 4:12

Today is the birthday of a woman who is revered as both an end-time prophetess and a founder of our church. Ellen Harmon was born on November 26, 1827, in Maine, USA. One day while she was walking home from school, a bully threw a stone that hit her in the face and left her unconscious for weeks afterward! When she finally regained consciousness, it became clear she would not be able to continue her education at school, so she stayed home and learned at her parents' side.

Bible stories reveal that many people give their heart to God when they are preteens. Ellen was no different. After going to a camp meeting when she was twelve, Ellen gave her heart to Jesus and was baptized two years later. She then attended meetings with her family to hear William Miller, a preacher God chose to share about His second coming. After Miller's prediction about when Jesus would come back did not prove to be accurate, Ellen began to earnestly study the Bible and pray with other young women.

During one of these prayer meetings, Ellen received her first vision from God. Guess how old she was? Seventeen! This experience launched her into a lifetime of ministry. She was a part of starting the Seventh-day Adventist Church as she and other young people discovered truths in the Bible that other churches were not teaching.*

Do you ever get discouraged and feel like the church is only for older adults? Be encouraged—the Adventist Church began when God called a teenage girl to preach His message! God has always used youth for big things, and He has an incredible plan for your life as well. He has called each of us to something special, and He wants you to be a part of the mission He started with seventeen-year-old Ellen.

---

* Arthur L. White, "Ellen G. White: A Brief Biography," The Ellen G. White Estate, updated August 2000, http://www.whiteestate.org/about/egwbio.asp.

Let's Get Along

Be kind to one another, tenderhearted,
forgiving one another, as God in Christ forgave you.
—Ephesians 4:32

She bit me!" "She scratched me!" "It's her fault. She started it!" "No, I did not! You did!" Back and forth, all childhood long. I have one sibling, a sister, and while we are as close as can be, and have been our whole lives, like all siblings, we had moments when we really did not get along at all. We would play favorites, trying to get our parents to take one person's side over the other. We would call names, saying nasty things to each other. We would argue, and sometimes even physically fight. I loved my sister very much, but in those moments of childish anger and rage, I could only think about getting even, not forgiving her.

The end of the year is always a time when family feuds tend to rear their ugly heads. In the midst of the celebrating, when an older sibling comes home from college or you get back from boarding academy, family drama usually pops up somehow. So how can you calm it down and choose to get along with your siblings or family members when you do not feel like it?

Sometimes taking a step back and going to another place in the house or outside can help you clear your head. Instead of retaliating when you get upset, take a moment to gather your thoughts and shoot up a prayer. God knows how frustrated we can get with one another, and He has sympathy for us. He can give you the forgiveness you did not know you had in you. He can help you hug it out instead of yell it out. He has enough love to go all the way around the table, even to that one family member you never seem to get along with. Give it to Him, and let Him calm your heart.

Give Thanks

Give thanks in all circumstances; for this is the will of God in Christ Jesus for you.
—1 Thessalonians 5:18

*L*iving a gratitude-filled life is one of the most rewarding things you can do for your mental health. Being thankful for the blessings you have will literally rewire how your brain chooses to think about the situations you encounter in your life. Having an attitude of thankfulness makes you a more mindful person, helps you care about your surroundings, forces you to pay attention to the best things in other people, and creates an atmosphere of happiness in every space you walk into.

Being thankful may not always be easy, especially since the world would rather have us grabbing desperately at selfish possessions. But the ability to be a thankful person no matter what situation you are in is powerful. As 1 Thessalonians 5:18 tells us, it is straight up the will of God for you! So try to change your attitude each day by choosing to be thankful.

What are some things you are thankful for today? Make a challenge for yourself this week: write down three things you are thankful for at the end of every day, and see how it affects your outlook on life. Here's a few to start you off today. Happy Thanksgiving!

I am thankful for _____

I am thankful for _____

I am thankful for _____

An unexpected blessing I am thankful for is _____

A person I am thankful for is _____

A place I am thankful for is _____

An experience I am thankful for is _____

A teacher I am thankful for is _____

Something God did I am thankful for is _____

Black Friday Clutter

Do not love the world or the things in the world.
—1 John 2:15

Stuff. It's everywhere! And with the piece of plastic in our wallet, we can buy the world. With online stores that ship for free in two days, we can buy anything we want and have almost instant gratification. Unless you are of the minimalist mind-set, you probably know how easy it can be to surround yourself with unnecessary things. If your parents still buy things for you, you can get anything you want and it will feel like it's free because you did not work to pay for it.

Wrapping our minds around the idea of letting go and having less can be tough, especially in a nation where buying in excess is glorified. How many times have you passed a store and saw something inside that caught your eye? How many times have you gone to a store to get one item and come out with far more?

Living in excess is not good for us, even though it might feel nice at first to surround yourself with all the latest and greatest trends. As the apostle John counsels: "Do not love the world or the things in the world. If anyone loves the world, the love of the Father is not in him. For all that is in the world—the desires of the flesh and the desires of the eyes and pride of life—is not from the Father but is from the world. And the world is passing away along with its desires, but whoever does the will of God abides forever" (1 John 2:15–17).

Imperishable Wreaths

Do you not know that in a race all the runners run,
but only one receives the prize? So run that you may obtain it.
—1 Corinthians 9:24

Touchdown! The thundering noise of people shouting and cheering, feet stomping and hands clapping, has reached 142.2 decibels, the current world record for the loudest crowd roar at a sports stadium, according to Guinness World Records. Sports ignites excitement in people around the globe. Watching your favorite sports team is thrilling. And when they do well, you cannot help but cheer along!*

You may have gotten into fights with friends over favorite sports teams or players. Passion for sports never seems to go away, and it has been around for thousands of years! The apostle Paul even talks about it in the Bible: "Do you not know that in a race all the runners run, but only one receives the prize? So run that you may obtain it. Every athlete exercises self-control in all things. They do it to receive a perishable wreath, but we an imperishable. So I do not run aimlessly; I do not box as one beating the air. But I discipline my body and keep it under control, lest after preaching to others I myself should be disqualified" (1 Corinthians 9:24–27).

During Paul's time on earth, the ancient Greek Olympics were very popular, and athletes would compete in them much like today. The winner of these Olympic Games would be given an olive branch wreath to wear like a crown, which Paul mentions in this verse as "perishable." He reminds us to always strive for eternal things, "running" through life focused on God instead of just what we can get from this earth. So as you continue forward in your relationship with God, make Him an even greater priority than your favorite sports team, since He always wins!

---

* "Loudest Crowd Roar at a Sports Stadium," Guinness World Records, accessed June 19, 2018, http://www.guinnessworldrecords.com/world-records/loudest-crowd-roar-at-a-sports-stadium.

7-Eleven Druggie

The second is this: "You shall love your neighbor as yourself."
—Mark 12:31

Gas stations are locations where curious characters can often be found. One day while I was paying for my gas, I think I witnessed a drug deal go down at my local 7-Eleven. After everyone else drove off, there was one guy left sitting against the wall of the building, in the cold, looking like he would fall over and pass out at any moment.

The Christian heart in me wanted to make sure he was OK, but the "you are-a-female-and-have-to-think-about-safety" side of me steered me away. So instead, I prayed, hoping he would be all right.

It left me wondering how the church could be better at helping these people. Have you ever seen someone clearly down and out on life and wondered what it would be like if they entered your church? How would people respond? Would they steer clear, or step up to help?

A wealthy young man once asked Jesus which commandment was the most important to follow. Here's how Jesus responded in Mark 12:29–31: "The most important is, 'Hear, O Israel: The Lord our God, the Lord is one. And you shall love the Lord your God with all your heart and with all your soul and with all your mind and with all your strength.' The second is this: 'You shall love your neighbor as yourself.' There is no other commandment greater than these."

Jesus was clear: Being a good Christian is not about following all the rules but about truly loving the Lord our God with everything in us and choosing to follow Him out of love. And part of that love means loving our neighbor, whoever that neighbor may be.

Do You Have Any Fish?

He said to them, "Cast the net on the right side of the boat, and you will find some."
So they cast it, and now they were not able to haul it in, because of the quantity of fish.
—John 21:6

One of the last miracles that Jesus performed on earth took place with His disciples after His death and resurrection. After He rose again, He would appear and go away in miraculous ways, not always traveling with them in the same way as during His earthly ministry. In John 21, the disciples were coming in from fishing all night. The day had just begun, with the sun starting to peek over the horizon. Jesus stood on the shore watching as His friends made their way toward the shore. They did not know it was Jesus on the shore, so He called out and asked whether they had caught anything. When they replied with a sad "No," He told them to throw their net on the right side of their boat. As they drug in the net that was now full of fish, it finally dawned on the sleepy John, "It is the Lord!" (John 21:7).

Peter was so excited to see Jesus that he put on his clothes and jumped into the water, frantically trying to get to Jesus as quickly as possible! When they reached the beach, Jesus had a meal already prepared for them. So they ate together for one of the last times before Jesus returned to heaven.

When you have come through the night, a time of darkness and fear, Jesus has not left you alone. You might not see Him yet, but He is standing there waiting for you to recognize Him. He has something great prepared for you, and He has miraculous things He will do for you. Sometimes the blessings come in the darkest times, when you have given up and think you will never hope again. Do not give up on Jesus. He will tell you the right time to throw your net on the other side of your problems. He will help you find a way out. And He will restore your strength on the other side.

How Long, Lord?

They cried out with a loud voice, "O Sovereign Lord, holy and true,
how long before you will judge and avenge our blood on those who dwell on the earth?"
—Revelation 6:10

The world we live in is not a friendly one. We are surrounded by chaotic displays of disaster on a consistent basis, whether natural or from human origins. Wars surround us, and sometimes it feels like God could care less. Or, even worse, sometimes it feels like He does not exist at all. How could a loving, caring, kind God let my loved ones die? How could He let these terrible things happen?

Grief is never easy, but it is an unavoidable part of human life on this planet. It is one of those things we have to deal with. Getting comfortable during pain or hardship is impossible. There is no way to rationalize the bloodshed on earth.

There is really only one way out: waiting for Jesus to come. And that is where we echo the cry of Revelation 6:10: "How long, Lord, before you will judge this terrible planet and stop this agony?" I do not know the answer. In fact, no one but God knows. And for now, we have to trust that He knows what He is doing and that He has it under control. Trust Him with your life, and He will get you through anything, both the good and the bad.

We Believe: The Millennium

"And he seized the dragon, that ancient serpent,
who is the devil and Satan,
and bound him for a thousand years."
—Revelation 20:2

*L*et's begin by reading how the Fundamental Beliefs of Seventh-day Adventists describes the millennium after Christ's return:

The millennium is the thousand-year reign of Christ with His saints in heaven between the first and second resurrections. During this time the wicked dead will be judged; the earth will be utterly desolate, without living human inhabitants, but occupied by Satan and his angels. At its close Christ with His saints and the Holy City will descend from heaven to earth. The unrighteous dead will then be resurrected, and with Satan and his angels will surround the city; but fire from God will consume them and cleanse the earth. The universe will thus be freed of sin and sinners forever. (Jer. 4:23-26; Ezek. 28:18, 19; Mal. 4:1; 1 Cor. 6:2, 3; Rev. 20; 21:1-5.)*

Revelation talks about a time after Christ's return to earth when we will be reigning in heaven with Him for a thousand years. This time in heaven will be unique because although we will be in a perfect heaven, sin will not yet be entirely destroyed. Satan will be stuck on earth, unable to leave.

When Jesus came to earth the first time, it was in human form, and He won the spiritual war forever through His death on the cross and subsequent resurrection. When Jesus comes the second time, it will be as our Lord and Savior, the one who has redeemed us from our sins. He will be coming to take us back to heaven with Him! When Jesus returns to earth the third time, to take back the earth from Satan once and for all and put the New Jerusalem on earth, we will go with Him to earth at that time. When we get to earth, Jesus will raise the dead who did not follow Him, and Satan will try to convince them to overthrow the Holy City. The fire of God's glory will destroy them all, but it will not burn forever! It will simply rid the universe of sin forever. As scary as it may sound, it is also hopeful because it means sin will be destroyed once and for all.

* Seventh-day Adventist Church, "The Millennium and the End of Sin," in *28 Fundamental Beliefs* (General Conference of Seventh-day Adventists, 2015), 11, https://szu.adventist.org/wp-content/uploads/2016/04/28_Beliefs.pdf.

Youth in the Bible: Mark

And there arose a sharp disagreement,
so that they separated from each other.
—Acts 15:39

The writer of the second Gospel in the New Testament, Mark, was an evangelist for Christ. He was a young person, and while he was not one of the disciples of Jesus, he learned under them and, because of their stories, was able to write his book and be a young minister of the gospel. Mark traveled with the apostle Peter, whose ministry probably inspired Mark in his quest for a deeper relationship with God.

So what can you, as a teenager, learn from Mark, a youth whom God used to write part of the Bible? Mark was eager to learn, and he listened closely to Peter's stories and sermons. Much of his book probably comes from the stories Peter told about Jesus' life and ministry. Mark was a cousin to Barnabas, and he began his ministry by traveling with Paul and Barnabas on one of their missionary journeys.

According to the few times there are stories including Mark in the New Testament, he may have had a hard time committing to being a traveling evangelist for God. Perhaps he felt God's call but was afraid to jump into full-time ministry. Paul got mad about this at one point, so he went one direction while Barnabas took his cousin Mark with him on his own missionary journeys: "And there arose a sharp disagreement, so that they separated from each other. Barnabas took Mark with him and sailed away to Cyprus, but Paul chose Silas and departed, having been commended by the brothers to the grace of the Lord" (Acts 15:39, 40).

Eventually, Mark chose to minister faithfully, though, because in his second letter to Timothy, the apostle Paul asks for Mark to come to him since he is so useful in ministry. Wherever you are at in your relationship with God and choice as to how to follow Him, be encouraged by Mark's story. He was a young person who ended up getting to write a part of the Bible! God used him on missionary journeys that went through many different countries. He was able to minister powerfully to people and teach them about God because he accepted God's call on his heart. Will you do the same?

Flat Tires

Therefore, we are ambassadors for Christ, God making his appeal through us.
We implore you on behalf of Christ, be reconciled to God.
—2 Corinthians 5:20

God knows that I need a little bit of prompting to do any sort of witnessing to strangers. Maybe you can relate! In church, where I know my role, it is easy to talk about God—it is a safe environment where people expect to hear about Him. But I have a hard time when I am out and about finding ways to witness and share about Him in settings where He normally is not talked about.

One time my car had a flat tire. There was some sort of screw stuck in it, so I had to take it to the tire store where I bought the tires to get it fixed for free. (Praise God for good service!) While I was there, it was very busy, and since I did not have an appointment, it took them a long time to get to my car. I was a little annoyed, but thankfully, I did not have anywhere I was supposed to be, so it was not a huge deal. Since I was sitting in the shop for so long, I started talking with the store manager who was working that day. He told me all about his life, his kids, and some of the struggles he was going through. Later it struck me: I was able to make a connection with this person in the community because of my flat tire!

A few months ago I got another nail in my tire, and it went flat again, so I had to take it back to the same store to get it fixed. The same manager happened to be working that day, so I had another connection point with this person and a chance to witness. Unfortunately, I was too shy. So God gave me one last chance—a third flat tire!

This time I was closer to a different store, but I was again able to witness. God practically threw the opportunity in my lap when a woman asked about my job, and we got to talking about God and church. I think God must have had a good laugh about all my flat tires—all of which were fixed for free. Maybe He lets me go over those nails to push me outside my comfort zone and give me opportunities to share about Him in places where He is not often talked about. Has God placed any nails in your path this week? Maybe He was trying to give you an opportunity to witness for Him. Do not be afraid to take advantage of the divine appointments He gives you!

The Wisdom of Solomon

At Gibeon the LORD appeared to Solomon in a dream by night, and God said, "Ask what I shall give you." . . . "Give your servant therefore an understanding mind to govern your people, that I may discern between good and evil, for who is able to govern this your great people?"
—1 Kings 3:5–9

People pray all the time. They pray for their food, before bed, and multiple times during church. But how sincere are our prayers? Do we ever actually expect that God will do something extraordinary because we asked it of Him?

Solomon lived his life in a constant tug-of-war between the enduring love of God and the sensual pull of lust, money, power, and fame. After making a treaty between his nation and the pharaoh of Egypt at the beginning of 1 Kings 3, he married the pharaoh's daughter. At that time, Solomon still loved the Lord greatly and was trying to follow in his father David's footsteps. So Solomon went to Gibeon to sacrifice to the Lord, and while he was there, God gave him a dream in which He offered Solomon anything he desired. Because Solomon asks for wisdom rather than wealth and power, God gave him all three. He was able to have the

wisdom to govern his nation well as well as a life of power and wealth. Although Solomon made some bad choices later on in his life, at this point, his heart was still aimed in the right place.

What do you typically ask God for? To help you ace a test or do well in a basketball game? Maybe you ask Him for healing for someone who is sick. What do you think would happen if you asked Him for wisdom, as Solomon did? We know God answered this great request. Imagine how your life would change if He answered yours! Take a moment right now to pray for something bold.

Hold Hands

"A new commandment I give to you, that you love one another:
just as I have loved you, you also are to love one another.
By this all people will know that you are my disciples,
if you have love for one another."
—John 13:34, 35

This world is a place where people are divided by everything. The divides range from the color of skin to political affiliation, from eating meat to eating vegan, from identifying as "conservative" or "liberal." Division also includes what sports teams you root for, the kinds of music or movies you like, and even which way you put the toilet paper roll on the dispenser! The things that seek to divide us are impossible to escape.

One way we can bridge these gaps is by holding hands with strangers—literally or figuratively. It involves supporting one another in hard situations and joyful moments. Community is extremely important in your Christian experience. Of course, your relationship with God is the top priority, but Jesus also encouraged His followers to belong to a community of believers. The early Christian church worked hard to figure out how to best support one another in the good times and the bad ones. If you want to have a sense of belonging in church or Adventism as a whole, seek that experience at the local church level. Support older members who have lost a spouse; hold their hand and pray with them. Laugh and sing with little children during Vacation Bible School and Sabbath School experiences! Intentionally become a contributing member of your church community, and see how it grows your faith.

It's a Look

"He must increase, but I must decrease."
—John 3:30

Photography is one of my hobbies. I enjoy learning how to take well-crafted photographs. Seeing the world through a camera lens changes your perspective and the way you view the world. And posting photographs to get those "likes"—well, we all know how that feels.

Do you ever find yourself counting your "likes" and comparing them to other people's? Do you scroll through the Instagram posts of famous models or photographers, trying to figure out what they have done to gain such a following? It's all in the look. Through social media, you can choose to portray yourself in any way you choose. You can be like some models who use sex to sell in the way they flaunt their body or show off their good looks. You can be a minimalist, running with themes of white in each photo. Or you could be like the millennial generation, using soft pinks, golds, and natural green plants to popularize your page. What is the image you try to portray?

While we all have become addicted to social media, we are still smart enough to know that the moments we post are only small snapshots of our daily lives. They are the well-groomed instances we want our friends to see and think we live these amazing, hilarious, outgoing lives. Does this striving for acceptance through a screen echo the loneliness of our hearts, and a society that could care less about the broken moments? Put down the screen and spend some time face-to-face with the people that really matter to you. Instead of videoing the moment for others to see, live it yourself first. Think about the image you portray to the world and why you want to be seen in that light. Try to find your validation in God's opinion of you instead of how many likes or views you get.

Coming Home

"And he arose and came to his father. But while he was still a long way off,
his father saw him and felt compassion, and ran and embraced him and kissed him."
—Luke 15:20

Luke 15:11–32 shares with us the famous story Jesus told about the prodigal son. Take time to read it now, then jump back into this devotion!

The younger of two sons, Sam (that is what we will call him for today), was getting tired of his position in the family and wanted to get out in the world and make his own way. So he asked his father for his inheritance early, took off, and traveled through the countryside to cities that had every sinful pleasure known to man. He indulged, he spent, he flashed his wealth for all to see. And after a while, his treasures were gone and he was left stranded and alone. The only way to survive was to take care of pigs, unclean animals according to Jewish society. Not only that, he was so broke he had to eat what the pigs ate. Finally, he humbled himself and realized that the servants in his father's home had better lives than he did—maybe, just maybe, his father would take him back as a servant and give him food and shelter. You know the story.

When Sam came home, how did his father treat him? Did he bring up past offenses, point out Sam's poor judgment, or send Sam to work with the servants? No! He instantly upgraded his status and took him back as his honored son. If you go to school away from your parents or live in a dorm and go home for the holidays, do you find that you sometimes struggle to get along with your family, even though you may be glad to see them?

Going home can be nerve-racking if you have a relationship that needs mending. Do not be afraid to be the first one to make things right with a family member you have a strained relationship with. Ask God to give you patience and kindness to deal with your family, and make an extra effort to build a stronger relationship with them. If there is something wrong between you, be the first one to step forward and make it right. God will honor your commitment to kindness. If you are the prodigal son coming home, unsure of what the welcome will be, trust it to God. He knows your heart, and He has everything under control.

Rotten Thoughts

Finally, brothers, whatever is true, whatever is honorable, whatever is just,
whatever is pure, whatever is lovely, whatever is commendable,
if there is any excellence, if there is anything worthy of praise, think about these things.
—Philippians 4:8

Would you eat a rotten apple? No! Of course not! That is disgusting! You would not use rotten apples to cook a pie, and you certainly would not offer them to guests coming to eat at your house either. Yet we live in a society that offers up "rotten apples" to us all the time, and it has become normalized.

The rotten apples may look like anxiety, discouragement, violence, chaos, or loneliness, all of which are very real problems that we face. But we must remember that just because we encounter a rotten apple does not mean we must eat it. Your mental health should be as important to you as taking care of your diet and not eating rotten apples!

While it is nearly impossible to avoid negative messages every day, breathing them in like the air you breathe is not healthy, or smart! Since we often put out what we take in, constantly being fed negativity will breed more negativity. Instead of always focusing on what is wrong with the world, take some time to focus on what God is doing here that *is* going well. Read the victory stories! Soak up the happy family time! Play with your pets! Get some fresh air and exercise! Spending time doing what you love is not only good for your mental health; it is great for your relationship with God as well. He wants you to live a happy and fulfilling life, full of purpose, even on this dark planet. He cares about you and loves you, so He does not want you to be full of negative information 24/7. Turn off the news and read a good book instead. Pay attention to the good things God is doing, and stop eating those rotten apples!

We Believe: The New Earth

And the ransomed of the LORD shall return and come to Zion with singing; everlasting joy shall
be upon their heads; they shall obtain gladness and joy, and sorrow and sighing shall flee away.
—Isaiah 35:10

The Fundamental Beliefs of Seventh-day Adventists describes the new earth like this: "On the new earth, in which righteousness dwells, God will provide an eternal home for the redeemed and a perfect environment for everlasting life, love, joy, and learning in His presence. For here God Himself will dwell with His people, and suffering and death will have passed away. The great controversy will be ended, and sin will be no more. All things, animate and inanimate, will declare that God is love; and He shall reign forever. Amen. (Isa. 35; 65:17-25; Matt. 5:5; 2 Peter 3:13; Rev. 11:15; 21:1-7; 22:1-5)."*

This is the last fundamental belief listed in Adventist doctrine. It gives hope just reading it! Imagine that scene: heaven, in all its glory, and all things—animate and inanimate—will be praising God and declaring His love!

In the new earth, we will finally have the joy of seeing our dead loved ones who accepted Jesus into their hearts during their life on earth. We will frolic across the fields without a worry in our minds. We will sing God's praises and shout about His love. We will never have to face sin, temptation, or anything evil ever again. It is a perfect picture of hope, joy, peace, love, and happiness forevermore.

You will no longer have questions about why certain people are not there, or why others are. God will have answered those. We will be in a state of unfathomable bliss, something we cannot understand while on this sinful earth. You will be able to rest in Jesus, finally and forever, never having to fear anything again. Imagine the best feeling you have ever had on this earth, a time when you were full of complete love, joy, and happiness, and it felt like nothing could go wrong. Heaven will be like that, but millions of times better! So do not lose hope while you are still struggling to get by on this earth. This is not the end. Thankfully, the end is beautiful and happy!

---

* Seventh-day Adventist Church, "The New Earth," in *28 Fundamental Beliefs* (General Conference of Seventh-day Adventists, 2015), 11, https://szu.adventist.org/wp-content/uploads/2016/04/28_Beliefs.pdf.

Where Is the Love?

I am feeble and crushed;
I groan because of the tumult of my heart.
O Lord, all my longing is before you;
my sighing is not hidden from you.
My heart throbs; my strength fails me,
and the light of my eyes—it also has gone from me."
—Psalm 38:8–10

Divorce. It rocked his world. After his parents split, he could not commit. Girl after girl, night after night. His heart was split in two. To mom or dad, who loved him more? How could they split if they loved him at all? Was it him? Had he done something? He feared never being able to love a wife of his own. He feared having children and causing them the same pain.

To the sons and daughters of divorce: You are not alone. It is not your fault. While you may always feel the split your parents made deep in your soul, your wounds can heal, and you can be restored. God knows you feel confused, lonely, and lost. God knows this has shattered your image of love.

God wants to restore that picture of love in your life. Even though it might feel impossible, give God a chance. Just because your parents separated does not mean you will follow in their footsteps. And most importantly, just because your parents divorced or your mom or dad left does not mean that God will leave you too. *God will never leave you.* And He will never stop loving you! You are His child, and no matter what, He is not going to disappear on you.

A True Friend

"As soon as he had finished speaking to Saul, the soul of Jonathan was knit to the soul of David, and Jonathan loved him as his own soul. . . . And Jonathan stripped himself of the robe that was on him and gave it to David, and his armor, and even his sword and his bow and his belt. And David went out and was successful wherever Saul sent him."
—1 Samuel 18:1–5

Jonathan was a prince, the son of King Saul. He was next in line for the throne, the next one who was supposed to rule the nation of Israel. And Jonathan was a fine gentleman with a kind heart and a loyal spirit, following God despite his father Saul's unfaithfulness to God. Yet when the prophet Samuel followed God's instructions and anointed David as the next king of Israel, Jonathan's chances at the throne were taken away from him. As he got to know David and started realizing God's plan, Jonathan knew that he was not destined for the throne he grew up believing would one day be his.

Jonathan's attitude toward God's choice was incredible. Instead of fighting against David, he graciously accepted God's plan and supported David in every way he could—even going against his own father to do so! Jonathan is the ultimate example of what humbly following God looks like. He did not chase after the fame and fortune of this world. He recognized who God was calling to the job, and he gave up his future throne without a quarrel and became a best friend to David. He chose to love instead of hate, to support and help instead of tear down and destroy.

How can you be like Jonathan? Do you ever get jealous of your friends when they do well at something, or get a job offer you wanted, or do better than you in sports? Try taking on Jonathan's attitude and see how it changes your friendships with those people. Choosing to love and be best friends even when you are in competition and choosing to celebrate their wins with them will make lifelong friendships and be rewarding in the end.

The Man With a Limp

"But you, take courage! Do not let your hands be weak,
for your work shall be rewarded."
—2 Chronicles 15:7

On a cold winter day, a man with a limp struggled to climb a hill. Snow blanketed the ground, and he hobbled painfully up the hill. When he reached the top, he turned around and went back to the bottom and started over again. For an hour this man trudged back and forth in the snow, each time trying to stand a little straighter and make his legs move a little smoother. His endurance was impressive, considering the obvious injury his leg had suffered. But what was more impressive was the mental grit he had to keep pushing on even though it was freezing outside.

What do you do when something has gone wrong in your life, when you have messed up in some way or someone has hurt you? Do you give up and stop trying or keep pressing on like this man? He had an injury that could not be easily fixed, but he pressed on and kept exercising his leg to help it regain its former mobility. Your heart is like that too. When it has been broken or you have done something to ruin its relationship with someone else, you cannot just give up. You must push on and keep trying, and in doing so you will gradually begin to heal.

Serious wounds, like a sports injury from basketball, usually take time to heal. You must go to a physical therapist for help and consistently do your exercises to get better. Likewise, wounds in your social circle also take time to heal. God will support you through it, but you need to trust that He knows the best path forward for you. When He shows you the next step to take, do not be afraid to follow His plan. He knows what He is doing!

Superman

"For God so loved the world, that he gave his only Son,
that whoever believes in him should not perish but have eternal life."
—John 3:16

The story of Superman is classic and has traveled around the world, exciting millions. If you have not heard the fictional story, the plot begins on a far-away planet called Krypton. It is a miraculous place, far more technologically advanced than Earth. However, it is about to be destroyed, so Superman's parents send him as a baby to planet Earth. There, he is raised by a farmer and his wife. While he is young, he discovers the source of his superhuman powers, and he becomes Superman, the hero who saves innocent civilians and fights against evil.

A heavenly father sends his only son to save the earth. He is raised by two human parents. His mission on earth is to fight for truth and justice out of love. It closely mirrors the story of Christ! Even though the story is not evangelistic, it can be used to show people that this fictional story actually happened in real life. God came down, saved humanity and the earth, and ultimately sacrificed Himself for us.

Sharing favorite movies, music, and books with friends is easy—you probably do it all the time! How often do you share your favorite view of salvation or experience with God? It might not seem as exciting as a Superman movie, but the reality is that the salvation plotline actually happened in an even better form! If you have a friend who is not a Christian but might be interested in learning more about God, find creative ways to share the story of Jesus with them. If they like Superman, maybe that is a unique place to start! There are hundreds of ways to witness to people, and different things will speak to different individuals.

Jesus Gives Me Peace

And the peace of God, which surpasses all understanding,
will guard your hearts and your minds in Christ Jesus.
—Philippians 4:7

This world is a traumatic place to be. Things happen that make life feel like it is spinning out of control and you cannot hold on any longer. In those moments, there is one thing you need: peace.

Today, ask Jesus for peace. He knows the trials this life brings, and He has peace for you that goes beyond even what your heart can see. When you feel lost in the storm, ask Jesus for peace in the turmoil. He calmed the seas once, and He can do it for you as well. When you feel lost or confused, ask Him for peace in the midst of it all. Jesus can give you clarity of mind and understanding for those moments of confusion. Ask for peace when you feel misunderstood. Jesus knows your heart, and He can smooth over any problem that arises between you and another person. If you have a friend that has not been getting along with you very well, ask for a sense of peace to be infused into your friendship.

When you go through loss—whether it is the loss of someone to death or the loss of a relationship or maybe the loss of a parent or sibling being involved in your life—ask Jesus for peace. Even though your heart may feel ripped from your chest, He is still there to cover the pain with peace. Jesus' peace is one which surpasses all understanding—it goes beyond what we can imagine, and it has power beyond what we expect. His peace can guard your heart when it is broken. His peace can transform your mind when it is overwhelmed. His peace can help strengthen your faith when you feel like you have none. Let His peace be your source of strength today.

Spiritual ADD

Do not be conformed to this world, but be transformed by the renewal of your mind,
that by testing you may discern what is the will of God, what is good and acceptable and perfect.
—Romans 12:2

While smartphones are convenient and useful inventions, they have created a complication for our spiritual lives. We are a bit more spiritually challenged in how we concentrate. It is hard to focus your attention during a

church service, so as a result, you look for the most entertaining form of church out there instead of what will foster a genuine connection with God.

There are some great ways to use technology and your smart devices to enhance your spiritual life. But on the whole, they lead to your attention being dispersed over many different things. When you read Ellen White's counsel about spending an hour talking to God in prayer, that sounds endless, does it not? And yet that hour could change your life.

While Sabbath is just one day a week, we almost need a sort of "Sabbath" from technology, where we intentionally put down the phone and turn off the distractions. Instead, choose to live in the moment with God, spend time enjoying His presence, and get used to the calm silence of not checking social media every time you are bored.

How else can we fix this spiritual disconnect? Intentionally connect with people in your church who are not smartphone users or social media posters. Do not use your phone as your alarm. Put it in another room so that when you go to bed and when you wake up you do something other than check social media. Write some letters instead of texting. You do not have to give up your smartphone completely, but do take some time away so that you can reconnect spiritually.

Little Lost Things

"Or what woman, having ten silver coins, if she loses one coin, does not light a lamp and sweep the house and seek diligently until she finds it? And when she has found it, she calls together her friends and neighbors, saying, 'Rejoice with me, for I have found the coin that I had lost.'"
—Luke 15:8, 9

Do you believe God cares about the little things in your life? Sometimes it seems like He is so far away, busy with the big problems of the world, like wars and famines, that He would not have time to care about everyday little problems. But God is so incredibly personal that He does care, even about the tiniest things!

My mom has a fitness tracker that she uses to track her activity and exercise throughout the day. It's very small, so it can easily be put in a pocket while you walk. One day during her devotional time, she felt impressed to go for a walk. She did not feel like it, so she put it off. Then she felt impressed again to go walk. Still not wanting to go, she ignored the thought. But she kept feeling impressed to get outside and walk. So finally she got up and went to grab her fitness tracker from the place she usually left it, but it was not there!

Thankfully, she remembered that she had left it in her pants pocket from the last time she used it. But, oh no! She had already started the first load of laundry, which normally would include that pair of pants! As she frantically searched through the laundry basket, she realized, much to her relief, that for some reason she had started a load with different types of clothes that day, so the pants were still in the laundry basket. Inside the pocket was her fitness tracker, right where she had left it, unharmed.

If that fitness tracker had gone through the wash, it would have been ruined. Thankfully, God impressed her to go for a walk, which prompted her to look for the fitness tracker. God does care about the little things! You can trust Him with every little moment of your life, no matter how insignificant it feels. And beyond that, He knows what you need before you even ask or realize it. So pay attention to those little impressions from the Holy Spirit—He might just save your phone from a watery death!

"Do We Have To?"

As each has received a gift, use it to serve one another,
as good stewards of God's varied grace.
—1 Peter 4:10

Do you enjoy volunteering? Usually, in high school you are required to have a certain number of volunteer hours per year. I remember once leading a group of kids in a volunteer project that was a requirement, and, oh, the groans that came from that group! While a few students were fine with the activity, the majority seemed to complain, talk about how they did not like what they were doing, and ask why we had to be doing this. As their leader, I wanted them to learn the value of service and the joy of giving to others. But I became worried the outreach would not go in that direction after all.

Volunteering is not always fun at first, but after the activity is done, participants usually feel good about the work they have done to help someone else. Thankfully, the kids who were volunteering felt this too after the activity was over. If you have a good attitude going into a service project, you are more likely to do better work, see good results, and even change someone's life!

What are some ways you can volunteer in your community or school? Does your church have a homeless outreach? Could you lead a canned food drive? How about collecting shoes for kids? Even reading to a grade school classroom can be meaningful! There are hundreds of ways to volunteer. Take some time now to write down a few ideas you have, pray about them, and talk to your youth leader about what you want to do.

The Magnificat

And Mary said,
"My soul magnifies the Lord,
and my spirit rejoices in God my Savior."
—Luke 1:46, 47

The beginning of Mary's journey to be the mother of the Son of God was not so glamorous. Think about what it would have been like for her, being engaged to marry a man named Joseph and then for everyone to see that she was pregnant! I am sure Mary told people about her miraculous visit from an angel announcing the virgin birth of the Messiah. But honestly, who would believe her?

Mary had to be incredibly resilient to put up with the shame and scorn that was placed upon her. Luke 1 tells us she went to live with her cousin Elizabeth while they were both pregnant with miracle babies. This chapter also carries a record of Mary's song of praise:

> And Mary said,
> "My soul magnifies the Lord,
> and my spirit rejoices in God my Savior,
> for he has looked on the humble estate of his servant.
> For behold, from now on all generations will call me blessed;
> for he who is mighty has done great things for me,
> and holy is his name.
> And his mercy is for those who fear him
> from generation to generation.
> He has shown strength with his arm;
> he has scattered the proud in the thoughts of their hearts;
> he has brought down the mighty from their thrones
> and exalted those of humble estate;
> he has filled the hungry with good things,
> and the rich he has sent away empty.
> He has helped his servant Israel,
> in remembrance of his mercy,
> as he spoke to our fathers,
> to Abraham and to his offspring forever."

And Mary remained with [Elizabeth] about three months and returned to her home (Luke 1:46–56).

Journey to Bethlehem

*In those days a decree went out from Caesar Augustus that all the world
should be registered. This was the first registration when Quirinius was governor of Syria.
And all went to be registered, each to his own town. And Joseph also went up from Galilee,
from the town of Nazareth, to Judea, to the city of David, which is called Bethlehem,
because he was of the house and lineage of David, to be registered with Mary, his betrothed,
who was with child. And while they were there, the time came for her to give birth.
And she gave birth to her firstborn son and wrapped him in swaddling cloths
and laid him in a manger, because there was no place for them in the inn.*
—Luke 2:1–7

Jesus' journey into the world began with a rough ride. Have you ever been to a "Journey to Bethlehem" play where you saw the whole story of Christ's birth? Because of the census, which Caesar Augustus decreed, Mary and Joseph had to travel from Nazareth, where they were living, to Bethlehem, where his ancestors came from. The time of the census could not have been worse—it was right before Mary was supposed to give birth! And so Jesus was born in poor conditions, likely a cave where the animals were kept, and placed in a manger where the animals fed from. The Bread of Life placed in a feeding trough— perhaps it was meant to be?

Though He was the King of heaven, He humbled Himself and was born to a carpenter and his pregnant fiancée. He was looked down on and treated poorly. But He learned at His parents' side and grew to be the Messiah the Father sent Him to be. Your family background might not be fancy. Jesus can relate! You do not need to come from a family of status to make a difference in your school, church, or community. Like Jesus, learn from those who teach you about God, read the Scriptures and study them, and let Him teach you. He will guide you into God's great purpose for your life!

Magi's Journey

Now after Jesus was born in Bethlehem of Judea in the days of Herod the king, behold,
wise men from the east came to Jerusalem, saying, "Where is he who has been born king
of the Jews? For we saw his star when it rose and have come to worship him."
—Matthew 2:1, 2

Wise men from the East studying Jewish prophecies does not seem to make a whole lot of sense. Why would non-Jews care about Jewish religious prophecies of the Messiah? And even if they studied them for curiosity's sake, what would prompt them to believe they were true and go to try to find this toddler king?

Many theories about the Magi exist, but a few interesting possibilities seem logical. While Daniel was in Babylon, he may have started a school of thought and science studying Jewish Scriptures. Perhaps there were still some Jewish descendants living in the area that had kept these teachings alive. Or perhaps they were just scientists who watched the stars and read broadly, and when they saw this prophecy come to life in the sky, they believed in the existence of God and the coming Messiah. Either way, no doubt when they saw the little child Jesus, they believed. Finally, they heeded the warning God sent in a dream to not revisit King Herod on their way home.

God is the Creator of the stars, and He used them like an arrow pointing to where Jesus was. And He was able to spread the message of the young Messiah through wise men from a far-off land. God often uses unexpected people or events to share His truth! Be on the lookout for what unexpected thing He might do in your life this Christmas.

Shepherds and Angels

And in the same region there were shepherds out in the field, keeping watch over their flock
by night. And an angel of the Lord appeared to them, and the glory of the Lord shone around
them, and they were filled with great fear. And the angel said to them, "Fear not,
for behold, I bring you good news of great joy that will be for all the people.
For unto you is born this day in the city of David a Savior, who is Christ the Lord.
And this will be a sign for you: you will find a baby wrapped in swaddling cloths
and lying in a manger." And suddenly there was with the angel a multitude of the heavenly host
praising God and saying, "

Glory to God in the highest,
and on earth peace among those with whom he is pleased!"

When the angels went away from them into heaven, the shepherds said to one another, "
Let us go over to Bethlehem and see this thing that has happened, which the Lord has made
known to us." And they went with haste and found Mary and Joseph,
and the baby lying in a manger. And when they saw it, they made known the saying that had
been told them concerning this child. And all who heard it wondered at what the shepherds told
them. But Mary treasured up all these things, pondering them in her heart. And the shepherds
returned, glorifying and praising God for all they had heard and seen, as it had been told them.
—Luke 2:8–20

The shepherds' role in Jesus' birth story is some of the first evidence of His countercultural life and ministry. Shepherds are a part of every Christmas pageant—kids love to dress up as them and play out the scene between the shepherds and the angels. But in Jesus' era, shepherds were at the bottom of society. Over time, shepherds earned a bad reputation, and Jewish leaders were prejudiced against them. Yet God chose to send the angel's announcement of the Messiah to lowly shepherds. He asked one of the most marginalized groups in society to go welcome the Savior of the world to earth! The message of the gospel is for everyone, not just the churchgoing folk. What can you do to share Jesus' message with someone from a marginalized group today? Write some ideas below:

_____

_____

_____

Joseph's Dilemma

And he called his name Jesus.
—Matthew 1:25

Merry Christmas! Today is a day of excitement and joy, spent with family and friends eating good food, laughing, maybe opening gifts, and celebrating Christ's first coming to earth. Before you do anything else, say a prayer of thanks to God for all He has done in your life this year, thanks for the family and friends in your life today, and a big thanks that He came to earth!

Matthew 1:18–25 describes how Joseph was told about the coming birth of Jesus and the dilemma Joseph faced:

> Now the birth of Jesus Christ took place in this way. When his mother Mary had been betrothed to Joseph, before they came together she was found to be with child from the Holy Spirit. And her husband Joseph, being a just man and unwilling to put her to shame, resolved to divorce her quietly. But as he considered these things, behold, an angel of the Lord appeared to him in a dream, saying, "Joseph, son of David, do not fear to take Mary as your wife, for that which is conceived in her is from the Holy Spirit. She will bear a son, and you shall call his name Jesus, for he will save his people from their sins." All this took place to fulfill what the Lord had spoken by the prophet:
>
> > "Behold, the virgin shall conceive and bear a son,
> >   and they shall call his name Immanuel"
>
> (which means, God with us). When Joseph woke from sleep, he did as the angel of the Lord commanded him: he took his wife, but knew her not until she had given birth to a son. And he called his name Jesus.

Joseph was a kind man, respectable and thoughtful. When Mary got pregnant, he assumed it was by another man, but he cared for her enough that he decided to divorce her quietly. He did not want to publicly shame her. But God's angel, Gabriel, told him what was going on, and Joseph graciously accepted the role of being Jesus' father on earth. He did not question God's request of him. God sometimes asks big things of us. Do not be afraid to say yes. He knows what He is doing, and He has made you with special talents, like Joseph, to tackle whatever is in front of you.

When Jesus Disappeared

After three days they found him in the temple, sitting among the teachers,
listening to them and asking them questions. And all who heard him were amazed
at his understanding and his answers. And when his parents saw him,
they were astonished. And his mother said to him, "Son, why have you treated us so?
Behold, your father and I have been searching for you in great distress." And he said to them,
"Why were you looking for me? Did you not know that I must be in my Father's house?"
And they did not understand the saying that he spoke to them.
And he went down with them and came to Nazareth and was submissive to them.
And his mother treasured up all these things in her heart.
And Jesus increased in wisdom and in stature and in favor with God and man.
—Luke 2:46–52

After Jesus' birth, not much is recorded about His early childhood years. The next major story we come to is this section near the beginning of Luke's Gospel that talks about him as a preteen at the temple. At twelve years of age, Jewish boys would go through a sort of rite of passage where they would be instructed in the Scriptures by religious teachers of the law instead of just their parents. However, Jesus' purpose there went beyond simple learning like other boys. He was realizing His mission as the Messiah and His place in those Scriptures that were being read.

The three days that Jesus' parents were looking for Him must have felt like torture to them. When Mary and Joseph walked in on the scene of Him speaking so wisely with the teachers, they must have felt a large sense of pride and relief at finding Him, and they certainly were also upset, as we see by Mary's words. But Jesus' first recorded words reveal that even as a preteen, He sensed God's call on Him.

Have you sensed God's call on your life? Often it comes in your teen years. God may speak to you through the Scriptures, through a Christian song, as an impression that convicts your heart and mind, or even through other people speaking truth into your life. Answer that call *this* year, during this break from school, when you can spend some extra time with God praying about it. And next year, live with purpose in the call He has given you!

I Can

But he said to me, "My grace is sufficient for you, for my power is made perfect in weakness." Therefore I will boast all the more gladly of my weaknesses, so that the power of Christ may rest upon me. For the sake of Christ, then, I am content with weaknesses, insults, hardships, persecutions, and calamities. For when I am weak, then I am strong.
—2 Corinthians 12:9, 10

Having self-confidence is an attractive trait. Maintaining a humble attitude while still being secure in who you are and who God has made you to be is something that will gain you deep friendships, make people feel comfortable around you, and help you navigate life.

So how do you become a confident Christian? It starts with your self-talk, the inner dialogue you have with yourself and God. If you say "I can do this," you are far more likely to succeed at something than if you tell yourself you cannot do something. If you believe in yourself and the gifts God has given you, you will be able to use those talents effectively for God's glory. Whenever you notice that you are defeating yourself by saying "I cannot," intentionally take a moment to say "I can!"

1. I am a child of God. He created me and made me for a purpose.
2. I am unique and gifted. There is no one else God made like me. I am special to Him.
3. I am confident in my God-given abilities. I can do this!
4. I am beautiful/handsome.
5. I am a person who is confident enough in myself to show love and support to other people who need it.
6. God will help me through this situation, and He will bring me healing.
7. I refuse to give up because God gives me the strength to keep going.
8. I matter. I am strong. I am capable. I am smart.
9. I choose peace, love, joy, kindness, respect, and hope.
10. I am loved.

As you head into the next year, make a goal of consistently spending time with God, of choosing to see yourself in a positive way, and of having an "I can" attitude!

The Areopagus

*Some of the Epicurean and Stoic philosophers also conversed with him. And some said,
"What does this babbler wish to say?" Others said, "He seems to be a preacher
of foreign divinities"—because he was preaching Jesus and the resurrection.
And they took him and brought him to the Areopagus, saying, "May we know what
this new teaching is that you are presenting? For you bring some strange things to our ears.
We wish to know therefore what these things mean." Now all the Athenians and the foreigners
who lived there would spend their time in nothing except telling or hearing something new.*
—Acts 17:18–21

Paul's spiritual journey was unique. He started out as Saul, an intense believer on one end of the spectrum, following the Jewish laws carefully and climbing his way up the religious power ladder. Then, after a miraculous encounter with Jesus on his way to persecute Christians in Damascus, he became an intense believer on the other end of the religious spectrum, becoming convinced of Jesus' divinity and preaching about His role as the Messiah. Saul's life was completely transformed—even going by the new name Paul as evidence of this!

So when Paul got to Athens, Greece, as a missionary for the gospel, he did not take his job lightly. Athens was a hub for intellectuals and the discussion of philosophy. As the philosophers listened to Paul preach, they found him intriguing. Since they had not heard much about this "Jesus" and His teachings, they were curious and wanted to examine this new religion and its ideas. So they brought Paul to the *Areopagus*, a place historically used for court trials and other important meetings—in this case, for philosophical debate and learning.

What is striking about this story is that even in such an apparently secular environment, there was still a thirst for knowledge and a curiosity about these new religious ideas. Today we may not have the same advantage of the "newness" of the gospel that Paul had since many areas of the world have had a taste of one form of Christianity or another. However, in the secular environments you find yourself in, many people are still curious about a God who would die for them. If someone asks about your beliefs, be willing to share. You are a missionary for God. Now go spread His message!

To the Unknown God

So Paul, standing in the midst of the Areopagus, said: "Men of Athens,
I perceive that in every way you are very religious. For as I passed along
and observed the objects of your worship, I found also an altar with this inscription:
'To the unknown god.' What therefore you worship as unknown, this I proclaim to you.
The God who made the world and everything in it, being Lord of heaven and earth,
does not live in temples made by man, nor is he served by human hands, as though
he needed anything, since he himself gives to all mankind life and breath and everything."
—Acts 17:22–25

oday, let's continue to journey with Paul through Athens as he addresses the Greek philosophers at the Areopagus. Creativity is essential when sharing the gospel. When Paul walked into Athens, he used everything he could to connect culturally with his listeners. He knew that they were curious about anything in the spiritual realm, and they had a tendency to believe in powerful beings beyond humanity.

As he walked onto the Areopagus, Paul mentioned the religious prevalence already in Athens. Paul had an open mind as he walked around Athens; he was not afraid to see what they held as a part of their religious identity, and he found an altar that said it was built "to the unknown god." Then Paul does something extraordinary. He claims this artifact boldly, saying that his God is the unknown god this altar is for. He preaches to the philosophers about the Creator, explaining that there is one true God above all else who made the world and gives life to all.

When you are questioned about your faith, what do you turn to? See if you can point to something familiar and use it to explain your faith in God. Be bold and preach the Creator even in secular areas where He is not typically talked about. His breath touches everything, and He will give you strength to witness for His glory. Ask Him for a divine appointment today to share His gospel!

Thirty-Fifth to Fifty-First Street Prayer

I thank my God in all my remembrance of you,
always in every prayer of mine for you all making my prayer with joy.
—Philippians 1:3, 4

Recently on the local Christian radio station, I heard the disc jockey talk about something she overheard her father-in-law say to her son. As they were talking, her father-in-law said, "I pray for you between Thirty-Fifth and Fifty-First streets!" She wondered what he meant, so she asked him later what the significance of Thirty-Fifth to Fifty-First streets was. He told her that he marks his commute every day by praying for every single member of his family along his route to work. On part of the drive, he will pray for his wife, other parts, he prays for his kids and then his grandkids. Each family member gets the same section of his commute every day, and Thirty-Fifth Street to Fifty-First Street belongs to her son. This grandfather developed an incredibly consistent prayer routine that has him praying for every family member every day on his way to work!

Consistency in your time with God makes such a huge difference in your connection with Him. If you want your relationship to grow as you enter this next year, do not neglect the time you have been spending with Him this year. Think of new ways you can spend time with Him that go beyond what you tried this year. Make 2020 a year of 20/20 vision! Develop clarity, focus on your relationship with Him, and make Him your top priority—the only lens you see the world through. Whether you develop a prayer path or plan like this grandfather or make your own new ideas for spending consistent time with God, be intentional about it. Write down a few of your ideas here, and put them into practice next year!

God's Calling

And so, from the day we heard, we have not ceased to pray for you, asking that you
may be filled with the knowledge of his will in all spiritual wisdom and understanding,
so as to walk in a manner worthy of the Lord, fully pleasing to him: bearing fruit
in every good work and increasing in the knowledge of God; being strengthened with all power,
according to his glorious might, for all endurance and patience with joy; giving thanks
to the Father, who has qualified you to share in the inheritance of the saints in light.
—Colossians 1:9–12

God has called you to be more and do more this year. He has placed a desire in your heart to serve Him in some way. You may have gone through some serious trials this year. You may have gone through wonderful triumphs! You may have experienced all the joys you could ever imagine or more tears than you thought were possible. Whatever the circumstance, God has still called you this year to draw closer to Him.

As this year is closing and another one begins soon, ask God to place an unshakeable faith in your heart. Do you feel Him convicting you of something or calling you though you are unsure where it will lead? Do not worry about failure. Trust Him, and have faith that He will see you through.

Just as the believers in Colossae read Paul's letter and realized they were being prayed for and encouraged in their walk with God, know that you have been prayed for as well. Even though I do not know your name and probably have never met you, I have prayed for you. I have prayed that everyone who picks up this book would be blessed by God and that He would help you grow in your personal relationship with Him. Be strengthened with His power. Have endurance, stay patient, be joyful, and give thanks to God. You will inherit the blessings God gives to all His followers!

Worries I Need to Pray For

Other Things I Need
to Talk to God About

People I am Praying For

Dear God,

What Is God Saying to Me?

My Plans to Get to Know God Like a Friend

Ways That God Has Shown Me
His Love and Care

Some of My Favorite
Bible Promises

Blessings I Am Thankful For

These Are My Spiritual Strengths

Things I Want to Accomplish
For God